Effie T. Battle
Gertrude Arquene Fisher
Myra Viola Wilds
and Others

SIX POETS OF RACIAL UPLIFT

AFRICAN-AMERICAN WOMEN WRITERS, 1910–1940

HENRY LOUIS GATES, JR. *GENERAL EDITOR*

Jennifer Burton *Associate Editor*

OTHER TITLES IN THIS SERIES

Elizabeth Laura Adams	*Dark Symphony and Other Works*
Charlotte Hawkins Brown	*"Mammy": An Appeal to the Heart of the South* *The Correct Thing To Do—To Say—To Wear*
Fanny Jackson Coppin	*Reminiscences of School Life, and Hints on Teaching*
Jessie Redmon Fauset	*The Chinaberry Tree*
Jessie Redmon Fauset	*Comedy: American Style*
Maggie Shaw Fullilove	*Who Was Responsible?* *Stories from* Half Century *Magazine*
Edythe Mae Gordon	*Selected Works of Edythe Mae Gordon*
Juanita Harrison	*My Great, Wide, Beautiful World*
Gertrude Pitts	*Tragedies of Life*
Anne Scott	*George Sampson Brite* *Case 999—A Christmas Story*
Mary Etta Spencer	*The Resentment*
Mary Church Terrell	*A Colored Woman in a White World*
Zara Wright	*Black and White Tangled Threads* *Kenneth*

Effie T. Battle
Gertrude Arquene Fisher
Myra Viola Wilds
and Others

SIX POETS OF RACIAL UPLIFT

Introduction by
Gayle Pemberton

G. K. HALL & CO.
An Imprint of Simon & Schuster Macmillan
New York

Prentice Hall International
London Mexico City New Delhi Singapore Sydney Toronto

G. K. Hall & Co.
An Imprint of Simon & Schuster Macmillan
1633 Broadway
New York, New York 10019

Library of Congress Catalog Card Number: 96-48714

Printed in the United States of America

Printing Number
1 2 3 4 5 6 7 8 9 10

Library of Congress Cataloging-in-Publication Data

Battle, Effie T.
Six poets of racial uplift / Effie T. Battle, Gertrude Arquene Fisher, Myra Viola Wilds, and others.
p. cm. — (African-American women writers, 1910–1940)
Includes bibliogrpahical references.
IBSN 0-7838-1431-3
1. American poetry—Afro-American authors. 2. American poetry—Women authors. 3. American poetry—20th century. 4. Afro-American women—Poetry. 5. Afro-Americans—Poetry. 6. Race awareness—Poetry. I. Fisher, Gertrude Arquene. II. Wilds, Myra Viola. III. Title. IV. Series.
PS591.N4B3 1996
811'.520809287'08996073—dc21 96-48714
CIP

This paper meets the requirements of ANSI/NISO Z39.48.1992 (Permanence of Paper).

CONTENTS

GENERAL EDITORS' PREFACE

The past decade of our literary history might be thought of as the era of African-American women writers. Culminating in the awarding of the Pulitzer Prize to Toni Morrison and Rita Dove and the Nobel Prize for Literature to Toni Morrison in 1993 and characterized by the presence of several writers—Toni Morrison, Alice Walker, Maya Angelou, and the Delaney Sisters, among others—on the *New York Times* Best Seller List, the shape of the most recent period in our literary history has been determined in large part by the writings of black women.

This, of course, has not always been the case. African-American women authors have been publishing their thoughts and feelings at least since 1773, when Phillis Wheatley published her book of poems in London, thereby bringing poetry directly to bear upon the philosophical discourse over the African's "place in nature" and his or her place in the great chain of being. The scores of words published by black women in America in the nineteenth century—most of which were published in extremely limited editions and never reprinted—have been republished in new critical editions in the forty-volume *Schomburg Library of Nineteenth-Century Black Women Writers*. The critical response to that series has led to requests from scholars and students alike for a similar series, one geared to the work by black women published between 1910 and the beginning of World War II.

African-American Women Writers, 1910–1940 is designed to bring back into print many writers who otherwise would be unknown to contemporary readers, and to increase the availability of lesser-known texts by established writers who originally published during this critical period in African-American letters. This series implicitly acts as a chronological sequel to the Schomburg series, which focused on the origins of the black female literary tradition in America.

In less than a decade, the study of African-American women's writings has grown from its promising beginnings into a firmly established field in departments of English, American Studies, and African-American Studies. A comparison of the form and function of the original series and this sequel illustrates this dramatic shift. The *Schomburg Library* was published at the cusp of focused academic investigation into the interplay between race and gender. It covered the extensive period from the publication of Phillis Wheatley's *Poems on Various Subjects, Religious and Moral* in 1773 through the "Black Women's Era" of 1890–1910, and was designed to be an inclusive series of the major early texts by black women writers. The Schomburg Library provided a historical backdrop for black women's writings of the 1970s and 1980s, including the works of writers such as Toni Morrison, Alice Walker, Maya Angelou, and Rita Dove.

African-American Women Writers, 1910–1940 continues our effort to provide a new generation of readers access to texts—historical, sociological, and literary—that have been largely "unread" for most of this century. The series bypasses works that are important both to the period and the tradition, but that are readily available, such as Zora Neale Hurston's *Their Eyes Were Watching God*, Jessie Fauset's *Plum Bun* and *There Is Confusion*, and Nella Larsen's *Quicksand* and *Passing*. Our goal is to provide access to a wide variety of rare texts. The series includes Fauset's two other novels, *The Chinaberry Tree: A Novel of American Life* and *Comedy: American Style*, and Hurston's short play *Color Struck*, since these are not yet widely available. It also features works by virtually unknown writers, such as *A Tiny Spark*, Christina Moody's slim volume of poetry self-published in 1910, and *Reminiscences of School Life, and Hints on Teaching*, written by Fanny Jackson Coppin in the last year of her life (1913), a multigenre work combining an autobiographical sketch and reflections on trips to England and South Africa, complete with pedagogical advice.

Cultural Studies' investment in diverse resources allows the historic scope of the *African-American Women Writers* series to be more focused than the *Schomburg Library* series, which covered works written over a 137-year period. With few exceptions, the authors included in the *African-American Women Writers* series wrote their major works between 1910 and 1940. The texts reprinted include all the works by each particular author that are not otherwise readily obtainable. As a result, two volumes contain works originally published after 1940. The Charlotte Hawkins Brown volume includes her book of etiquette published in 1941, *The Correct Thing To Do—To Say—To Wear*. One of the poetry volumes contains Maggie Pogue Johnson's *Fallen Blossoms*, published in 1951, a compilation of all her previously published and unpublished poems.

Excavational work by scholars during the past decade has been crucial to the development of *African-American Women Writers, 1910–1940*. Germinal bibliographical sources such as Ann Allen Shockley's *Afro-American Women Writers 1746–1933* and Maryemma Graham's *Database of African-American Women Writers* made the initial identification of texts possible. Other works were brought to our attention by scholars who wrote letters sharing their research. Additional texts by selected authors were then added, so that many volumes contain the complete oeuvres of particular writers. Pieces by authors without enough published work to fill an entire volume were grouped with other pieces by genre.

The two types of collections, those organized by author and those organized by genre, bring out different characteristics of black women's writings of the period. The collected works of the literary writers illustrate that many of them were experimenting with a variety of forms. Mercedes Gilbert's volume, for example, contains her 1931 collection *Selected Gems of Poetry, Comedy, and Drama, Etc.*, as well as her 1938 novel *Aunt Sarah's Wooden God*. Georgia Douglas Johnson's volume contains her plays and short stories in addition to her poetry. Sarah Lee Brown Fleming's volume combines her 1918 novel *Hope's Highway* with her 1920 collection of poetry, *Clouds and Sunshine*.

The generic volumes both bring out the formal and thematic similarities among many of the writings and highlight the striking individuality of particular writers. Most of the plays in the volume of one-acts are social dramas whose tragic endings can be clearly attributed to miscegenation and racism. Within the context of these other plays, Marita Bonner's expressionistic theatrical vision becomes all the more striking.

The volumes of *African-American Women Writers, 1910–1940* contain reproductions of more than one hundred previously published texts, including twenty-nine plays, seventeen poetry collections, twelve novels, six autobiographies, five collections of short biographical sketches, three biographies, three histories of organizations, three black histories, two anthologies, two sociological studies, a diary, and a book of etiquette. Each volume features an introduction by a contemporary scholar that provides crucial biographical data on each author and the historical and critical context of her work. In some cases, little information on the authors was available outside of the fragments of biographical data contained in the original introduction or in the text itself. In these instances, editors have documented the libraries and research centers where they tried to find information, in the hope that subsequent scholars will continue the necessary search to find the "lost" clues to the women's stories in the rich stores of papers, letters, photographs, and other primary materials scattered throughout the country that have yet to be fully catalogued.

Many of the thrilling moments that occurred during the development of this series were the result of previously fragmented pieces of these women's histories suddenly coming together, such as Adele Alexander's uncovering of an old family photograph picturing her own aunt with Addie Hunton, the author Alexander was researching. Claudia Tate's examination of Georgia Douglas Johnson's papers in the Moorland-Spingarn Research Center of Howard University resulted in the discovery of a wealth of previously unpublished work.

The slippery quality of race itself emerged during the construction of the series. One of the short novels originally intended for inclusion in the series had to be cut when the family of the author protested that the writer was not of African descent. Another case involved Louise Kennedy's sociological study *The Negro Peasant Turns Inward*. The fact that none of the available biographical material on Kennedy specifically mentioned race, combined with some coded criticism in a review in the *Crisis*, convinced editor Sheila Smith McKoy that Kennedy was probably white.

These women, taken together, began to chart the true vitality, and complexity, of the literary tradition that African-American women have generated, using a wide variety of forms. They testify to the fact that the monumental works of Hurston, Larsen, and Fauset, for example, emerged out of a larger cultural context; they were not exceptions or aberrations. Indeed, their contributions to American literature and culture, as this series makes clear, were fundamental not only to the shaping of the African-American tradition but to the American tradition as well.

Henry Louis Gates, Jr.
Jennifer Burton

PUBLISHER'S NOTE

In the *African-American Women Writers, 1910–1940* series, G. K. Hall not only is making available previously neglected works that in many cases have been long out of print, we are also, whenever possible, publishing these works in facsimiles reprinted from their original editions including, when available, reproductions of original title pages, copyright pages, and photographs.

When it was not possible for us to reproduce a complete facsimile edition of a particular work (for example, if the original exists only as a handwritten draft or is too fragile to be reproduced), we have attempted to preserve the essence of the original by resetting the work exactly as it originally appeared. Therefore, any typographical errors, strikeouts, or other anomalies reflect our efforts to give the reader a true sense of the original work.

We trust that these facsimile and reprint editions, together with the new introductory essays, will be both useful and historically enlightening to scholars and students alike.

INTRODUCTION

BY GALE PEMBERTON

The poetry collected in this volume belongs to a particularly difficult and pivotal time in African-American historian called the nadir. The term was coined by African-American historian Rayford Logan to designate the years between 1877 and 1915.[1] The era began when President Rutherford B. Hayes, in 1877, withdrew federal troops from southern areas occupied since 1865, thus ending Reconstruction. By the nadir's end in 1915, the United States was a player in international politics, priming to enter Europe's Great War, adjusting to a faster pace of living brought on by industrialization and urbanization. The nadir meant black struggle against white backlash to Reconstruction—a backlash that brought on a virtual whirlwind of racist legislation at all governmental levels, vigilantism, lynching, and other forms of white supremacy that strengthened the grip and range of Mr. and Mrs. Jim Crow. In the year 1892 alone there were 255 reported lynchings.

The era was a transitional one, with a changing of the guard in black American leadership and personality. Sojourner Truth had died in 1883, Martin Delany in 1885, Frederick Douglass in 1895, Harriet Tubman in 1913, and Booker T. Washington in 1915. A new generation replaced the older one, continuing the struggle against injustice, violence, and hypocrisy with new tactics and different politics to meet a different age. This new generation included such figures as W. E. B. Du Bois, Ida B. Wells, William Monroe Trotter, Mary Church Terrell, and Marcus Garvey. Where and how black Americans lived also changed, with a movement away from the dominant rural South to an urban South and North. Northern cities such as Chicago, Detroit, New York, and Philadelphia were rapidly developing large black communities.

The poetry of Effie T. Battle, Gertrude Arquene Fisher, Bettiola Heloise Fortson, Christina Moody, Maggie Pogue Johnson, and Myra Viola Wilds is a reflection of the era, and a testimony by the women who wrote it of the value of black life in a time of despair. As Ann Allen Shockley writes, the agonies of the period "strengthened the awareness of blacks for the need to promote black history and pride in race."[2] These six women wrote in relative obscurity, publishing their work in the second decade of this century. They joined an illustrious company of black men and women—many of whom began writing in the 1880s—who articulated the confidence and dreams, the fears and hopes of a people barely half a century out of slavery. It was an era of the poetry and fiction of Paul Laurence Dunbar, of the stories of Charles Chesnutt, of the poetry, essays, music, and lyrics of J. Rosamond and James Weldon Johnson, of the eloquent feminist passion of Anna Julia Cooper, of the illuminating fiction of Frances Ellen Watkins Harper, and of the prophetic and versatile genius of W. E. B. Du Bois.

As Paula Giddings notes in her landmark *When and Where I Enter: The Impact of Black Women on Race and Sex in America*, during this era black women had to "confront and redefine morality and assess its relationship to 'true womanhood.'"[3] This "cult," as it was called, was both an outgrowth of and reaction to increased industrialization in American society. White women, if true to the cult, were to be mistresses of their homes, guardians of culture, acquiescent and unassertive bystanders to events outside of their homes and, of course, to maintain an appropriate daintiness and modesty. Such a concept would easily separate white middle-class women from poor white, black, and immigrant women whose labor was absolutely necessary for the survival of their families and themselves. On an even more pernicious level, the cult of true womanhood collaborated with ideologies of black inferiority, cultural Darwinism, and the legacy of white male sexual oppression of black women to invent a picture of black women as immoral, licentious, and lazy. Giddings charts the many ways that black women went about both defending their names and challenging the criteria of "true womanhood."

Black women had other battles, not the least of which were with black men, who placed issues of women's oppression on back burners, at best, in their efforts to counter the effects of the nadir and to forge a fulfilling vision of the future. As Anna Julia Cooper in *A Voice from the South* noted, black men were "not yet prepared to concede" to the reality that black women had significant words and vision for the "great social and economic" questions of life.[4]

The poems of Battle, Fisher, Fortson, Moody, Johnson, and Wilds disclose these many tensions and issues in black women's lives. What the women share is their desire to undo stereotypes of black inferiority as they affirm virtues of familial love and devotion, piety, and respect for God and country. They announce themselves as members of the middle-class, as "true" black women, with leisure and idle time on their hands to compose verse. All of the women wrote in what might be called the age of Paul Laurence Dunbar. His influence is apparent particularly in the attempts at dialect poetry and its romanticized and sometimes nebulous nostalgia for a rural and safe black bygone day. But the poets also know Dunbar the romantic, Dunbar the poet of fair ladies and public figures.

As Dickson D. Bruce Jr. notes, most of the black poets of this era were innovative neither in form nor content. The subjects and the modes of expression were derivative. He says that "in poetry, this meant that virtually all of the work conformed to regular patterns of rhythm and rhyme and that much of it used the kind of imagery also found in the works of white poets appearing in popular American newspapers and magazines."[5] What becomes noteworthy in this volume then is not the quality or freshness of the poetry, but rather its emphatic proclamation of self-worth, dignity, and membership in a community of upstanding and proud black people.

The poets and poetry are interesting too because of the class assumptions at the core of the writing. In a time when a large percentage of black Americans were poor, illiterate, and consigned to some kind of peonage, these women celebrate their middle-class status. Their message to whatever audience reads them—black or white—is that their poetry is normative, representing the highest aims of black people in general. The responsibility of these poets, as they see it, is to glorify black uplift as they also define it. God and Christian faith, country, community, family, education, decency, and the poet's contemplations are the appropriate subjects for their verse-making.

These women are unknown poets. What we know of their lives comes from the very brief prefaces and forewords of their poetry volumes. In no way should they be considered literary artists. Each was engaged in a form of "race work," using poetry as others used petitions, speeches, boycotts, and when possible, ballots to change the woeful condition of black people. Unable to use more direct political means for reasons that probably had to do with opportunity, education, temperament, religion, tradition, and psychology, each chose poetry writing to uplift the race. And by doing so, each poet did her part to counteract the ubiquitous imagery of black people as ugly, filthy, craven, and beastly.

The power of this poetry volume is in its totality, in what racial uplift led six women to do. Only a handful of the poems are well crafted or successful from a purely literary perspective. The importance of the volume is its revelation of just how passionate was the desire of many black people to participate in the long and arduous movement from slavery to freedom. At the end of the twentieth century, it may be difficult for many readers to have a palpable sense of black life so close to the end of slavery, and under siege. And it might be impossible for others to understand what could drive a person to believe that a privately published volume of poetry could mean anything in the face of the nadir. But it should not be difficult to reckon with these notions. The events of this century and its racial history show just how indispensable any kind of united or collective action is in the quest for equality and equity. These poets saw their writing as an expression of vision shared by other black people that would help sustain and encourage their progressive movement toward an ever elusive place called freedom.

What follows are brief introductions to each poet. As there is so little biographical information, the poems become a means of understanding the poet. The work of Effie T. Battle and Gertrude Arquene Fisher is examined first. They share a common small-town background and published slight volumes. Next, Myra Viola Wilds and Maggie Pogue Johnson are discussed. Both women lived in cities, but were raised in rural areas, and there are certain similar resonances in their work. Finally, poetry from the two youngest poets, Bettiola Heloise Fortson and Christina Moody, is examined. They grew up one more generation removed from slavery than the other four poets of the volume, and in the case of Moody, there are signs of real poetic ability.

EFFIE T. BATTLE

What we know of Effie T. Battle she tells us herself in the foreword to her one poetry volume, *Gleanings from Dixie Land*. It is commonly assigned the publishing date of 1914 and we are told that the typesetting and presswork were "done by Students of the Tuskegee Normal and Industrial Institute, Alabama" ([2]). Undated, but written from Okolona, Mississippi, Battle's foreword ushers her readers into her poetry by evoking a well-known, stereotypical image of the South. She writes, "For me the sunny skies, the balmy air, the budding trees, the smooth green lawn, the blushing flowers have always had a subtle charm. When only a child it gave me pleasure to try to paint the beauties of Nature, as shown forth in fair Dixie-land, in little verses" ([3]). She ends the foreword with a classic apology. It is clear that she knows poetic convention, and like thousands of other poets she apologizes for her lack of talent and has a simple wish for her readers: "Should the spirit of these simple lines serve to touch a human life and draw it a little closer to Nature's heart and thus to Nature's God, then this humble effort shall not have been in vain" ([3]). Battle's gleanings—those bits and pieces of poetry drawn over time—suggest a slow pace of life and the leisure time to fashion verse.

There are only fourteen poems in the volume, and Battle honors her pledge to write of her region. The first poem, "To Okolona," is also a classic apology, fourteen stanzas long, where the poet claims not to have the skill to celebrate her town appropriately. Okolona, about twenty miles south of Tupelo and near the Alabama border, has always been a Mississippi hamlet, but for Battle, this site, perhaps that of her birth, deserves lasting praise:

Little Prairie City fair,
    Nestled 'mid the bowers
Of thy stately elms and oaks,
    Decked with grass and flowers.

Will the muses tune my voice
    Now to chant thy story?
Shall my feeble pen now paint
    Pictures of thy glory?

(5)

It is not really Okolona, however, but a past and a comfort with nature that Battle memorializes. From the vantage point of the second decade of the twentieth century, the Okolona of old, this rural and southern place, looks good:

'Tho upon thy humble streets
    Rise no stately towers;
For thee no "skyscrapers" bold
    Grace thy simple bowers.

But a breath of sweet content
    Rests within thy borders;
And thy people all are free
    From strife and disorders.

(6)

Battle's nostalgia here is without racial content or allusion, and is consistent with the drift of sentimental popular literature of the times. There is none of the gloominess of Edwin Arlington Robinson's New England rural life here, but rather more of the midwestern folk voice of James Whitcomb Riley, or the remembrances of South Carolinian Sidney Lanier. Battle appears quite unwilling to use her poetry as a base for commentary on race relations.

Even a poem such as "To the Little Maid from Porto Rico"—a narrative of a homesick young woman at Tuskegee Institute—refrains from any direct racial commentary. The young woman longs to return to friends and family, has almost completed with her plan of study, and is content with the progress of her work. But there is something in the calm of the night that induces her reverie. The narrator tells us:

I understood the longing,
  I knew full well the pain;
Who does not dream of time when he
  Shall touch his shore again?

Who does not long to breathe the air
  Of land that gave him birth?
Who does not sometimes see in dreams
  That "Dearest spot on earth"?

Yes, though afar we wander,
  In distant lands may roam,
The dearest place will always be
  Our own fair Home, Sweet Home.
(12)

Had Battle's poem been part of the New Negro Movement that followed it by a decade, there might be grounds to read a romanticized vision of Africa in these final stanzas. But there is nothing to suggest that Battle is thinking of anyplace else but Okolona.

Battle's poems are of familiar topics—the seasons, time, friendship, and war. Her "A Tribute" to Booker T. Washington was composed, we are told, after seeing Washington's body lying in state on November 16, 1915. The poem lacks the traditional elegiac stanza or heroic quatrain form, but it contains standard imagery in lauding Washington's founding of Tuskegee Institute.

How hard he's labored day by day;
    How toiled he in the night;
To Ethiopia's dusky race
    To bring a ray of light!
(19)

In "To Woman" Battle provides her version of true womanhood. "What a mission Heaven gave thee!" opens the second stanza (23), and she enumerates the ways that woman, as helpmate, mother, and moral center, drives the world, as reinforced in her final lines, "Everywhere thy feet may plod; / Help to lift a dear humanity / Just a little nearer God!" (24). By accepting prescribed roles for women in this poem, Battle declares black women a part of the equation, even though they remain unnamed. She is, in Dickson Bruce's words, "polite" to be sure, and she is eager to prove that a black writer can generate universal feelings through verse.

GERTRUDE ARQUENE FISHER

In 1910 the Foley Railway Printing Company of Parsons, Kansas, published Gertrude Arquene Fisher's *Original Poems*. Fisher's photograph faces the copyright page: high-collared white embroidered dress, friendly and serious face gazing straight at the camera.* Clearly, Gertrude Fisher had a mission in creating her original poems, and her foreword, entitled "Progress of the Negro Since 1865," gives us a hint of her determination. She opens with "I feel that the Almighty who is interested in all the great problems of civilization, is interested in the Negro problem. He has carried the Negro through the wilderness of disasters, and at last put him in a large open place of liberty" ([5]).

What follows suggests an acquaintance with the writings of Booker T. Washington (and perhaps those of Thomas Jefferson) as Fisher affirms what she sees as Negro progress since the Civil

* The photograph of Fisher referred to here was regrettably of such inferior quality in our source that it could not be reproduced. —Ed.

War, while exonerating the institution of slavery. "Slavery, while a curse," she writes, "has been a redeeming institution to the American Negro. It was a necessary evil to prepare us for this most advanced civilization of the world" ([5]). Fisher clearly treads on dangerous ground, as she has gone much further than Washington in the tenor of her accommodationist reasoning. But like him, she expresses confidence that the Negro's progress is uninterrupted, spiraling upward, and in the natural order of things. Echoing Thomas Jefferson's defense of Americans to European critics in his *Notes from the State of Virginia*, Fisher writes, "It is true that we have produced no skilled master mechanics or speculators. These are beyond our reach and reserved for later growth; but we have today (in this Inter state literary association of Kansas and the West) men and women of recognized ability" ([5]). The ten poems that follow are designed to stand as proof positive of this advancement.

Fisher's first poem continues her foreword. Entitled "Fifty Years Ago the Negro Was Asking These Questions," this dialect poem functions as another version of her declarations of Negro progress. Careful, once again, to make sure no whites are ruffled by her assertions of black progress, she continues to sanction a racial hierarchy that consigns blacks to the bottom rung, where any kind of racial equity or equality is safely tucked away into a far distant future. "Have you heard the news, / Dat gwine round de town, / Da say white folks is planing, / To turn we niggers down" is her opening verse ([6]). The usage of being "turned down" is evocative here, suggesting not so much a suitor's rejection as that of a club "black-balling" someone for membership. Before the Emancipation, Fisher tells us in this poem, whites were ready to send blacks away. What redeems the situation for blacks are Abraham Lincoln and education. A trustworthy white man, "Mas Si," tells the poem's narrator,

> If you educate your children,
> Teach them what the white child know,
> Then they will make good citizens,
> And they won't have to go.
>
> ([6])

Fisher affirms that success has occurred. The reason is simple, as she ventures a prayer, "May the Almighty God *continue* this progress until we shall stand shoulder to shoulder with the highest civilization and culture of The World." ([7]; emphasis added.)

As Okolona, Mississippi, served as the axis of Effie T. Battle's world, Parsons, Kansas, is the celebrated home of Gertrude Arquene Fisher. "Texas" is a migration story, from a troubled place to "the old state of the free"—Kansas—which holds her undying loyalty. "Yes I went back to Texas, / My birth place to see, / But little old Parsons, Kansas, / Is good enough for me" ([13]). She celebrates her school in "Hopson Normal Institute" and provides aphoristic messages in her "Christmas Day" and "Original Poem with a Moral."

The other poets in this volume are careful to present black life in a positive light, filled with Christian virtue, but Fisher takes on stereotypes of the lazy and womanizing black man in "'Taint No Use You Begging Me," "Dat High Brown Gall," and "Whar's Yo Been." Her narrator is overworked and hungry in the first, cheated on in the second, and furious in the third. Whether Fisher wrote autobiographically is not known, but her concern with badly treated women in these three poems suggests that her desire to vent certain emotions outweighs the lofty and ambitious assumptions of her prose and poetry forewords.

Effie T. Battle and Gertrude Arquene Fisher memorialized small towns, simple virtues, and common frailties. Self-published, they present themselves as part of the uplifted and uplifting vanguard of black Americans born after slavery's demise. They are forthright and hopeful, but cautious. In the case of Gertrude Fisher, what might be considered safe ground is nonetheless shifting.

MYRA VIOLA WILDS

What we know of Myra Viola Wilds is limited, but quite significant. Wilds is presented as a phenomenon and a novelty because she wrote *Thoughts of Idle Hours* after illness caused her to become totally blind. Under her name on the title page reads "blind verse writer" and her preface provides the reader with the details. A dressmaker, she suffered from eye strain and overwork and contracted a severe illness in 1911. "On March 10th, 1914, at 3 a.m. I awoke out of a sound sleep and wrote my first poem, 'Sunshine,'" writes Wilds ([6]), and for nearly a full year afterward, she wrote the poetry collected in this volume. Addressing the implicit question from her audience, Wilds authenticates her work, noting that she wrote each verse in her own hand, despite her blindness, and then gave it to her husband, who transcribed it into a book. This testimony, juxtaposed with her photograph—standing proudly behind an ornate dining-room chair, her body in a classic military at-ease pose, her sightless gaze oblique—denotes seriousness and fortitude befitting a poet of uplift.

Wilds's poetry exemplifies her era. Her home is Philadelphia, and some of her idle hours are filled with thoughts about her city. A number of poems are dedicated to various people living there, including one to the city statistician ("Beloved by all the friends he knew, / And to his duty stood quite true; / On him the city could rely / To raise her standard bright and high" [14]). But an even greater number of poems honor a bygone, rural world. In this, Wilds is consistent with much popular verse of her time, but the nostalgia also reveals the influence of Paul Laurence Dunbar. Wilds, more than any other poet in the volume, is in his debt. "The Hoop Skirt," "A Racoon Chase," "Basket Meeting Day," "The Organ Master," and "The Ladies' Sewing Bee," among others, are dialect, pastoral poems, humorous and commonsensical. Her "Elsie" ("She was fair, / With golden brown hair"), "The Best Family," "Nature," "Bessie," and "A Man of the Heart" are also Dunbaresque. Wilds lacks Dunbar's occasionally brilliant syncopation and sprung rhythms, but she has a touch of his humor and maintains clean rhymes, as in "Superstitious Sam on the War."

Now, dah ain't no use in talkin',
  Somp'em will hap'en shoe's you born;
If de folks don't stop dare fighting,
  Gable shore will blow de horn.

Den dar'l be no use in stop'in'.
    Fur dey won't have time to pray;
Fur when Gable blows that mighty horn,
    Dar'l be de judgment day.

(25)

The use of dialect, the nostalgia for real or imagined times past, the celebration of her local community, the aphoristic quality of the verse all show the degree to which Wilds sees herself as a proper female poet, expressing personal views as well as those of a middle-class black population concerned with racial uplift. Her "Our Exposition," which commemorates an exposition celebrating the fiftieth anniversary of the Emancipation Proclamation, is an example of the public, uplift poetry that is an important part of *Thoughts of Idle Hours*. Not as accommodationist as Fisher's poetry, Wilds's verses nonetheless share a view of Abraham Lincoln as emancipator, suggesting a divine hand behind his actions.

Bring your trades of skill and labor,
Bring the work of next door neighbor,
Show the nations our progressions,
Since Lincoln set us free.

At our coming exposition
Let us have a disposition
To go up and onward ever,
In the rights of Liberty.

He who rules the world and nations,
Truly signed the proclamation,
Show the nations our progressions,
Since Jesus set us free.

(50–53)

The poem conforms to the view that behind the actions of mortal men—when justice is to be served—is the guiding hand of the Deity.

Only once is Wilds explicit about the state of black life in her time. In "A Yoke of Oppression" there is rare anger.

> We've obeyed our rulers,
> We've fought for our land;
> We've planted the vineyards,
> We've gone at command.
> But a yoke of oppression we yet still feel,
> A yoke that oppresses our common weal.
>
> Be not discouraged, go on to the end;
> Be brave men of valor, be women and men,
> And the yoke of oppression that is weighing us down,
> Some day, like a boomerang,
> May turn and rebound.
>
> (40)

Less a threat than a hope for retribution, these lines nevertheless reveal a tone unusual in Wilds's poetry and that of others in this volume. This deviation from the norm of the polite also suggests the levels to which the process of writing poetry can be a means of masking indignation toward white America.

MAGGIE POGUE JOHNSON

Maggie Pogue Johnson is easily the most prolific and the best-known writer in this volume. Johnson was born in Fincastle, Virginia, probably in the 1880s. She was educated at the Virginia Normal and Industrial Institute in Petersburg and married Walter W. Johnson, a doctor from Staunton. They had one son, Walter Jr., to whom she dedicated the 1951 *Fallen Blossoms* volume. She was known primarily as a composer, writing both lyrics and music.[6]

Maggie Pogue Johnson's 1951 *Fallen Blossoms* is a composite of her 1915 *Thoughts for Idle Hours* and a slightly earlier *Virginia Dreams*. The poetry runs the gamut from standard topics of the day and dialect poetry—the essence of this volume—to love poems and verse that commemorate institutions and individuals. In her foreword to *Fallen Blossoms*, she writes that she hopes "you," the reader, "may find some idle moments in which you may enjoy reading these three books in one and that in reading, you may find a line or a verse which may light up within you a spark of inspiration to kindle a love anew for all mankind and help make this a better world in which to live" ([ix]). Johnson's poetic practice of creating uplifting verse is designed to elicit a similar response in her readers.

Her topics are conventional for the most part. *Thoughts for Idle Hours* opens with a glorification of mothers, "Somebody's Mother." In this poem there is always a mother to help the beggar, the wayward young woman, the reckless boy, and the poor. "Was there ever a word so sweet / To sister, husband or brother, / That every demand could meet, / And in form so simple as mother?" (4) She writes of roses and of soldiers leaving their loved ones, a dedication to Booker T. Washington and dialect poetry on weddings and obstreperous children.

In Johnson's poetry, it is possible to find many currents of the popular poetry and women's culture of her day. The nadir also corresponded to one of the most fertile periods of temperance organization, and "The Drunkard's Dream" is a twenty-five-stanza, nineteenth-century Gothic poem, with the narrator sure he has murdered his wife and daughter: "Yes, I killed my wife, / Yes, I killed my child— / My child, a girl of eight— / Yet am I crazed or wild?" (*Thoughts* 10). The answer is neither; he is drunk. He is redeemed at the end, having only dreamed his crime, and he reforms.

"The Hero of Afric's Wild" is the narrative of an old African chieftain, long a slave, who lives to see the Emancipation. Johnson's old slave comments on his life and death,

> "For way in Afric's sunny wild
> Our fathers, true and brave,
> Would lose each drop of blood
> Before they'd be a slave.

"And let me die, Oh! die so happy!
And tho' I've been a slave,
Before my people get the message,
I'll be happy in the grave.
(*Thoughts* 16)

Johnson certainly was not alone in romanticizing Africa, and "The Hero of Afric's Wild" obviously has held on through years of "slave's disgrace" in order to die in freedom, which was his birthright in Africa.

Johnson, like her sister poets in this volume, celebrates the provincial and unsophisticated. The reader is not surprised when at the end of "Jim's Wife Buys a Car," an automobile adventure convinces her that "Show's my name's Jinny Spar / I finds dat we is way too poe / To ebah own a car" (*Fallen* 107) "Aunt Cloe's Trip to See Miss Liza Kyle" is a humorous story of a country woman seeking to dress in style when she gets to New York City. But Aunt Cloe's efforts fail miserably, and Miss Liza Kyle refuses even to admit that she knows her.

She wid dem city friens,
Didn't want to own
Precious Ole Aunt Cloe,
But I followed her right home.

. . . .

She sent de sarvents in,
Said dey, "Dar's some mistake,
Lady, you'se missed de number,
We's skeered we's most disgraced."

I flung my shoes right in der face,
"No police in de lan
Kin git me out ob here,
Right here I takes my stan.

"Ef dis am de greetin dat you git,

When you come in style,
I'll war ole clos de nex time
To see Ole Liza Kyle."
(*Thoughts* 23)

"Miss Liza Kyle" becomes "Ole Liza Kyle" by the end of the very long poem, and although humorous, it reinforces the sentimentality and nostalgia of popular poetry and images from this era. The poem celebrates the provincial and is at its core anti-urban.

Many of Johnson's poems in *Thoughts for Idle Hours* and *Fallen Blossoms* are long narratives—either in a folk, aphoristic mode, or lofty and concerned with universal verities. Her "Poet of Our Race" in memory of Paul Laurence Dunbar is an example of the magisterial quality of much of her verse:

Thy tho'ts with rapture seem to soar
So far yea far above
And shower a heavy down-pour
Of sparkling glittering love

Thou with stroke of mighty pen
Hast told of joy and mirth
And read the hearts and souls of men
As cradled from their birth
(*Fallen* 123)

Similar poems are devoted to the memory of George Washington Carver ("The Unknown Child"), to Booker T. Washington ("The Lad Without a Name") and to James Weldon Johnson ("Poet Laureate"). She also wrote many memorials to the less famous. Johnson evidently could compose poetry quickly, at the behest of friends and associates. Her "There Is No Death" was composed two hours before the Memorial Service of the Woman's Auxiliary to the National Medical Association in Cleveland in 1942 in memory of two people whose deaths had just been reported to the group. And according to the preface of the poem, "In Memory of Rev. C. B. W. Gordon, Sr." was composed an hour before his funeral service.

Johnson wrote more patriotic poems than the other poets although the theme is pervasive in this volume. Christina Moody had written "The Negro's Flag and Country" stating unequivocally her allegiance to the Stars and Stripes. Johnson is as fervent. "The Negro Soldier" says,

> I volunteered to answer to my Country's call
>   Where ever I am needed I must go
> I'll give my blood and even should I fall
>   'Tis that my Country may be safe I know
>
> (*Fallen* 76)

Her "Thoughts of a Soldier," "America," and "Our Country's Call" all celebrate patriotism, although these poems have no allusion to black people or their lives.

It is obvious that the poems about America or the United States function in a way similar to the expression of Christian faith and devotion. Without irony, Johnson and the other poets here depict black Americans as determined, good citizens, cherishing all of the nation's values. Implicitly—and more rarely explicitly—the message is that blacks deserve much more than they have received. This is the case even when the poetry suggests that opportunities for advancement and uplift are abundant, as in Johnson's "The Negro Has a Chance."

> 'Tis true they lived one life
>   Thro' out the darkened age
> When 'mid events full of strife
>   They wrote upon Life's page
> In darkest hours of the night
>   Their souls would seem entranced
> Wondering if some time in life
>   The Negro'd have a chance
>
> But now those days are gone
>   And on Life's page are blank
> And sons of ages newly born

Are being placed in rank
Just as they file in line
To make a slow advance
They read in front this sign
"The Negro Has A Chance"
(*Fallen* 101)

Johnson's philosophy of uplift may also have meant celebrating dreams as reality. This would function as an encouragement to her black brothers and sisters.

Maggie Pogue Johnson was the most successful of the poets in this volume, success being a measure here of pages and length of career. There is no information to date about other published or unpublished works by Battle, Fisher, Fortson, Moody, or Wilds. Within what appears to be a wide circle of middle-class black America, Johnson's poetry and music found a small audience.

BETTIOLA HELOISE FORTSON

The *Mental Pearls* of Bettiola Heloise Fortson are poems and essays on the Negro participation in world wars and contributions to world civilization. Fortson is unequivocal in asserting the reason for her verse and prose book. "My purpose," she writes, "is to furnish some information concerning the Negro, which the white man has failed to print in his many text-books." *Mental Pearls* was created "with the hope that it may assist in promoting a literary uplift of all who may have access to its pages" (iii).

The preface by the "Authoress" and introductions by John W. Robinson, pastor of St. Mark Methodist Episcopal Church in Chicago, and the publisher and editor Julius F. Taylor provide the only information we have about Fortson. One of the younger poets in the volume, Fortson was born in Hopkinsville, Kentucky, on December 29, 1890, and grew up with relatives in Chicago. She graduated from high school there, learned the "feather trade from Mme. Lambert," and began her own millinery business. According to Taylor, Fortson was a part of the dramatic reading circuit in and around Chicago, which gained her "recognition in the poetical field" (8). Taylor goes on to describe the twenty-five-year-old as "an ardent suffragette and club worker."

Bettiola Fortson is a product of the twentieth century. She is not as decorous as Battle or Wilds, nor does she find a home with racial stereotypes or nostalgic visions of the past. Her intent is both literary and political; she celebrates black life and castigates white America for its racism. She opens her volume, however, with a paean to "Mother," which is more a sign of good form than an original poem: "Who touches first our tiny lips / Then gently lays our heads / To rest, upon the pillow slips? / Mother." (13) However, immediately following "Mother" is "Brothers," a narrative poem dedicated to "the Jones brothers of Mississippi who lost their lives defending the Negro Women's Virtue in that State, Oct., 1913." (14) Fortson also says the event "attracted much attention among many Northerners who advised the writer to publish the same."[7]

"Brothers" details the true story of a tragedy in black and white. The incident is one of hundreds of lynchings and mob violence that has been lost from the pages of history—perhaps because it was never entered. However, blacks in Chicago in 1913 knew a version of the story. Fortson would have been exposed to the *Chicago Defender*, one of the longest running and most successful black newspapers. The *Defender*'s headlines were filled weekly with news of black heroes and heroines, success and tragedy in black America, particularly from the Midwest and the South, and outrages and misdemeanors of all sorts. The *Chicago Defender* in 1913 called itself "A fearless HONEST CHAMPION of the People." It boasted of getting "the real truth" of lynchings and other crimes against blacks to counteract the wire stories that invariably deemed the lynching victims guilty. "Sweet Home" Chicago was due north on the Rock Island Line—the railroad immortalized in song by Leadbelly—and a final destination for many a black southern emigrant from the deepest reaches of Mississippi, Alabama, and the rest of the South. Northern blacks had their battles against racism to wage, but during this era, eyes were frequently cast on the intractability of southern white racism and the violence that attended it. Estimates vary and there is no way ever to know the exact number, but between 1882 and 1899 more than 2,400 blacks were lynched, and between 1901 and 1914 there were 1,100 reported lynchings, almost all of them in the South.[8] It is not surprising, then, for the young suffragette poet and essayist Bettiola Fortson to find inspiration among both the famous and the anonymous who fought for black dignity.

Fortson's Fred Jones and his unnamed brother in the poem were, in the *Defender*, Walter and Will Jones. Walter Jones sought out Thead Grayson, a white man, and shot him. Miss Aiken, Walter's fiancée, also died in the gun blast, as she lay next to Grayson. The newspaper, like Fortson, suggests that Grayson had used his power as a white man to coerce Aiken into the relationship. After the shooting, the brothers retreated to a cotton mill, and held off a large mob for ten hours before running out of ammunition. They allegedly killed 65 people, almost all of them white. The mill was set on fire and they were burned to death. The *Defender*'s "anonymous" reporter noted that the wire services had represented the brothers as crazed and drunken, but wondered how drunk men could be such accurate shooters. For Fortson and the *Defender*, the act of Walter and Will Jones was of supreme bravery.

> If you search the deeds of record
>   Two names I'm sure you will trace;
> Who died to protect the virtue
>   For the women of their race.
>
> (16)

With an irony that still reverberates today, Miss Aiken's "protection" could not keep her alive.

In addition to honoring the Jones brothers, Fortson penned a sonnet entitled "To Champion Jack Johnson," and the poems "Dunbar," "A Generous Heart" (dedicated to Madame C. J. Walker), "Sonnet" for Booker T. Washington, and "Queen of Our Race," dedicated to Ida B. Wells-Barnett. In the latter poem, Fortson reinforces the dichotomy, found elsewhere in this volume, of North as progressive and South as benighted.

Side by side with the whites she walked,
Step after step the Southerners balked,
But Illinois, fond of order and grace,
Stuck to the black Queen of our race.

. . . .

To-day the grand old march is o'er,
There are many white women sore;
Because of their prejudice to trace
The dignity of the Queen of our race.

. . . .

Page after page in history you'll read
Of one who was ready and able to lead,
Who set the nation on fire with her pace
And the Heroine will be the Queen of our race.

(27–28)

Bettiola Fortson's essays, "The Part Played by Negro Soldiers in the Wars of the World" and "Contributions of the Negro Race Toward the Advancement of Civilization," are catalogues of black achievement. Her litany begins with Clitus, half-brother of Alexander the Great: "[W]hen Negroes were in the minority, in numbers, the patriotic spirit burned within their souls and thus made them heroes" (45). She ends with Ida B. Wells. The dual function of the essays is similar to that of the poems. Fortson—adhering to the eighteenth-century doctrine that literature should teach and please—reminds her black audience of their ignored and insulted history. She also proclaims and celebrates this history to an ignorant and frequently arrogant white audience. Her final word is a poem, "Facts," where she writes,

Of the Negro Race half has been told.
    Here upon earth where men are tools—
But the other half is covered with gold,
    By the Throne of Him who over all rules.

Some day the blank page of history
    Will be filled with your many deeds:
And to this world be a mystery,
    So don't stop scattering the seeds.

(62)

Hoping, believing, seeking, Fortson creates herself as one of the guides to understanding black life. Her youthful exuberance and energy are obvious from each page of *Mental Pearls*.

CHRISTINA MOODY

The youngest poet in this volume is also the most talented. *A Tiny Spark* was published in 1910, when Moody was just sixteen years old, and it is driven on dialect poetry. But there is variety of voice and rhythm, tone and coloring in her work. Moody makes herself a part of the tradition of lady poets by telling the reader that she wrote her poetry "in my leisure hours, as an expression of the author's varying states of mind, or for the gratification of friends" ([3]). She underplays her ability and in a classic apology in the first poem, shows an adept hand at dialect while she claims incompetence.

> Don't criticize my writing
> Cause I ain't well trained you know
> I hab al-ways been so sickly
> Dat I haben had much show.
>
> Don't laff and ridicule me
> Cause 'twill make me feel ashamed.
> For I knows dat I ain't great
> Nor neither have I fame.
>
> (7)

In several poems Moody shows her interest in the reality of slavery. "The Love of a Slave Mother" actually is haunting, and for contemporary readers, suggestive of Toni Morrison's Sethe of *Beloved*—the brilliant novel suggested by the experience of Margaret Garner and her documented attempt to kill her children rather than allow them to be consigned to slavery. In "The Love of a Slave Mother" we witness a scene of sacrifice, love, and loss.

Just between the dawn and daylight
    Down by the Swany River shore
Crept a slave mother with her child
    Clasped to her bosom tight.

She looked upon her and whispered
    "So Mas'er was gwine to sell you
And we's done run away.
    No Mas'er won't see us no mo'
T'will de break of Judment day."

(8)

Happy endings were rare for the real slaves who sought to escape, and so is the case here. Moody's touch is delicate, and does not compete with the overpowering sadness and tragedy of the slave mother drowning with her child.

In "The Depth from Whence We Came" Moody again takes on slavery, this time proudly asserting her heritage as she celebrates the uplift of the race in her own times. In the first verse, "My fore-parents were slaves, / I'm not ashamed to say; / Though many a one disdains the fact, / And fain would drive it away" (21), Moody does more than hint at the denial at the core of many black Americans of her generation and of those who followed concerning the slave past. But in her hands the triumph over slavery is an indication of strength and power. She ends the poem,

He shook the dust from his shoulders,
    And stood face to face with the world
He has proved his grit and courage
    Though rocks at him were hurled.

He grasped every opportunity
    And rose in spite of all,
Whenever duty demanded him
    He did not need be called.

You have risen, oh Mother Race,
    So be thou not ashamed,
Let the once cursed name of Negro
    Stand for the word of Fame.

(22)

Christina Moody has a range of narrators: daughters, grandmothers, women, men, and children. These personae give breadth to her verse; she can be humorous, as in "Chillun and Men," with an overworked mother wondering why "Chillun and men, chillun and men; / When a 'oman gits married / Then hur trobles begin" (11). And she is sentimental without being too maudlin in "Alone"—a nineteenth-century genre piece of death poetry. Here a young woman has seen her parents and her brother die. "No mamma to read by the fireside, / No brother to kiss and chide, / No more smiles from father / I wish that I too had died" (16). If nothing else, the poem reinforces the pervasiveness of illness and death in times when mortality rates were higher and average life expectancy was much shorter than today.

"Mary Lue's Lover" is a humorous love story in which Moody shows her understanding of rhythmic variety in the refrain. The poem begins

> Sambo he aint true
> Bo! Ho! Bo! Ho!
> He's gone to loving little Miss Drew
> Jest de thing I thought he'd do.
> Bo! Ho! Bo! Ho!

The second stanza begins the variation

> I aint crying fur him you know
> Oh! Oh! Oh! Oh!
> But he hurt my feelings so
> I aint gwine speak to him no mo.'
> Oh! Oh! Oh! Oh!
>
> (30)

There are *teehes*, *oh dears*, *oh mes*, and *oh mys*. Convention tells us the ending before we get there—that the narrator will forgive and welcome Sambo back—but there is also some fun in getting there.

The broader range of subject matter and style highlights Christina Moody's "idle hours" poetry. This young woman from Washington, D.C., might well have been a convalescent, a hint given in "To My Dear Reader," or she may have been robust. But she had a young talent that could have been honed into a more mature and confident one. Imagine Christina Moody as a Harlem Renaissance poet.

Effie T. Battle, Gertrude Arquene Fisher, Myra Viola Wilds, Maggie Pogue Johnson, Bettiola Heloise Fortson, and Christina Moody were black women writing, finding through sentimental verse a means of creating an image of themselves, of black women, and of black people in general that defied the stereotypes. The fixation with idle time and leisure; the reinforcement of religious faith; the celebration of motherhood, family ties, and patriotism are, like sentimentality, an assertion of value and worth in an oppressively racist society. As Paul Laurence Dunbar had done with his dialect poetry of the turn of the century, these poets sought to create a black world that seemed safer, simpler, and easier than the often harsh environment in Dayton or New York or Chicago during the nadir.

Myra Viola Wilds went from being a sick and blind former seamstress to a poet, expressing joy in her husband, in the lives of her Philadelphia neighbors, and in memories of her Mount Ollie, Kentucky, childhood. Maggie Pogue Johnson could publish poetry in 1915 and reissue it with new work in 1951, having witnessed nearly half a century of what she certainly would have deemed black progress. Effie T. Battle and "Gertie" Fisher, from smaller towns, had smaller visions, but no less energy in creating their verse. Christina Moody, somewhere in Washington, D.C., placed her teenage self into the personae of mothers, grandmothers, and sons in evoking black life that she appeared to love. Bettiola Heloise Fortson set out forthrightly to correct the books and tell truths of black life. Such spunk and fortitude make these poets and their work a historical inheritance of merit. And this volume provides a published forum for their poetry that they certainly could never have imagined.

NOTES

[1]Rayford Logan, *The Negro in American Life and Thought: The Nadir, 1877–1906* (New York: Dial, 1947).

[2]Ann Allen Shockley, *Afro-American Women Writers, 1746–1933: An Anthology and Critical Guide* (New York: Meridian, 1988), 282–83.

[3]Paula Giddings, *When and Where I Enter: The Impact of Black Women on Race and Sex in America* (New York: Bantam, 1984), 85.

[4]Anna Julia Cooper, *A Voice from the South* (New York: Oxford University Press, 1988), 135.

[5]Dickson D. Bruce Jr., *Black American Writing from the Nadir: The Evolution of a Literary Tradition, 1877–1915* (Baton Rouge: Louisiana State University Press, 1989), 12.

[6]Frank Lincoln Mather, ed., *Who's Who of the Colored Race: A General Biographical Dictionary of Men and Women of African Descent*, vol. 1 (Chicago: Memento Edition Half-Century Anniversary of Negro Freedom in the U.S., 1915; reprint, Detroit: Gale Research Company, 1976), 157.

[7]See the *Chicago Defender* 8, no. 40, Saturday, October 4, 1913, p. 1.

[8]John Hope Franklin, *From Slavery to Freedom* (New York: Knopf, 1967), 439. See also Ida B. Wells, *On Lynchings: Southern Horror, A Red Record, Mob Rule in New Orleans* (Reprint, Salem, New Hampshire: Ayer, 1990).

GLEANINGS FROM DIXIE LAND

EFFIE T. BATTLE

Typesetting and Presswork done by Students
of the Tuskegee Normal and Industrial
Institute, Alabama

Foreword

For me the sunny skies, the balmy air, the budding trees, the smooth green lawn, the blushing flowers have always had a subtle charm. When only a child it gave me pleasure to try to paint the beauties of Nature, as shown forth in fair Dixie-land, in little verses. Later on, whenever a little time could be snatched from the pressing duties of life, it was my delight to indulge in these day dreams of Nature and Human Life. Encouraged by friends I sent some of these productions to a few of the best papers and to my surprise they were commended by the editors and published.

Friends are now asking that I collect and publish the writings of earlier days in book form. Many of them have been destroyed as, until recent years, no effort was made to preserve them. In the present booklet I am giving the reader an introduction to the book of these poems which will be published later. Should the spirit of these simple lines serve to touch a human life and draw it a little closer to Nature's heart and thus to Nature's God, then this humble effort shall not have been in vain.

THE AUTHOR.

Okolona, Miss.

Gleanings From Dixie Land

TO OKOLONA

Little Prairie City fair,
Nestled 'mid the bowers
Of thy stately elms and oaks,
Decked with grass and flowers.

Will the muses tune my voice
Now to chant thy story?
Shall my feeble pen now paint
Pictures of thy glory?

Nature blessed thee, little vale,
With her richest treasures;
Sunny skies and singing birds
Add to thy rare pleasures.

While to those less favored lands
Winter still is clinging,
Springtime comes to smile on thee,
Flow'rs and sunshine bringing.

What a proud look thou dost wear
In thy Springtime glory,
Buttercups and Hyacinths
Telling thy glad story!

How we love thee, little vale,
How our hearts are beating
With devotion full and deep,
As we chant this greeting!

Then the Summer comes to bring
Lilies, pinks and roses;
Waving grain and tempting fruit
Thy fair field discloses.

Then comes golden Harvest time
To thee treasures bringing,
Making all thy people glad
As thy praise they're singing.

'Tho upon thy humble streets
Rise no stately towers;
For thee no "skyscrapers" bold
Grace thy simple bowers.

But a breath of sweet content
Rests within thy borders;
And thy people all are free
From strife and disorders.

'Tho far from thy peaceful walks,
Sometimes we may wander
Still to thee will mem'ry cling,
Of thee we will ponder.

Little city of our birth,
Home of merry childhood,
Dear to us are all thy lawns,
Birds and flow'rs and wildwood.

Would that with a poet's voice,
I might sing thy story;
Would that with a bolder pen,
I might paint thy glory!

But this simple lay of mine,
Is a feeble token
Of the love my heart now feels
For thee, Okolona.

TO THE BLACK MAN

(**As published** in the Southwestern Christian Advocate,
New Orleans, La.)

Muses, lend me your aid,
  Help me tell the story,
Tune my feeble voice to sing
  Of the Black Man's glory.

Not of Slavery's darkest night
  Would I now be telling,
Notes of sadness and of gloom
  I would not be swelling.

Not of prejudice and wrongs
  Round him sometimes plying,
Not of clouds, as black as night,
  O'er him sometimes flying.

I would sing a brighter day,
  That o'er him is dawning;
I would paint a fairer scene,
  Tell of Hope's bright morning.

I would tell the story true
  Of how he now is rising
Out from Ignorance and Sin—
  See him upward striving!

Of the houses and the lands,
  That he now is gaining,
Of store-houses and of banks,
  Where he now is reigning.

See him now behind the bar,
As a lawyer pleading,
In the pulpit, at the desk,
On his race still leading!

But Ethiopia's dusky son,
Stop not here to ponder;
Of the laurels you have won,
Do not pause to wonder.

Every nation of the earth,
Your footsteps are eyeing,
All the forces of the age
With you now are vying.

Falter not 'though 'bove your head
Gloomy night seems pending;
'Though through craggy rocks and mire
Oft your path is tending.

Through the darkness and the gloom,
Hope's bright ray is shining;
And the heavy clouds above
Have their silver lining.

Ever upward on your way,
Onward, upward scaling,
Till you reach the dizzy heights
Where Right is prevailing.

JUNE

(As published in The Springfield (Mass.) **Republican.)**

Nature blushes 'neath the gaze
Of the ardent sun,
Earth is teeming o'er with praise,
Summer has begun!

Roses now are open wide,
Fragance fills the air;
Breezes kiss the lovely face
Of the lily fair.

See the dewdrops on the grass,
Sparkling in the light,
When the brilliant sun appears,
Chasing off the night!

What fair visitor is this,
Who has come to earth,
Bringing with her birds and flow'rs,
Sunshine, joy and mirth?

List, upon the floating breeze,
Comes the birdie's tune,
As he answers back to me:
" 'Tis the rosy June!"

SPRING

(As published in The Springfield (Mass.) Republican.)

Earth has changed her winter garment
  And has robed herself in green;
Easter lilies deck her bosom,
  Modest violets, too, are seen.

Buttercups stand out all golden,
  Hyacinth's bells begin to ring;
Fragrance comes from sweet narcissus,
  All the birds now chirp and sing.

Nature seems so full of gladness,
  That her face breaks in a smile,
As the sun with ardent glances,
  With his rays doth her beguile.

Father, may our hearts be ever
  Full of sunshine—free from care,
And though spring may change to summer,
  May we e'er find gladness there.

TO THE LITTLE MAID FROM PORTO RICO

The eve was calm and lovely,
  The moon in splendor gay,
Cast down upon Tuskegee
  Its most entrancing ray.

'Twas in the quiet hour
  When brilliant Day had flown,
And in her place Night serene
  Held sway upon the throne.

The hum of busy workshop
  Could now be heard no more;
The class-room now was empty
  And closed was office door.

Great throngs of happy faces
Could be seen here and there;
And strains of music soft and sweet
Were floating on the air.

I gazed from out my window
Upon this scene so fair,
And thought I found at last a place
That knew no pain or care.

I listened to the merry laugh
And foosteps light and free,
As students from their evening meal
Came forth so merrily.

And as I gazed upon them,
Methought I heard a sigh;
And turning quickly, chanced to see
A little maid close by.

And as I turned upon her
She wore a pensive smile,
And in her eyes the tear-drops
Were glistening the while.

And ready came my question:
"What grieves thee, little maid?
While all around is bright and fair,
Why dwell in Sorrow's shade?"

Her answer quickly came to me
Touched with a foreign air:
"I am from Porto Rico;
My heart tonight is there.

Three years have passed since I saw
My own dear native land;
Three years have passed since I pressed
My father's trembling hand.

I bade good-by to home and friends
To seek a training here;
To fit myself to serve in turn
My home and people dear.

I have performed my duties well,
A record fair I've made;
My future prospect now seems bright
I know not why I'm sad.

But yet 'mid all this scene so fair,
I dream of days of yore;
I long to see my friends again
And touch my native shore.

Just one more year of study here
And then, my course complete,
Back to my island home I'll go
And friends again I'll greet."

I understood the longing,
I knew full well the pain;
Who does not dream of time when he
Shall touch his shore again?

Who does not long to breathe the air
Of land that gave him birth?
Who does not sometimes see in dreams
That "Dearest spot on earth"?

Yes, though afar we wander,
In distant lands may roam,
The dearest place will always be
Our own fair Home, Sweet Home.

CHILDHOOD

Childhood days are golden treasures,
  That doth brighten every life;
Oh, how precious is their mem'ry
  In the after years of life!

Childhood paints the sky with wonders,
  Fills the air with myriads bright;
Finds perfume in every flower,
  Dreams the earth a world of light.

Childhood sees not earth's rough places,
  All its paths are filled with flow'rs;
In the cloud it sees the rainbow,
  And forgets the time of showers.

In its realm it knows no falsehood,
  On the face sees but the smile;
Innocence is its companion,
  Fancy doth its hours beguile.

Memory, keep within thy casket
  These fair scenes of childhood bright;
And in hours of gloom and sadness
  Bring these visions to my sight!

Like the brilliant hues of sunlight,
  Doth the clouds with silver line,
So through cares and disappointments,
  These fair visions will entwine.

DREAMING

Deep in my heart there comes today,
A longing to be far away
From pain and sorrow, grief and care,
Where all around is bright and fair.

I sit alone at close of day
And watch the sun's departing ray;
A sweet sad hush comes over all;
The day is done; the shadows fall.

The bird flies homeward to its nest;
All nature seeks a bed of rest.
But I sit here sad and alone,
My hope is past; my dream has flown.

'Twas only a short while ago
When o'er me brilliant skies did glow;
Earth seemed a haven of delight,
Where all around was gay and bright.

Then Fancy's smile did on me beam,
As I lay wrapped in this sweet dream;
Reality then to me spoke;
His rough hand touched me; I awoke!

I gazed around in mute surprise;
No beauty now before my eyes;
The dreams of Fancy fade away,
Reality now holds stern sway!

In paths that once were strewn with green,
Today the bare rough rocks are seen!
Where yesterday were cloudless skies,
Today the angry storms arise!

But shall I give up in despair,
  Because my life is full of care?
Is there not something I can do
  To cheer some heart, some hope renew?

Awake! my soul, thy dream is o'er,
  And gone are fancies evermore;
But Duty's field before thee lies,
    And on thee blessings yet shall rise!

TO A VIOLET

The morn was bright and lovely,
  And all around was fair;
The dew was on the roses
  And fragrance filled the air.

I strolled among the flowers,
  Their sweetness to inhale,
For life needs to be brightened
  With flow'rs from hill and dale.

And as I strolled among them,
  I plucked this one of blue;
And wondered what the world would be
  If all the hearts were true;

True as the lowly violet,
  Blooming upon the ground,
Giving forth joy and sweetness
  To all the air around.

MUSINGS ON THE WAR IN EUROPE

Europe's air is full of terror,
Darkness chaseth off her day;
Hear her groans and see her tremble,
As grim Mars holds her in sway!

O'er her hamlets, towns and cities
Bomb and cannon burst amain,
Pouring forth Death's awful torrents
Over valley, hill and plain.

And the God of war is raging
On the bosom of the waves;
Now the sea, once calm and peaceful,
Tells its tale of soldiers' graves.

Now the Dove of Peace sits sadly
Drooping, pining on her bough;
O'er her head the sable mantle
Of the night is hanging now.

Dove of Peace, sit not so sadly,
With bowed head and drooping wings!
Hark, from out the raging conflict,
How the note of Hope now rings!

Providence works out her wonders
In a strange, mysterious way;
And tomorrow there'll be sunshine
Where dark shadows reign today.

Know thou that the blackest darkness
Cometh just before the morn;
And in hours of bitter anguish
Children of sweet Peace are born.

O'er the groans of dying soldiers,
  O'er the din of shot and shell,
Providence to man rebellious
  A new message now will tell.

For when Europe stands in silence
  On her bloody battle-plain,
Sees the flower of her manhood
  By the hand of Mars there slain,

Sees the noblest blood of empire
  Flowing there upon the ground,
Painting all the streams in crimson,
  Tainting all the air around;

When she sees her lovely cities,
  Where Prosperity should reign,
Laid in waste and clothed in ashes,
  And her people bowed in pain;

And when at her feet there kneeleth
  Mothers weeping for their sons,
Wives in mourning for their loved ones,
  Victims of the battle's guns,

Then fair Europe's heart will sicken
  And she'll hate the ways of Mars;
Then she'll groan in bitter anguish
  O'er the heaps and ruins of wars.

Then with vengeance in her bosom,
  She will grasp her sword again
And in one last deadly conflict
  By her hand Mars shall be slain!

As she stand there, all triumphant,
  With the tyrant at her feet,
Dove of Peace, she'll turn to thee then,
  Thy note to her will be sweet.

Thou canst breathe thy tender message
Deep into her troubled ear;
Thou canst soothe her wounded bosom
With thy note so sweet and clear.

Then the world will wake to bless thee
And thy night will pass away;
All thy pathway will be brightened
By the sun's most brilliant ray.

Wake then, Dove of Peace, from sadness!
Lift thy head and swell thy breast!
To thee man will soon be turning
And thy name will soon be blest!

A TRIBUTE

(Composed at Tuskegee, November 16th, 1915, after seeing the body of Mr. Washington lying in state in his chapel.)

A solemn hush hangs over all
Tuskegee's pine-clad hills;
A mist of sadness, soft and dim,
The air around us fills.

Full many an eye is filled with tears,
Full many a heart's in grief;
And Sorrow Grim now holds full sway
From which comes no relief.

A mighty chief has fallen now,
A leader, brother, friend,
Who to his fellow-man stood out
A ready hand to lend.

Full many a year ago there came
To him a happy dream,
From Alabama's barren hills
A vision bright did gleam.

He saw an institution grand
  Rise by some fairy wand;
He saw tall buildings grow in state
  As if by magic hand!

And out upon the verdant lawns
  He saw a happy band
Of youth, who came eager to train
  The head, the heart, the hand.

And as he gazed still others came
  From lands across the sea;
From rocky heights, from grassy plains,
  From island and from lea.

He saw them in the class rooms large,
  He saw them all about;
He heard the clanging of their tools
  From busy shops ring out.

He heard the Dixie songs they sang
  In voices clear and sweet;
He heard the marching firm and strong
  Of eager, ready feet.

And then, alas, did he awake
  To find the vision flown;
To find around him empty space
  And all the beauty gone!

But in his mind a purpose strong
  Did quickly make its way;
And though before him mountains rose,
  That purpose came to stay!

How hard he's labored day by day;
  How toiled he in the night;
To Ethiopia's dusky race
  To bring a ray of light!

They heard his voice throughout the land,
For Negro youth to plead;
His hand was ever hard at work
To fill his brother's need.

. . . . .

And now again he falls asleep
To bask in happy dreams,
To drink he to his weary soul
From Eden's crystal streams!

He round him now his mantle draws
In one last sweet repose;
And from his labor, pain and care,
His weary eyelids close!

But though he sleeps in silence there,
Still through Time's endless age,
The world will pause to honor him,
Tuskegee's chief and sage.

And poets yet unborn shall rise
To sing his endless fame;
And nations shall come forth to bless
And honor his fair name!

TO A FRIEND

No, you can never know, my dear,
The joys you bring to me,
When weary with the cares of life,
Your smiles bid shadows flee.

You share my sorrows and my joys,
You drive away my tears,
Your cheerful face brings love and light,
Wherever it appears.

FATHER TIME

(As published in the National Negro School News, Tuskegee, Ala.)

All blessing on thee, Father Time!
Thou art the theme of prose and rhyme,
O let me now thy praises sing;
For, Time, thou art a mighty king.

Thy golden scepter sways o'er all,
Before thee kingdoms rise and fall;
Still never weary on thy way,
Thou speedest on from day to day.

By thy command comes lovely Spring,
The flowers bloom, the birds all sing;
Then while all nature seems in tune,
In comes the rosy face of June!

Oh! how delightful is the scene,
When earth is all arrayed in green,
Bedecked with Summer roses rare,
Sweet pinks and waving lilies fair.

Say, Father Time, now pause awhile
And let us bask in Summer's smile,
And linger 'neath her cooling shade!
Oh! why should summer roses fade?

But no! Once more thy scepter sways
And now comes in September days,
Earth's verdant robe is changed to gold,
The flowers fade, the year grows old.

Thou ploddest on with steady tread,
November's snow-flakes brush thy head,
Around thee blows the chilling blast
Until the Old Year breathes his last.

Yes, Father Time, thou art a king,
And well of thee let poets sing,
For thou doth hold a rightful sway
And thy commands we must obey.

The robust forms with sparkling eye
Before thee slowly fade and die,
The strong man droops, his strength decays
As o'er him pass thy fleeting days.

By thy command loved ones must part,
The eyes grow dim, and sad the heart;
Then to the heart bowed down in grief
Thy soothing balm brings sweet relief.

Still ever on thy ages run,
What others dare not, thou hast done,
Well might thy praises tune this rhyme,
O Prince of Rulers, Father Time!

March on, O King! march on thy way,
Still o'er us let thy scepter sway
Until we reach the Golden Shore
Where friends and loved ones part no more.

TO THE OLD YEAR

A solemn hush broods over all,
  And fierce December heaves a sigh;
Behold upon his snowy couch
  The Old Year lies down to die!

His mission now on earth is o'er,
  His locks once gold are silver now,
His eyes once bright are weak and dim
  And furrows sit upon his brow.

Farewell, Old Year, thy work is done,
  Thou hast performed thy duty well;
Thine hour is past, thy race is run,
  Now go thy way, and fare thee well!

TO WOMAN

Woman, frail 'tho mighty creature,
Fairest handiwork of God,
What a wilderness that place is
Where thy feet have never trod!

What a mission Heaven gave thee!
Oh, what power is in thy hands!
Sin and sorrow, gloom and sadness
Hie away at thy commands.

Thou canst hold the world enchanted
With the power of thy spell;
Thou canst make thy sphere a Heaven
Or can change it into Hell.

In thine arms the tiny infant
On whose face there is no guile,
Finds its store of joy and gladness
In the brightness of thy smile.

Later on in childhood's trials
'Tis the mother he doth seek;
All the clouds around him vanish
When unto him she doth speak.

As he nears the walk of manhood,
In the parting of the way;
'Tis the loving mother's counsel
Comes to him as guide and stay.

What is home without the woman?
What is man without her aid?
What's the school without her presence?
By her help the church is made.

You will find her by the bedside
  Of the outcast racked with pain,
Soothing all her woes and sorrows
  Bidding her take hope again.

In the time when War's dark mantle
  Casts its shadows o'er the land,
How the wounded, dying soldiers
  Greet the touch of her warm hand!

And the sailor, home returning
  From his rough and rugged sea,
Soon forgets the storms and dangers
  When her kind face he doth see.

Not a place in all the wide world
  From the hovel to the throne,
But a woman's hand is needed,
  But a woman's voice is known!

  Not a crisis, not an event,
  But the woman plays her part,
Plays it with a gentle firmness
  That doth win the world's great heart.

On, then, woman, on thy mission!
  Scatter darkness, banish pain;
Cheer the lonely, raise the fallen,
  Bid the world take hope again!

Carry sunshine, carry gladness,
  Everywhere thy feet may plod;
Help to lift a dear humanity
  Just a little nearer God!

Extracts From Letters Received

You owe it to your talent and your race to publish your poems in book form.

Dr. R. E. Jones,
Editor Southwestern Christian Advocate,
New Orleans, La.

I am returning your poems, both of which possess great merit. You have decided talent for verse and I would advise you to cultivate it.

Rev. B. F. Riley,
Author "The White Man's Burden."
Birmingham, Ala.

Have read your poem, "Spring," in the Springfield Republican. It is a gem. I am glad you are contemplating the publication of your poems. Be assured beforehand of my hearty co-operation in the distribution of the books.

The Springfield Republican, as you know, is one of the greatest papers of the nation and a compliment from that source is much to be appreciated.

Rev. Sutton E. Griggs,
Author "Pointing the Way," "Wisdom's Call," etc.
Memphis, Tenn.

Mrs. Battle is often styled "The hardest worker and one of the most scholarly of Negro women of Mississippi." Her poems are now being widely published and are attracting much attention.

The Southwestern Christian Advocate.
New Orleans, La.

My dear Mrs. Battle: It is very gratifying to read your collection of verses. They are smooth and graceful, always highminded and clear, reverent to all truth and goodness and appreciative of all beauty and true aspiration. In writing them you are doing your country a service, and as a citizen I thank you, while as a friend I congratulate you.

Yours truly,
(Signed) George W. Cable,
Northampton, Mass.

Mrs. Battle has an individual gift of melody and the ability to express much fine appeal. She is at her best as a poet of Nature.

Springfield Republican.

Sketch From the Life of the Author

Born at Okolona, Mississippi, of poor but intelligent parents. Early home an old Southern homestead of rare natural beauty. As a child, showed strong love for Nature's beauties around her. Entered Rust University, Holly Springs, Mississippi, at age of thirteen. Held first honors for scholarship for six years. Inclination to verse composition encouraged by Northern teachers. Verses published while in school. Won prize for composing hymn and $15.00 prize for essay in an Inter-Collegiate Contest of Freedman Aid Schools. Graduated in 1900 at age of 19, one of the youngest college graduates of the Freedman Aid Schools. Taught at the Meridian Institute, Meridian, Mississippi. In 1903 was married to Wallace A. Battle, and with him has worked twelve years in building up the Okolona Industrial School, one of the best of the younger schools of the South. Has written poems for some of the best papers and magazines, among them the Springfield Republican, and Southwestern Christian Advocate. In June, 1914, published "Gleanings from Dixie Land," as an introduction to a book of poems to be published in Boston later. Booklet has the commendation of some of the country's strongest literary men.

The first edition of the booklet having been so heartily received, Mrs. Battle has added a few of her recent compositions and published the present edition while engaged in some work and study at Tuskegee.

ORIGINAL POEMS

ORIGINAL POEMS

BY

Gertrude Arquene Fisher

Parsons, Kansas

PRICE 50 CENTS.

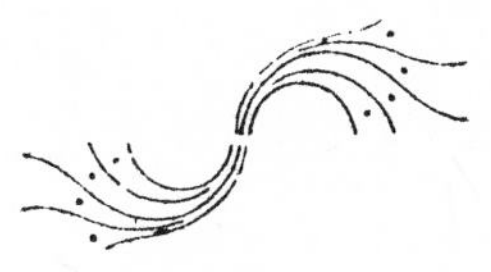

FOLEY RAILWAY PRINTING COMPANY
PARSONS, KANSAS

PROGRESS OF THE NEGRO SINCE 1865

I feel that the Almighty who is interested in all the great problems of civilization, is interested in the Negro problem. He has carried the Negro through the wilderness of disasters, and at last put him in a large open place of liberty. When, we take into consideration all the circumstances, coupled with the fact that when cut loose from slavery in 1865 it was a matter of root hog or die. Think of what our condition was in 1865 and what it is today. That we are progressing, there can be no doubt notwithstanding the fact that there are lowering clouds and muttering thunders and the doors of opportunity do not swing wide yet there is every indication of a day coming that we shall stand shoulder to shoulder with the highest civilization and culture of the world. Slavery, while a curse, has been a redeeming institution to the American Negro. It was a necessary evil to prepare us for this most advanced civilization of the world. Fifty years ago the Negro was asking these questions. Forty-four years ago the Negro had nothing. Forty-four years ago the proclamation of emancipation was issued.

From that eventful day onward the mighty aspiration of the ex-slave for education and material development has written a new page in the history of the world's progress. It is true that we have produced no skilled master mechanics or speculators These are beyond our reach and reserved for later growth; but we have today (in this Inter state literary association of Kansas and the West) men and women of recognized ability. We have produced soldiers, poets, artists, teachers, lawyers and doctors. The number may not reach that of the white man but the beginning has been made. These achievements have been wrought by us under the most adverse conditions. We realize that the bottom is crowded and there is more room at the top. So we are pressing onward and upward.

FIFTY YEARS AGO THE NEGRO WAS ASKING THESE QUESTIONS

Have you heard the news,
Dat gwine round de town,
Da say white folks is planing,
To turn we niggers down.

I can't read or write,
But I know I's got a soul,
And it nearly breaks my heart,
To know we's got to go.

We don't bother white folks,
We haven't got a show,
We tends to our own business,
I don't see why, we's got to go.

We got no education,
But what we know we know,
And maybe dat's de reason,
Dat we's got to go.

Da hasn't sot no time,
We may be here two years or more,
In dat time, I'll find out,
Why we Niggers is got to go.

I've thought of another way,
Mas Si is an honest white man,
I'll ax him why we's got to go,
And find out all I can.

Says I, Mas Si, will you tell me?
Why we Niggers is got to go,
Says Si, they are uneducated,
And you people are to slow.

If you educate your children,
Teach them what the white child know,
Then they will make good citizens,
And they won't have to go.

There will be an emancipator,
With firmness in the right,
He will issue the proclamation,
That will give the Negro's right.

Then you must educate your children,
And they will have a show,
They will make good loyal citizens,
And they won't have to go.

Since that refined period, the Negro has proven that he has the elements that make him a fit part of this great country. There are those among us who have reached fame in nearly all the avenues of life. The Negro achievements have been marvelous.

Since the Negro gained his freedom,
He has proved himself a hero,
We are climbing up the ladder,
And we ainter gwiner go.

We have Lawyers, we have Doctors,
Teachers and preachers also,
These host of noble women,
And we ainter gwinter go.

Abraham Lincoln, Abraham Lincoln,
'Twas he who fixed it so,
We can stand and tell the world,
We don't have to go.

The Negro achievements have been marvelous and the heights are still beyond. We are slowly rising and day by day hopes grow brighter. May the Almighty God continue this progress until we shall stand shoulder to shoulder with the highest civilization and culture of The World.

GERTIE.

SISTER HANNAH JONES

Had you ever stop to think—about
Gabriel blowing his horn
There'll be lots of good people
That will wish they had never been born.

2

It will be a waking up feeling
And some of you will get mad
But there'll be no time to argue
So you just as well be glad.

3

I ask sister Hannah Jones
What road was she traveling on
She said honey I's gwine to heben
Gwine dar as sho as you born.

4

I ask her to tell me her experience
She said honey hit de same ole tale
Hit's prars dat take you to heben
You can neber travel by rail.

5

I said keep on sister Hannah
I love to hear you talk
I know you are a christian
I know it by your walk.

6

She said sometimes dis road am hard
Sometimes I's up, sometimes I's down
But I keep er praying honey
Just to war dat shining crown.

7

I want's to prove by faith
Dat I's a chile ob God
Now ef dis road was al'us smothe
To prove dis wouldent be hard.

8

I wants to wurk fur Jesus
I aint gwine wid a empty han
I's gwine ter talk fur Jesus
As I jurney thru dis lan'.

9

Now I's an ole member
I started long years ago
And Jesus is my shepard
And I lub's him more and more.

10

I tries to obey de good book
Do I don't know how to read
But wit' de pure in heart
God seems to plant a seed.

11

Dis seed it seem to sprout
And teach me right from wrong
Yes honey I's gwine to heben
Gwine dar as sho you born.

12

But Honey don't get discouraged
If you should find
Some other christian spersence
Dat ain't de same as mine.

13

Fur we all have difference sperence
And wid some de road am hard
Just member dis der honey
Dat we're serving de same God.

14

Well sister Hannah I'll ask
Once more and for all
When and where were you
When you heard the Savior call.

15

Well mine ware in de ole way
But in de new way you'll find
Dat God will answer your prayers
De same as he done mine.

16

But I'll tell you as yo ax me
Hit was when I ware sixteen
De day my sins was washed away
Was de brightest I eber seen.

17

I ware a wicket sinner
I ware so mean and vile
I felt de need of a Saviour
I wanted to be God's chile.

18

So I goes down to de ole barn
And gits down on my knee's
And say Oh come heah Jesus
And heah me ef you please.

19

I jus kept on praying
And den I heah, a voice say
Your sins air all forgiven
Fur Ive washed dem all away.

20

Hit been nigh on to forty years
Dat I's been serving God
I's neber got tiahed yet
Sometimes do dis road am hard.

21

Now this is ole time religion
They have made many changes I see
But that ole time religion sister Hannah got
Is good enough for me.

GERTRUDE ARQUENE FISHER.

TEXAS

My folks left Navasota,
When I was only three,
For they were bound for Kansas,
The ole state of the free.

2

When we arrived in Denison,
My Father got a job,
He said I'll stick right here,
This kind of work ain't hard.

3

We lived in Denison, six years,
And the day sister Maggie was eight,
We started again on our journey,
To see the ole free state.

4

We made Parsons our home,
And we have been doing fine,
But some how or other,
I got Texas on my mind.

5

I wanted to recall those by gone days,
Those days of long ago,
When I was down in Texas,
And the boys all called me Jo.

6

Well kind friends I must say,
Time brings many a change,
I went back to Texas.
But Texas ain't the same.

7

I find down in Texas,
That the people draw a line,
And ever time you look around,
You can see the Negro sign.

8

Yes I went back to Texas,
My birth place to see,
But little ole Parsons, Kansas,
Is good enough for me.

GERTRUDE ARQUENE FISHER.

CHRISTMAS DAY

Christmas Day is almost here,
We haven't time to pause,
Children its just a few more days,
And there'll come a Santa Clause.

2

Go to bed early on Christmas eve,
And hang your stocking high,
For when you get as old as me,
Santa will pass you by.

3

Yes, I am too old for Santa Claus,
He'll never visit me again,
But should I live to see Christmas Day,
I'll be happy just the same.

4

So kind friends one and all,
On Christmas you must pray,
For Jesus died to save the world,
And he was born on Christmas Day.

5

We must always strive,
To love one another,
Do all the good we can,
And never hate our brother.

6

For Jesus died to save the world,
That we may live again,
Oh! bless the name of Jesus,
Who bore those dreadful pain.

7

We must be careful how we judge,
And live a christian true,
We must pray for one another,
And be careful what we do.

8

After death comes judgment,
And a consultation before the throne,
It is there that we shall know,
Just as we are known.

9

So let us pray to Jesus,
Who was born on Christmas Day,
We must bless the name of Jesus,
We must bless the Christmas day.

GERTRUDE ARQUENE FISHER.

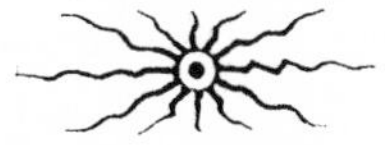

HOPSON NORMAL INSTITUTE

Breathe soft and low O whispering wind,
While I think of my old school days,
While I think of Hopson Institute,
Breathe soft and low Oh wind I pray.

2

As I gaze upon the portrait,
Of prof. D. W. Bowles,
My minds reflect backward,
Reflects to days of old.

3

Yet Prof. Bowles lies calm and still,
He sleeps beyond life woe and wail,
Beyond the fleet of sailing clouds,
Beyond the shadows of the vale.

4

But the ole familar frame stands,
Where he use to teach—no more,
It is our institute,
But the home for the friendless poor.

5

There are men and women here today,
Who on that ground have trod,
There are some who live in other towns,
And some beneath the sod.

6

We use to sing such good ole song,
And the Lord's prayer repeat,
I never knew its meaning then,
But now it sound so sweet.

7

Since then many voices have been hushed,
So many souls have gone for aye,
So many hands that I've touched,
Are folded over hearts of clay.

8

There were no trees upon that ground,
To cut my sweet hearts name,
Never less by me dear one's,
Are remembered just the same.

9

Farewell to thee ole Hopson,
You are the home of the friendless I know,
But I'll always call the Hopson,
Tho you'll be my school no more.

GERTRUDE ARQUENE FISHER.

'TAINT NO USE YOU BEGGING ME

Taint no use you beggin me,
Cause I ain't comin back,
You got no money, you got no job,
I want a man dat's got de sack.

2

Dis way livin don't suit me,
One week plenty to eat livin high,
Next week not a bite in the house,
Starving to death bout to die.

3

I don't like to live dis way,
And I think it is a sin,
That I don't get nothing to eat,
Only every now and then.

4

Well what ef I is fat,
You don't see dat I eat,
Why man you are lying,
You is only fed me twice dis week.

5

What do you specks for me to do,
Well you must be a specking fool,
Now you just keep on specking,
And see if I don't do some speckin too.

6

You specks for me to wash,
You specks for me to cook,
You specks for me to scrub,
Now Nigger don't you recon,
I specks dat I aught to have some grub.

GERTRUDE ARQUENE FISHER.

ORIGINAL POEM WITH A MORAL.

I knew a poor little girl,
That herd cows every day,
And as she passed along the streets,
She heard people say

2

Look at the tom boy,
Oh look at the guy,
It made her feel sad,
But she would not cry.

3

She had a poor mother,
And she was trying her might,
To keep the wolf from the door,
She thought honest work was right.

4

One day she went home and said,
Mother dear what shall I do,
People laugh and scorn me,
And they know I am helping you.

5

My child said her mother,
Let them laugh but you press on,
Kind words will never be said of you,
Until you are dead and gone.

6

And this world is like a stage,
Each one has to play,
So let them talk my darling,
But heed not what they say.

7

That little girl would go to school,
And when recess came,
She stood alone on the play ground,
And the children would call her names.

8

Said a little girl barely six,
I 'ont pay wid 'ou,
'Ou is a poor ole tash,
And 'ou is a tow boy too.

9

The little girl never said a word,
She simply folded her arm's,
She thought of what her Mother had said,
To do thy self no harm.

10

She herd cows faithfully five years,
At her the people did hollow,
But while they were making fun,
Her Mother was saving the Dollar.

11

Her Mother took in washing,
The city payed the rent,
Out of five years' earning,
Five Dollars was all she spent.

12

Her Mother carried an insurance,
Five thousand on her life,
And often she would say,
My child some day you'll be alright.

13

One day her Mother took sick and died,
And she was left alone,
She said Oh Lord, What shall I do?
I have no friends, I have no home.

14

But after the funeral was over,
People came by the score,
And the one's that use to make fun of her,
Will never make fun no more.

15

For she live's in a mansion of her own,
And she can truly say,
A girl that use to make fun of me,
Is one of my servants today.

16

And the little girl of six that said,
I 'ont pay wit' 'ou,
Is exceedingly glad to speak to her,
Or stoop to unloose her shoe.

17

Now that is the way people are today,
The one's they talk about,
Is far their superior,
And you will find it out.

18

And here is another thing,
That each of us should know,
That how to attend to our own business,
And let other people's go.

19

MORAL

For there is so much good in the worst of us,
And there is so much bad in the best of us,
Until it hardly behoves any of us,
To talk about the rest of us.

GERTRUDE ARQUENE FISHER.

DAT HIGH BROWN GALL

Honey you is gettin' tiahed ob me,
And I's gwin'er leave dis place,
I sho can't stand to see you,
Smiling in dat high brown's face.

2

I know you is gwine'er miss me,
Deed you will,
I got a chance to get me a high yaller too,
And I speck I is.

3

Oh guone Nigger don't talk so smart,
Dat's what I say about you,
I's trying to treat you right,
And dis is de way you do.

4

Thare's other men right now,
Waiting fur your place,
But you is done disgusted me,
With all de Nigger race.

5

And ef dis is what you call love,
I don't want none in mine,
Nigger didn't you know you was lying,
Told me you gwine lub me long as de sun did shine.

6

You must been ludding to your farthers' son,
And not de sun above,
Had me fooled all dis time,
Believing in your love.

7

I wouldn't care so much,
But heah what greaved my mind,
When I acused you ob dat gall, you said,
Chocolate drops for me, I wouldn't have a high Brown.

8

Man I ain't gwine have no more trouble,
With you nappie concerns,
So you go get your high brown,
You've lost your home, there is nothing stering.

9

I just dare you to hit me,
I know I ain't high Brown,
But if you hit me de day you have to serve,
On the county road will make you loose your mind.

GERTRUDE ARQUENE FISHER.

WHAR'S YO BEEN

Look heah, What yo keep axing me whar I been,
I ain't gwine tell you a thing,
I ain't axed you whar's you been,
I ain't ax you if you heah de bell ring.

2

You might know I's been wher I was,
And I was whar I's been,
Ef twarnt for a pity I'd pisin you,
But I know twould be a sin.

3

Whar is you been, Whar is you been,
Is you taking care ob me,
Ef you'd leave dat gambling room,
Den you could see—Whar I's been.

4

Keep on loosing you money dat way,
Some ob dese days while you trying to make leben,
Dat Katy train gwine carry me away,
And I's gwine leab on No. seben.

5

Dat am de nearest to seben leben,
Dat you'll ever make,
You call yo self a gambling man,
And can't buy ole chuck steak.

6

Oh go long man and sell your papers;
Or keep on guiling, I don't care,
Dat Nigger call for three square meals a day,
And he don't bring a dimes worth here.

7

Look heah Nigger I's gwine tell you sometin'
I's gwine leave heah some cold day,
And you is gwine come and can't get in,
And Nigger dis chile is gwine be warm where she is,
And you, you ragged rascal you gwine freeze to death
    trying to find out,
Whar I is been.

GERTRUDE ARQUENE FISHER

A GUILTY CONSCIENCE OF A SINNER

Leaf by leaf the roses fall,
After day comes night,
Each day bring about a change,
That is sometimes wrong and sometimes right.

2

As the preacher stood in the pulpit,
And before the text was read,
He noticed a man in the congregation,
Who sat with a hung down head.

3

Kind friends give me your attention,
Was what the preacher said,
Am I born to die,
Was the text the preacher read.

4

The preacher said, Am I born to die,
To lay this body down,
The man never said a word,
He sat as if spell bound.

5

Oh sinner man can you say,
With your soul it is well,
Or will you go on stumbling,
Stumbling down to hell.

6

A guilty conscience need no accusor,
For the way of the transgressor is hard,
Repent, believe and be baptized,
And prepare to meet thy God.

7

Then the choir began to sing,
All the way my Savior leads me,
And just before the hymn was finished,
The sinner man could see.

8

The guilty conscience of that sinner,
Was overflowed with joy,
He told of all the crimes he'd committed,
When a boy.

9

He said I want you all to pray,
Pray that I live right,
I've been a wicket sinner,
I've sinned all through life.

10

I remember when a boy,
My Mother made me pray,
But I strayed from her dear teaching,
The day she was layed away.

11

Now I have no loving Mother,
She sleeps beneath the sod,
But I pray that I shall meet her,
On the other side with God.

12

Confess oh guilty conscience,
And hold your light up right,
For many a guilty conscience,
Will read this sinner plight.

GERTRUDE ARQUENE FISHER

THOUGHTS OF IDLE HOURS.

Myra Viola Wilds

THOUGHTS OF

IDLE HOURS

BY

MYRA VIOLA WILDS

BLIND VERSE WRITER

ILLUSTRATIONS BY

LORENZO HARRIS, ARTIST

PHILADELPHIA PA.

Nashville, Tenn.:
National Baptist Publishing Board
1915.

DEDICATION.

To him of all on earth, most faithful,
"My Husband," I affectionately dedicate' this little volume.

PREFACE.

Total Blind and Limited Education.

I send out my first litle book, "Thoughts of Idle Hours," trusting it may find kind, considerate friends. Should I live to finish the second edition, I hope it will be a great improvement over this my first. I was born at Mount Ollie, Ky., a little country place. I lost my eyesight from overwork and eye strain at my occupation, dressmaking, in the year 1911. For three years afterwards, I went through a very severe illness. On March 10th, 1914, at 3 a. m. I awoke out of a sound sleep and wrote my first poem, "Sunshine." In eleven months and seventeen days afterwards, I had written the contents of this book. The question has often been asked, who writes your thoughts for you, since you are blind? I will answer here. Every line and verse in this little volume has been composed and written with my own hand notwithstanding the loss of my eyesight.

A copy of each verse I retain in my own handwriting, after this, they are copied in a book by my husband. I beg your kind consideration of the plain, simple verses herein:

I do not seek Wealth, Fame or Place,
Among the great ones of my race,
But, I would pen in letters bold!
Some thoughts! perhaps to cheer the soul.

Myra Viola Wilds

CONTENTS.

POEMS.

"SUNSHINE."

To C. Garfield Fox, of "The Philadelphia Record."

Like the sunshine, in the morning,
 As it falls upon the field,
Let our hearts be bright and happy,
 And to sorrow never yield.

Let all sadness turn to gladness,
 And our path will brighter be;
He who loves us is above us,
 And our way can plainly see.

9

"A THANKSGIVING PRAYER."

Our land has been fruitful,
  Thou hath given us food,
Clothing and shelter,
  And blessed us with good.

We have sown and gathered
  The ripe golden grain;
Thou hath sent us the sunshine,
  The clouds and the rain.

We've gathered in store
  The gifts from Thy hand;
There is peace and plenty,
  Throughout our broad land.

From the homes of the brave,
  In the land of the free,
We bow, Blessed Father,
  In Thanksgiving to Thee.

For mercy, O Lord,
  We humbly beseech Thee;
For the nations at war,
  In the lands across the sea.

Restore to us, Father,
  Thy love, and thy peace,
Oh Thou, King of all kings!
  Cause this cruel war to cease.

10

"THE EARLY MORNING."

In the early mist of morning,
As the day is slowly dawning,
Hear the rustling of the leaves
In the gentle summer breeze.

See the flowers lift their heads,
From their peaceful little beds,
Smiling sweetly, bright and gay,
Cheering thousands by their stay.

See the pansy's big bright eyes,
Peep at you in sweet surprise;
And the violet dipped in dew,
Says she has a kiss for you.

The pink rose turned a crimson red,
At the words the violet said;
The lily stood so pure and white,
Blushing sweet, then took her flight.

All day long the gentle breeze,
Scampered with the flowers and trees,
Till the sun which shown so bright,
Left for home and said good night.

11

"DEWDROPS."

To I. Underhill.

Watch the dewdrops in the morning,
  Shake their little diamond heads,
Sparkling, flashing, ever moving,
  From their silent little beds.

See the grass! Each blade is brightened,
  Roots are strengthened by their stay;
Like the dewdrops, let us scatter
  Gems of love along the way.

MY THOUGHTS.

Many thoughts had I!
And away they would fly,
From the east to the west,
Seeking some place to rest.

Through the woodland and trees,
In the soft summer breeze,
By the silvery stream,
For awhile they would dream.

Like a flash of the eye,
Off again they would fly;
As a bird seeks a nest,
For its young ones to rest.

In a garden they flew,
Where the sweet violets grew,
And sought for a kiss,
From her lips sweet with dew.

Then onward they went,
With love in the heart,
And stopped for a rest,
In the galleries of art.

The artist could see,
Love had set them at rest;
And he painted for me
The one I loved best.

May my thoughts never roam,
From the place where I met
The dearest of all,
One sweet violet.

To Hon. Edward James Cattell, Statistician of the City of Philadelphia, Pa.

A master mind was his,
In the art of calculation;
So swift, his thoughts were wont to fly
Throughout the whole creation.

The city had appointed him
To note her great progression;
And keep a tab on everything
She had in her possession.

He could tell about the city,
From the first day of its birth;
Her many parks and buildings,
And every cent she's worth.

His friends would gladly gather 'round.
To hear his late review,
About the city and its needs,
And what they hoped to do.

Beloved by all the friends he knew,
And to his duty stood quite true;
On him the city could rely
To raise her standard bright and high.

"LITTLE YELLOW BABY."

(This poem was composed and written June 8, 1914, and made its first appearance in the Philadelphia Record, July 13th, 1914. Since then a new verse has been added and the top line changed.)

Little yellow baby,
  With dimpled hands and face,
Where'd you get that dirt from?
  You're surely a disgrace.
Look at these sticky fingers
  My suger bowl, I know,
Old Shivery Slinkum
  Will catch you sure.

Don't grab me by the apron;
  I saw him peeping then.
And when the door is open,
  He's going to walk right in.
Don't let old "Slinkum" get you.
  Well then you best be good,
Or else I'll let him take you
  And chop you up for wood.

Dinah, bring the basin;
  Wash his face and hands.
Don't you dare to whimper;
  Sit up! Goodness lands!

Dinah, bring the basin;
Wash his face and hands.
Hush! don't dare to whimper,
Sit up! Goodness lands!

16

Eyes a little drowsy—
  Looking kind o' weak;
Little yellow baby,
  I'll rock you off to sleep.

Whimpering little baby,
  Hush! Now do not weep!
Tender eyes shall guard thee,
  While you are asleep.

Pleasant dreams attend thee!
  Angels near thee keep,
Little yellow baby,
  Sleep! Sleep! Sleep!

"A SONNET."

I've tried in vain to write a sonnet,
My mind was on a brand new bonnet;
I could not write a line.
Thoughts would come and then they'd go,
I found the task no better so,
I stopped it for a time.
At last I took my pen again,
And tried to make that sonnet plain,
And off my thoughts went flying;
My mind you see was all upset,
About that pretty bonnet.
My thoughts would fly, no use to try,
I could not write a sonnet.

A LULLABY—"LITTLE CURLY HEAD."

Come, little curly head,
Bright eye'd baby boy;
  Mammy's gwine to rock you to sleep.
Close dem eyes now,
Mammy's little love and joy,
  Hush, now! Go to sleep.

Mammy's gwine to buy you
A brand new rocking horse,
  And a pretty kite and string,
A little jumping jack,
And a pretty pussy cat.
  And a mocking bird that sings.

Mammy don't care
If your little face is black;
It's just the sweetest face I know.
Dem pearly teeth so white,
And sparkling eyes so bright
  They follow wherever I go.

Off to sleepy land!
Is Mammy's little man,
  Dreaming of his games and toys.
The pretty kite and string,
And other little things,
  And the many fights he'll have among the boys.

"ELSIE."

She was fair,
With golden brown hair,
As the autumn leaves,
In an October breeze,
From a child of three, .
She was happy and free,
As a lark on the wing,
In the young budding spring,
As the years rolled by,
On her I'd rely.

But alas! one day,
Carl took her away,
To be at his side,
His wife and his bride;
He a youth of good taste,
With manner and grace of a prince;
He was grand,
Just the right sort of man,
For Elsie, my friend,
I trust to the end.

THE LITTLE GERMAN BAND.

I had stopped down at the corner
To hear the little German band,
Playing "Away Down South in Dixie"
And "A March Through Georgia Land."

When I spied my mother coming,
With a broad strap in her hand,
O! I never stopped to look back
At that little German band.

Home I went a-running,
Just as fast as I could go;
In a closet hid myself,
My heart was full of woe.

When mother found me, there at last,
There was no use to cry;
I climbed up to the transom door,
And tried my best to fly.

She hauled me down, with might and main,
And then I tried to run;
I'll never watch a German band,
For strapping ain't no fun.

"THE BEST FAMILY."

The best family I knew,
Now honest and true,
Was a family of ten,
Both women and men.

It's seldom you pick
A family who stick
So closely together,
As the family of Kix.

The father and mother,
Were faithful and true;
And their children were reared
With the rod that was due.

An honor were they,
Each boy and girl;
And the kindest of friends,
That I had in the world.

"THE BABE THAT'S DARK AS NIGHT."

They've sung about the yellow babe,
The brown one and the white,
But the little babe I love the best
Is the one that's dark as night.

You see he has such sparkling eyes,
Bright as they can be;
He looks so cute and cunning-like,
When'er he smiles at me.

He's just the funniest little scamp
You'd find for miles around;
I love to jump him on my knee,
And trot him off to town.

"Dot Tanny now?" he said to me,
His little heart was full of glee;
When from my pocket wide and deep,
I pulled him out a candy sheep.

'Twas fun to see his big bright eyes,
Beam out with joy and glad surprise,
He laughed and jumped and ran and peeped,
Until he almost fell asleep.

It filled my heart with great delight,
To see that babe as dark as night,
A-sleeping sweet in slumber deep,
Still holding tight his candy sheep.

"NATURE."

Nature in the earth has slumbered,
  Through the chilly winter's blasts;
Beasts have sought their caves for shelter,
  Till the ice and snow have past.

Birds have sought a land of sunshine,
  Through the southern fields they roam;
Making merry with their singing,
  Winter o'er, they come back home.

Spring is near, the streams are swelling,
  Nature, too, is on her way;
Birds and beasts are fast returning,
  All the world seems bright and gay.

"SUPERSTITIOUS SAM ON THE WAR."

Things are getting mighty tangled,
In de world des latter days;
And dey sends your thoughts a-flying,
In a thousand different ways.

Well, de world is just as bright,
As it's always been to me;
But dar's something wrong, my brud'r,
Just as wrong as wrong can be.

Dah's de nations of de earth,
Dey ain't satisfied to stay;
In de worl' so full and fruitful,
Where dey haves it all de'r way.

Now, dah ain't no use in talkin',
Somp'em will hap'en shoe's you born;
If de folks don't stop dare fighting,
Gable shore will blow de horn.

Den dar'l be no use in stop'in',
Fur dey won't have time to pray;
Fur when Gable blows that mighty horn,
Dar'l be de judgment day.

"THE HOOP SKIRT."

You can talk about the new style gowns,
And high-heeled boots they wear,
The puffs and curls and other things,
That fashion now call hair.

But you ought to seen my mother,
In her hoop skirts, bless her soul;
With her waterfall of cotton,
Dyed black as furnace coal.

I remember standing by her,
In those good old fashioned days;
While her hoop skirt bobbed and noddled,
In a dozen different ways.

Thinking how she'd ever stop them,
When she sat her down to spin,
While a-standing there a-thinking,
Deacon Jones come walking in.

Good morning, Sister Mandy!
Said the deacon with a bow;
Is John at home? I come to see
If he'll go and help me plow.

THOUGHTS OF IDLE HOURS

I am sorry, said my mother,
  John has gone in town today,
With some chickens, eggs and butter,
  And a load of new mown hay.

Have a chair, my mother offered;
  Now when John comes back from town
I'll remember 'bout the plowing,
  And will sure to send him round.

Thank you, said the deacon,
  Well, I guess I'll have to go;
Mother's hoop skirt bobbed and noddled,
  As she stood there in the door.

Give my love to Sister Sally,
  Mother called out with a smile;
Tell her Sunday is baptizing,
  Up the road here 'bout a mile.

Brother Jasper will preach the sermon,
  In the morning, and at night
We will have another brother
  By the name of Isaiah White.

Then she sat down to her spinning,
  In her usual pleasant way,
Singing sweetly, "Roll on, Jordan,
  Till that bright and happy day."

THOUGHTS OF IDLE HOURS

After all I think that fashion,
  With its funny styles and ways,
Will welcome back the hoop skirt,
  Of those good old-fashioned days.

"A RACOON CHASE."

Ike and me, just him and me,
Went on a racoon chase.
Over hill and dale we found the trail,
But lost it in our haste.

Said Ike to me, that coon you see,
I think went up that 'simmon tree;
Said I to Ike, well, I'll be bound,
I'll climb that tree and fetch him down.

Oh, no! said Ike, just let him be,
That coon is wise as you and me;
We saw his shadow on the ground,
That scamp was slowly sneaking down.

I called to Ike to bring the dogs,
I'd chase that coon behind some logs;
He called old Roscow, Nero, too.
That coon got out and fairly flew.

As far as me and Ike could see,
That scamp ran up another tree;
The dogs, they ran and jumped and bound,
And tried their best to bring him down.

I looked at Ike,
Ike said to me,
That coon can have that 'simmon tree.

"BASKET MEETING DAY."

(This scene was taken from a little place in the hills of Kentucky called Mount Ollie, not far from my birth-place.)

Time was drawing mighty near,
To basket meeting day,
Down at Mt. Ollie where they say
The yearly spread is laid.

Every buggy in the town,
Wagon, cart and dray,
Had been engaged for weeks ahead
For basket meeting day.

Sis Hannah Brown, who always led
In everything that's great,
Sent word to all her friends around,
To start in and not wait.

There's cakes to bake and pies to make,
Peach preserves and jam,
Biscuits brown and hoe cakes too,
Perhaps a dozen hams.

The chickens, when it comes to them,
They took the cue and flew;
For miles around no fowl was found,
What would the preacher do?

The chickens when it came to them,
  They took the cue and flew;
For miles around, no fowl was found,
  What would the preacher do?

THOUGHTS OF IDLE HOURS.

The great eventful day arrived,
  They came from miles around,
From Johnson's place and Thompson's place,
  And lots of folks from town.

The day had started bright and fair,
  As anyone could wish;
The deacons they were on the grounds,
  To help on with the rush.

By twelve o'clock the yard was full,
  No room for man or beast;
The church was full and wagons full,
  Where would they spread the feast?

The meeting house was quite too small,
  To hold the surging crowd;
And Parson Sparks had had his pulpit
  Moved out in the yard.

He mounted high and took his stand,
  And then began to speak;
My text said he shall be this day
  "The shepherd and the sheep."

I have prepared on my right hand,
  A pasture for the sheep,
And on my left a stopping place,
  Where sinners come to weep.

He mounted high and took his stand,
  And then began to speak;
"My text," said he, "shall be this day,
'The Shepherd and the sheep.'"

33

Come right on up and take your place,
  The parson gave command;
And all at once the surging crowd
  Had marched on his right hand.

"Praise the Lamb!" a brother cried;
  And then the shouting started;
High in the air flew hats and hair,
  For heads and hair had parted.

They shouted in and shouted out,
  Till almost time for dinner;
The parson cried, "Now friends, sit down,"
  I cannot find a sinner."

Take your seats," he said again;
  And with his hand he waved.
"I find no goats are here today,
  There is nothing but the saved.

"Brother Pierce, please come up front,
  And take the day's collection;
Now, friends, each one must do his best,
  That it may bear inspection.

"Deacon Dodd, please start a hymn,
  With plenty money in it;

Praise the Lamb! a brother cried;
And then the shouting started.
High in the air flew hats and hair,
For heads and hair had parted.

(Hymn.)

I been listening all night long,
 I been listening all day;
I been listening all night long,
 To hear some sinner pray.

"Come right on up, don't sit and wait,
 It's almost time for eating;
At any rate it's growing late."
 Thus ends our basket meeting.

"THE ORGAN MASTER."

(To Mr. John A. Lively, Philadelphia, Pa., February 9th, 1915.)

We've got a great big organ
 At the church down where I go;
And you ought to hear the music,
 Playing softly, sweet and low.

They've as fine an organ master
 As is found in any town;
When he starts that organ singing,
 You got to lay your burden down.

I have often sat and listened,
 As he played along the keys,
At the music softly sighing,
 Like a gentle summer breeze.

Made you think about the angels,
 With their golden harps and wings;
And the mighty songs of Zion,
 That the Christian people sing.

There is music in that organ!
 When Brother Lively plays
He sends the keys a-running
 In a dozen different ways.

Then he'd strike the chords so gently,
  In a kind o' solemn way;
And play the sweetest music,
  As the people bowed to pray.

BESSIE.

Gentle in nature, modest and shy,
With a sparkle of hope in her pretty bright eyes.
Hope was the anchor she carried each day,
With courage and vigor she made her own way.
Her duties were many, to all she was true,
A dear, loving mother, with bright daughters two.

"A YOKE OF OPPRESSION."

We have been free, yes, fifty years!
From shackles and chains,
But not from tears,
The bloodhound has gone from the cabin door,
The slave master haunts our steps no more;
But a yoke of oppression we sometimes feel,
A yoke that oppresses our common weal.

We've obeyed our rulers,
We've fought for our land;
We've planted the vineyards,
We've gone at command.
But a yoke of oppression we yet still feel,
A yoke that oppresses our common weal.

Be not discouraged, go on to the end;
Be brave men of valor, be women and men,
And the yoke of oppression that is weighing us down,
Some day, like a boomerang,
May turn and rebound.

JACK AND I.

Jack and I went out for a walk,
Along the seashore for a pleasant talk,
As we sat on the sand,
By the sad, sad sea,
There Jack gave his heart
And his love all to me.

Said he, "Mary, I love you,
I give you my all;"
Said I, "Jack, don't be foolish,
Love rises and falls.
"Like the waves of the sea,
They are never at rest;
It is hard for you, Jack,
To tell who you love best."

"Now, Mary," said Jack,
"If you don't believe me,
I'll throw myself out
In the wild raging sea."

"Oh! Jack," said I,
"Don't do that for me,
For how on earth
Could I live in the sea?"

THE LADIES' SEWING BEE.

An invitation come for me
To join the ladies' sewing bee,
Which meets at Kitty Paxtons,
On Thursday next, the message said,
And Sally Simpson there will read
A paper on relaxtion.
That sewing bee may be all right
But it requires the best of sight
To make such little stitches;
The only ones that I could make
Would be perhaps a patch to take
And sew on Dollies breeches.
But then you know I had to go
No way to get around it,
When I got there, well I'll declare
I'll tell you how I found it.
The room was filled with tables small,
And chairs pushed back clear to the wall,
And ladies sitting 'round it.
This sewing bee, well now you see,
Was quite a brand new thing to me;
When I went in a lady said,
"Have you your thimble, needle and thread "
Not yet, said I, I come you see
To join the ladies sewing bee.
Your name, please. "Sue T. Horner."
Well now, please take that seat in the corner.
Well, the way those ladies looked at me

I was sorry I joined that sewing bee.
At last I was given an apron to make
While the ladies were discussing the way to make cake;
I tried my best and could not sew,
And had fully made up my mind to go
When Kitty Paxton rose and said,
Now, ladies, we'll have the paper read.
Well, Sally Simpson looked too sweet,
Gowned in white from head to feet;
As she arose she looked at me,
'Twas then a quarter after three.
Now, ladies, she said, before I start
I hope no one here will have to depart.
My paper today is on relaxtion,
Which requires much thought and action.
Now relaxtion is this, don't go to pieces,
If Dinnah falls down and breaks all the dishes;
Don't wind yourself up to the highest pitch
Throw Dinnah and the dishes all down in the ditch,
Then sit back and laugh in serene relaxtion.
Don't give a thought to the scene or the action.
The ladies all voted the paper was good,
And said they would try to obey if they could.
"Ladies," said Kitty, "we've been greatly honored,
We'll have a paper next week by Miss Sue T. Horner."
Speaking of me "who sat in the corner."
The work was all finished Kitty gave them to make
Then the ladies sat down to their tea and cake;
It is nice to go to a sewing bee,
But I doubt again if they ever see me.

THOUGHTS.

What kind of thoughts now, do you carry
  In your travels day by day
Are they bright and lofty visions,
  Or neglected, gone astray?

Matters not how great in fancy,
  Or what deeds of skill you've wrought;
Man, though high may be his station,
  Is no better than his thoughts.

Catch your thoughts and hold them tightly,
  Let each one an honor be;
Purge them, scourge them, burnish brightly,
  Then in love set each one free.

"WHEN YOU FEEL A LITTLE BLUE."

When you feel a little blue,
Kinder good for nothing, too,
And you try your best to rouse yourself and can't,

Think about the busy bee,
As he flies from tree to tree,
Then stop and take a lesson from the ant.

At the very peep of day,
They are up and on their way,
Toiling on until the setting of the sun.

When the harvest days are o'er,
And they've gathered in their store,
They can rest because their work has been well done.

45

"THE CHORUS."

TO ARTHUR E. BIRCHETT.

He had gathered in the singers—
  From the East and from the West,
The very best of singers,
  Who could stand, the hardest test.

The Leader, skilled in music,
  Was a man, who knew a tune,
From the plain old fashioned Jew harp,
  To the humming bird, in June.

He'd got them all together,
  And started them to train
Bass, alto and soprano;
  Then, the high-toned tenors came.

"Everybody" joined the chorus
  When Director Birchett led;
Why, the folks just kept on singing—
  Till they nearly lost their head,

Some of them, had long been singing,
  'Fore the Leader here was born,
Some I guess, will keep on singing—
  Until Gabriel blows the horn.

The Leader, mounted high the stand,
  And calmly stood and looked;
Order! said he; the chorus now
  Please take your singing books!

And turn to No. Thirty Three!
The "Singers keep their eyes on me.
The bass, will start, right over here;
Now! Sing your words, with ease, and clear

The Lead Bass, he had lost his place
Was singing way behind,
Alto and Tenor, stopped at once—
Sopranos kept on trying.

The Leader, beat and banged! his stick,
Sopranos, now were flying!
The Lead Bass could not find his place,
There was no use in trying,

At last the Leader got their ear
Their hearts were trembling now, with fear,
He looked them squarely in the face,
Said he: Such stuff is 'er real disgrace.

Then, all at once, that mighty chorus!
Sang out, as if the Heavenly Host"
Had struck their harps' of gold,
The music! Oh! 'twas sweet to hear,
It seemed to bring Salvation" near
As on and on, it rolled!

The Leader stood with smiling face;
Pleased it seemed, was plain,
For weeks and months, he'd labored hard,
His work was not in vain.

"EZIKEL'S FIRST DEGREE"

Ezikel Jones was on the list,
  To take the first degree,
On Friday next the message ran,
  A quarter after three.

Poor Ziek he could not sleep that night,
  No! not to save his soul,
He dreamed he saw a billy goat—
  And climbed a greasy pole.

The appointed day Ziek got there late,
  A quarter after four,
He heard the balls arolling loud,
  Upon the second floor.

Ezikel Jones! was called out loud,
  He answered, "Here am I,"
Please come up front the master said,
  Poor Ziek! made no reply.

You see this pole? Now Brother Jones,
  It's mighty hard to climb,
Take off your coat and necktie too,
  Now start, but take your time.

There is twelve degrees, the master said,
  You'll find them on the pole,
Many a man has gone up there,
  And never had a fall.

Ziek looked right shy,
And all at once, he heard a brother call,
The goat is there, Now! Brother Jones,
To catch you if you fall.

The goat eyed Ziek and Ziek the goat,
And then he eyed the pole,
How could he climb a greasy pole,
And never have a fall.

He started up, his foot slipped back,
The goat was drawing near,
To turn back now would never do,
His heart was full of fear.

He took one step and slipped back two,
Poor Ziek was almost crying,
He could not climb that greasy pole,
There was no use in trying.

So down! he come right on the goat,
They round the room went flying,
They caught the goat and found poor Ziek,
They really thought him dying.

When Ziek revived more dead than live,
He was a sight to see,
He'd lost his coat and necktie too,
But had the first degree.

HE DIDN'T STOP TO THINK.

Ike Johnson loved a fair young girl,
  Her name was Lucy Prim,
He thought the whole wide world of her,
  And she the same of him.

He took Bill Jones to call one day,
  Which always breaks the link,
He left them there to chat awhile,
  But he didn't stop to think.

Mister Jones he liked the girl,
  And there he told her so,
Just twenty seconds by the watch,
  Before he had to go.

He asked that he might call again,
  Miss Lucy looked at him,
She told him yes and gave a smile,
  Then Ike come walking in.

Jones thanked her and he took his hat,
  And then he went away,
From that time on no thought had Jones,
  But of his wedding day.

Poor Ike his days were numbered,
  Jones did not care a wink,
The trouble about the whole thing was,
  Ike didn't stop to think.

"THE GIRL WHO DOES NOT CARE."

The girl who says she does not care a snap about a man,
Will do her level best you know,
To catch one if she can.
Of course she has no time to waste,
On Harry, Tom or Ned,
Their words were vain,
She had no ear for anything they said.

Such fun you know to come and go,
And do just as you please,
No one to boss or make you cross,
One lives in greatest ease.

How years rolled by, she knew not why,
Her life was sad and lone,
Her friends were few and those untrue,
She longed to have a home.

Very late in life she became the wife,
Of a man who lived on a farm,
She had the garden to hoe, and no place to go,
But to gather the eggs from the barn.

Now girls be wise, "Do you realize,
How time is slipping away,
When Tom comes round don't turn him down,
It may be your last chance for a day.

"OUR EXPOSITION.

Our Exposition at Richmond, Va., 1915, Colonel Jiles B. Jackson, Promoter.
To Commemorate the Fiftieth Anniversary of Emancipation.

At our coming exposition,
Let us have a disposition
To expose the best we have,
That is good and great to see.

Bring your implements of wonder!
Tear the chain of doubt asunder,
Show the nations our progressions,
Since Lincoln set us free.

At our coming exposition,
Let us have a disposition
To expose the arts and crafts
That are made by you and me.

Bring your trades of skill and labor,
Bring the work of next door neighbor,
Show the nations our progressions,
Since Lincoln set us free.

At our coming exposition
Let us have a disposition
To go up and onward ever,
In the rights of Liberty.

He who rules the world and nations,
Truly signed the proclamation,
Show the nations our progressions,
Since Jesus set us free.

"THE OLD-TIME RELIGION."

Give me dis ole time religion,
Give me dis ole time religion,
Give me dis ole time religion,
It's good enough for me.

Look heah, Brud'er! don't sing dat way.
Dah ain't no ole time religion today;
Dar's a new time kind da's got of late,
A bran new style right up to date.

You go's up now and takes de preacher's han',
And steps right over in de promise lan';
Dar's no use fur to pray, or to speak of a shout,
Fur nobody'll know what you'r' talking about.

Dar's nothing fur to do but to set right down,
Put on your robe and try on your crown;
Den wait fur de chariot to de golden shore;
No use fur to moan and pray no more.

Dar now! Brud'er, I'm sorry fur to say,
Dar ain't no ole time religion today.

"DEACON JONES"

Deacon Jones was a real good man,
As deacons ought to be;
He had one wife, as the Scripture says,
Instead of having three.

He taught a class in Sunday school,
With vigor, might and force;
He said no drunkard in the church
Could join the heavenly host.

Across the way sat Deacon Dodd,
His face all in a frown;
And tried his best to read so loud,
The deacon's words he'd drown.

"Not a drop," said Deacon Jones,
"A Christian ought to take;
No matter what your troubles are,
Not for his stomach's sake"

Deacon Dodd, he saw no harm,
In just a sip or two;
If water 'round was hard to find,
To quench the thirst 'twould do.

When Deacon Jones went home from church,
His heart was clear and clean;
He'd told them 'bout King Alcohol,
And pictured well the scene.

THOUGHTS OF IDLE HOURS

At night he sought his peaceful bed,
  To rest his weary feet;
Outside the snow was falling fast,
  And turning into sleet.

Next day when he awoke,
  Snow covered all the ground;
And from a cupboard, dark and high,
  He pulled a bottle down.

He opened it, in haste he did.
  And looking quickly 'round,
"I see no harm," said he, "to drink
  When sleet is on the ground."

"A FOOLISH MAN."

A foolish man came riding by,
A wise man said, your horse will die.
Said the fool, if he dies,
I'll tan his skin,
And if he lives, I'll ride him again.

57

"SPRING."

Oh! What joy and peace and cheer,
Fill our hearts, when spring is near;
Gone is winter's chilly blast,
Birds and flowers return at last.

Butterflies in dresses gay,
They, too, have started on their way;
Spring is here! Now let us cheer,
The happiest days of all the year.

58

"LOOKING BACK."

Looking back I see myself,
  A child just five years old;
I'd climb up in my papa's lap,
  When mom began to scold.

He'd hold me on as best he could,
  And then he'd let her fuss;
He did not mind how much she talked,
  Just so she didn't cuss.

And then he'd jump me up and down,
  And tell me 'bout Bo Peep,
Who wandered all around the town,
  And could not find her sheep.

And then he said that poor Jack Spratt,
  He had to eat the lean;
That old Mrs. Spratt, she ate the fat,
  Because she was so mean.

But oh! my mother overheard
  My father tell me that;
From that time on he ate the lean,
  And mother ate the fat.

"DOWN IN THE COUNTRY."

Down in the country where we lived,
  The girls and boys were happy;
There was no mamma nor any papa,
  But just plain mam and pappy.

'Twas Uncle Joe and Aunt Maria,
  Uncle Ned and Jerry;
All day long was one sweet song,
  The heart was always merry.

The boys and girls joined in the sport
  Of baseball, kites and marbles;
And when at church the boys sung bass,
  The girls they'd always warble.

Then after school it was the rule
  To see-saw, jump and swing;
The boys spun tops and played hip-hop,
  In fact did everything.

Such happy days and country ways,
  Indeed it was a pleasure;
The greatest joy without alloy,
  And lots of time for leisure.

"THE WANDERING SHEEP."

Sheep without a shepherd,
  Over the mountains roam,
Weak and worn, bruised and torn,
  Wandering far from home.

Helpless! Shelterless! Wandering!
  "The wolf" can find his prey;
No hand to guide, no place to hide,
  Wandering all the day.

Father, who loves the wandering sheep,
  Bring them into the fold!
They know not, Lord, what snares await,
  Shelter them from the cold.

61

"A MAN OF THE HEART."

To My Friend, Edward Barber.

Give me a man who has a heart,
  To feel another's pain;
Who'll lift a brother from the earth,
  Help him his steps to gain.

Give me a man, who has a heart,
  To bravely stand for right;
When foes assail on every hand,
  Out in the thickest fight.

Give me a man, who has a heart,
  To meet a world of frowns;
With smiling face and courage bright,
  To lift up one who's down.

"AS YOU GO FROM HOME TODAY."

As you go from home today,
Think it out upon the way;
Have you left a kiss for mother,
A loving smile for sister, brother?
Have you bade a kind goodbye,
With your spirit bright and high?
If you have the day is bright,
And the heaviest burden light.

As you go from home today,
Think it out upon the way;
Have you done your very best,
Will your work now stand the test?
Have you conscientious been
In your dealings with all men?
If you have the day is bright,
And the heaviest burden light.

As you go from home today,
Think it out upon the way;
Have you rid your soul of sin?
Are you pure and clean within?
Have you bid the devil go,
Gave him not the slightest show?
If you have the day is bright,
And the heaviest burden light.

"HE IS RISEN."

Christ our Lord was hung on Calvary,
For the sins of you and me;
That from sin and condemnation,
Jew and Gentile should be free.

Jesus Christ our Lord is risen,
On the third day as he said;
There beside the empty prison,
Roman soldiers lay as dead.

Early in the dawn of morning,
"Mary" sought her Lord with tears;
Look! Behold, He is risen!
See the tomb! He is not here.

He has risen from the prison,
Bear the tidings far and wide;
Jesus Christ, our Lord, is risen,
On this glorious Easter tide!

If in Him we die from sin,
We shall also rise again;
Death no more can have its sway,
Jesus took the sting away.

TO J. J. PEARCE.

I shall not forget your friendship,
  When the days were dark and drear;
When in trouble, pain and sadness,
  We could find you always near.

I am a prisoner in the darkness,
  Never more may be set free;
But your sympathy, kind and tender,
  Makes the world so bright to me.

As I wait here in the shadow,
  Kindly thoughts shall be of thee;
Praying that the darkness vanish,
  And your pleasant face to see.

"NEW STYLE TUNES."

To Mr. W. H. Marlow.

They've got a lot of new style tunes,
For old-time hymns today;
Why! you never hear a single hymn
Sung in the old-time way.

You never hear them singing
"Am I a soldier of the cross?"
If you did, you'd never know it,
For the tune has long been lost.

O! I'd love to hear the tunes once more,
Like mother used to sing;
"And shall I fear to own his cause,
Or blush to speak his name?"

And then that old familiar hymn,
"And, am I born to die?"
She'd sing that hymn, so high and sweet,
'Twould almost reach the sky.

And then she had another song
About the Judgment day,
"And sinners plunged beneath that flood,
Washed all their sins away."

These new time tunes may be all right,
For high-tone folks to sing;
I'd rather hear the old-time tunes,
Like mother used to sing.

UNCLE JOSHUA'S BIRTHDAY DINNER.

News had spread throughout the town,
About a birthday dinner
Uncle Joshua Crow was going to have,
And invite both saints and sinner.

He didn't exactly know his age,
He thought 'twas ninety-seven;
He said he'd have one great big time,
Before he went to heaven.

Uncle Joshua was a kind old man,
Well-known around the village;
His trade was picking rags and bones,
And other privileges.

Everybody in the town
Received an invitation;
And all began at once to make
Elaborate preparations.

In fact the little town itself
Was decorated grand;
Ike Simms was there,
And had on hand his pickaninny band.

The festal day at last arrived.
It surely was a pity;
To see the folks crowd in that room
From countryside and city.

Uncle Joshua! greeted them one and all.
  Hypocrites, saints and sinners;
When all had had their turn at him,
  He invited them out to dinner.

Such shaking hands and bowing down,
  And great congratulations,
Such crowds were never seen before,
  Not in this generation.

Uncle Joshua greeted them, one and all,
  Hypocrites, saints and sinners;
When all had had their turn at him,
  He invited them out to dinner.

The table man! Don't say a word!
  Was loaded down with chicken;
Young spring shote and o'possum, too,
  And lobster still a-kicking.

Cakes and pies, why sakes alive!
  Peanuts, dates and candy;
Blackberry roll and peach preserves,
  Hush! a jug of apple brandy.

Dinner o'er they cleared the floor,
  That music sure was singing;
Miss Dinah Diggs and Uncle Josh
  Come down the floor a-swinging.

He swung Miss Dinah up and down,
  Uncle Joshua's feet were flying;
And then he turned her round and round,
  Miss Dinah was almost crying.

Dinner o'er they cleared the floor,
That music sure was singing;
Miss Dinnah Diggs and Uncle Josh
Come down the floor a-swinging.

The music played, the people swayed.
  Hypocrites, saints and sinners;
'Twas almost day when they went away,
  From Uncle Joshua's birthday dinner.

"PITY."

Do not stand back and pity me,
If I have fallen in the sea;
If thou hath love, jump in and see,
If you can help to rescue me.

"AS I PASS BY THE WAY."

Keep not your roses,
For my dead, cold clay;
Scatter them along as I pass by the way.

Speak a kind word,
While I'm with you today;
Give me a smile as I pass by the way.

The fairest flower that blooms in the day,
Will avail me but naught,
When I've passed away.

Give me the love that I long for today,
Scatter the flowers
As I pass by the way.

"TOILING."

Year after year, in toil and pain,
Striving a bit of gold to gain;
Laboring on from day to day,
On earth to live, in stores we lay.

When at last we've gained the gold,
And troubles o'er us no more roll,
Then time steps in and bids us go,
Our days on earth shall be no more.

Others left shall take our place
With braver runners in the race;
Yet toil shall be the lot of man,
It is the Master's great command.

Lay not in store great bags of gold,
But heap up treasures for the soul;
By sweat of brow thy bread shall earn,
Long as the lamp holds out to burn.

"THE WAR IN EUROPE, 1914."

See the world in great confusion!
  Stop and think oh, mortal man!
Friend and foe alike are losing,
  Thousands fall on every hand.

Why this needless cause of battle?
  Who can answer? No, not one;
Nations, like dumb driven cattle,
  Fall as grass before the sun.

Oh! the world so vast and fruitful
  Why not here content abide?
He who owns the lands and waters,
  Will from us no good thing hide.

"O, MIGHTY SEA!"

O, Mighty Sea! Thy mournful sound,
  Forever I can hear;
O, tell me what thy troubles are,
  What burdens doth thou bear?

Forever hath thou mournful been,
  What sorrows fill thy breast?
Thy tossing billows never cease;
  Hath thou no time for rest?

Perhaps a message now you bring,
  Up from the mighty deep;
Of loved ones, near and dear to us,
  In watery graves they sleep.

O, restless sea, now pray tell me,
  What message do I hear?
I'll wait beside thy mighty waves,
  And will thy tidings bear.

"THE THOUGHTS OF MAN."

The thoughts of man are seed of nature,
  They grow as wheat, for good or ill;
In planting thought take care to scatter
  Seed of love in deep good-will.

Then watch it grow each day and hour,
  Kissed by the sunshine of the soul;
The seed you've sown will grow in power,
  The fruit it bears will ne'er grow old.

"THE BEAUTIFUL WORLD."

The beautiful world, the grass, the trees,
The sweet smelling rose,
The gentle breeze.

The fish of the sea, the birds of the air,
The little tom-tit and the grizzly bear,
Each in its class is a beauty, you see,
In this grand old world for you and me.

The beautiful world, the ice and snow,
The silvery lakes where the rivulets flow;
The rocks and caves, the shells of the sea,
In this grand old world for you and me.

The beautiful world, the mountains and hills,
The wide spreading plains, the valleys and rills,
The beast of the field, the fowl of the air,
In the world there is beauty everywhere.

"CLIMBING UP"

Do not climb so fast, my brother,
  Take your time and go it slow;
Stop and meditate a little,
  Stop and think before you go.

Then when starting do not hurry,
  Take it slowly as you climb;
Stop awhile and rest a little,
  Start again but take your time.

When at last you've reached the summit,
  You will have no vain regrets;
For you've measured well the journey,
  And each difficulty met.
        Take it slow.

"STOP AND THINK."

Just stop and think a moment,
  When the way seems rough and steep;
When trials, pain and sadness,
  Fill your soul with sorrows deep.

When the mighty waves of trouble,
  O'er you like the billows roll;
Turn your lamp up bright, my brother,
  Take a look into your soul.

"WAITING IN THE SHADOW."

I am waiting in the shadow,
 For the coming of the light,
Bright and cheerful, I am waiting.
 Fearing not the darkest night.

Oh, what peace and consolation,
 As I wait here by the way!
Thinking of the joys awaiting,
 When the mist has rolled away.

Oh, the hand that leads and guides me!
 Sure will help me all the way,
Through the daylight and the darkness,
 While I wait here by the way.

FALLEN BLOSSOMS

Lovingly

Maggie Pogue Johnson

Sheller[illegible]

FALLEN BLOSSOMS

By

MAGGIE POGUE JOHNSON

Each fragrant blossom helps us live and hope and trust
But soon for us a life it gives and crumples into dust

Printed by
The Scholl Printing Co.
Parkersburg, W. Va.

Faithfully dedicated to

My Son

WALTER W. JOHNSON, JR., M.D.

FOREWORD

I have had so many requests from friends for copies of my first book, "Virginia Dreams" and for my second book, "Thoughts For Idle Hours" and since I did not have a second edition of these books published, I decided to combine "Virginia Dreams" and "Thoughts For Idle Hours" with my third book "Fallen Blossoms". Hoping that you may find some idle moments in which you may enjoy reading these three books in one and that in reading, you may find a line or a verse which may light up within you a spark of inspiration to kindle a love anew for all mankind and help make this a better world in which to live.

A Bit About the Author

The author, Maggie Pogue Johnson, is the daughter of the late Rev. Samuel Pogue, a Baptist minister and the late Lucie Jane Pogue. She was born in the town of Fincastle, Virginia. She was the 8th—in a family of twelve children, five of which were teachers, two physicians, one druggist, one minister, one farmer and two died while very young.

She attended the public school in her home town after which she attended Virginia State College, Petersburg, Virginia, from which she graduated. After teaching school in her home town two years, she married Dr. Walter W. Johnson, of Staunton, Virginia, who was a practicing physician in the town of Covington, Virginia.

To this union one son was born, Walter W. Johnson, Jr., who was a Senior at Virginia State College at the time of his father's passing and is now a practicing physician in Covington, Virginia, having taken up his father's work.

Several pageants and plays have been written by the author and a number of songs all of which have been used on various programs but only one of which has been published, entitled "I Know That I Love You"; others have been accepted for publication. She was made mention of in "Who's Who In The Negro Race" and also several years ago in "The Negro In Virginia".

Ten years after the passing of Dr. Walter W. Johnson, Sr., she married Dr. John Wesley Shellcroft, a lifelong friend of her late husband. They reside in Parkersburg, West Virginia.

FALLEN BLOSSOMS

MUSING

Thou canst not judge what I should write
For muses swarming thro' the night
Always tell me what to say
In their own peculiar way
Thou canst not tell me what to say
For muses always have their way
And e'en though much unseen
Allow no one to come between

WE PRAY

Our Father who hast spared us thro' the night
To see the dawning of another day so bright
We thank Thee with our heart our soul our mind
That Thou to us would ever be so kind

Thus morning noon and night to Thee we pray
To have Thy angels stand in grand array
And ever let that glorious happy band
Protect America our native land

We pray Oh God! for all the lands on earth
For those who've dwelt within from birth
We beg Thee stop that devastating hand
From slaying precious souls thro' out the land

We know Oh God that sin has bro't this dearth
On all the lands of this our precious earth
But Thou hast said Thou wilt for-give
If we have faith to look and live

We pray Oh God that thro' out all the land
Those with faith will form a sacred band
To fight with swords and bombs of prayer
And free our land from ev'ry earthly care

Dear Father thus again we make our plea
To beg that this our land again be free
For peace and love and freedom once again
We beg and ask this in thy name—Amen

RASTUS LEARNS TO DRIVE

We'd got our bran new flivver
En Rastus Abe en me
Was drivin bout de city
As happy as cud be

Rastus nevah driv befo
I tho't he larned right fas
Case in a couple hours or mo
He'd done tuk on de task

Abe dont notice nuffin
He jis seemed to flop
But I had seed dat our car
Passed ebery-ting dat stopped

I says den jis to me-sef
"Ole Rastus sho kin drive
He's passed eberyting I see
As sho's Ise alibe

Odder flivvers stood in line
Like dey cud'n go
But Rastus he was mekin time
Like eny-body know

Ebery-time we passed a light
　　Dat's shinin bright en red
De leasman gibes a hollah
　　But on by Rastus sped

I tho't deys cheerin him
　　But at de nex red light
A whole line ob po-leas-mens
　　Was standin lef en right

On to de car dey jumped
　　But Rastus nebah stopped
Leasmen on de side
　　Leasmen on de top

Leasmen on de running bode
　　Leasmen on de hood
　　Callin out to Rastus Stop!
　　As ef ole Rastus cud

Dey rode on fifteen miles or mo
　　When de flivver it did stop
Leasmen bust into de doe
　　Wid a mighty flop!

"Thirteen months in jail!
　　For not stopping at the light
Six evading the police
　　I never saw the like"

"Mr. Leasman let me splain
　　As sho as I do libe
I clar dis am de fus time
　　I has ebah driv

Dat man he torch me how to drove
　　But beliebe me Mr. Cop
He showed me how to run the road
　　But nevah how to stop

3

En ef dis gas had not runned out
Dis flivver'd nevah changed it's bout
Case doe it's runnin fas en soun
I nebah larned to turn aroun"

FATHER TIME

Father Time you are so weary look so old
Yet if the story of your life were told
One could see just why your life
Of twelve long months could be so full of strife
Could be so full of worry full of care
Would each month had thought to take it's share

You started out a babe so full of zest
Seemingly prepared to with-stand any test
Youth is so innocent it has no dread
Not e'en enough to stop and think ahead

But now your long twelve months are spent
You are so weary worn and ready to repent
That you did not warn each month ahead
Just what might come and what to dread

January started out so sweet and young
With welcome words on every tongue
February a little slack—
Trying to hide the ground-hog back

March so frisky with her airs
April with her showers—prepares
The healthy body of the ground
That violets and tulips may be found

May comes in with queens and dances gay
June with weddings all along the way
July with celebrations gay and hot
Putting independence on the spot

August fixes out her resting spot
Where folks may rest while weather is so hot
September brings her leaves of red and gold
And autumn and her beauty are fore-told

October brings her cooling breeze
Making leaves all clatter on the trees
November fixes out her day of thanks
December comes with Santa and his pranks

And thus the year is spent Oh Father Time
Each month with it's own whims and varied clime
And now for you we drop a parting tear
On this the ending of your year

THE BUCKET AND CHAIN THAT HUNG IN THE WELL

Take me back to the old home town
Where folks weird stories tell
Where near the house is always found
The bucket and the well

Where still around the home place
Is seen the old arm chair
The rocker that my mother used
And the narrow winding stair

The fire place the grate
The hearth all painted red
The chimney where the swallows roost
The big four poster bed

The lace around the mantel
A cushion on each chair
The ash cake in the fire place
And each expects his share

Supper then is ready
Each one eats a spell
Then comes a cooling bucket
Of water from the well

The old well seems to whisper
Tales of long ago
Within it's rocky surface
Where cooling waters flow

The bucket tells of by-gone days
Ne'er to come again
As up and down the wind-lass
Pulls the rusty chain

The chain sings a song with the rust of the years
While the bucket in turn o'er flows with tears
The link between them has held quite a spell
And each makes it's turn each day in the well

Oh! bucket of oak Oh! rusty chain
You sing your song with a sweet refrain
As up and down on your journey you go
Quenching the thirst of those you know

You're firmly linked for you never part
And it seems you should rest a spell
But the bucket replies "Oh have a heart
I hang around in the well

You've hung around for many years
You've cheered many folks and washed away tears
You've given to some refreshing showers
Tho you hang in the well thro passing hours

In the days of going up and down
You with your chain have won a crown
As years go by many will tell
Of the bucket and chain that hung in the well

WHOSE GAME

I nevah liked to fight 'tis true
    I aint nevah picked on you
I warns you now in plenty time
    Dont you dare to cross dat line

I aint nevah said you'se mean
    I aint nevah dared to dream—
De ugly tings you'se cuzin me
    Dis heah aint no coward's plea

I aint skeered of any kid
    Dont you dare to tech dat lid—
Of de pot dat's bilin dair
    I'll fling yo remnants in de air

I killed dat rabbit skint him too
    En jis to tink de likes ob you—
Come to claim him bilin hot
    While Ise got him in de pot

Now you dare jis cross dat line
    Ef you wants to see me shine
I'll beat you 'till you'se black en blue
    I dun got enuf of you

LIVE FOR ME

Live for me and let your life be clean and true
    Live for me and others will not laugh at you
Live for me for life at most is drear
    Live for me you'll not regret it dear

Live for me your life will be one grand sweet song
Live for me the days and years will not seem long
Live for me yes live and ever chant and sing
Live for me the years with joy and ecstacy will ring

Live for me the sun will shine so bright
Live for me my burdens will seem light
Live for me I will not scold nor chide
Live for me and be my happy bride

Live for me and let our two lives blend
And peace and joy and hope to other lives we'll lend
Live for me the world will not be cold and drear
Live for me you'll not regret it dear

WHEN THE CIRCUS COMES TO TOWN

Chillun git yo wuk all done
Taint no time fer play
Better min me now my son
Case 'morrow's Circus Day

Dar's gwine to be good times I know
Dey cums from near en far
En Mandy's gwine to see dat show
You heah? she'll be right dar

Dar wont nobody duk dat day
Case 'taint no time I know
Dat you cud gibe dat kin ob pay
To keep folks from a show

No indeedy when de sign
Is pasted on some stables
Folks begin to git der dimes
As fas as dey is able

Dey mite be poe wid out a cent
I clar it show is funny
But eberyting has paid der rent
En got der Circus money

En Ole man Si and Jimmy Gray
En Hester Jones en Ike
Is all in town at peep ob day
I nebah saw de like

En too old grandpa Henry Diggs
Was nebah knowd to fail
To cum in wid his one hoss rig
Wid lemonade fer sale

Voice a quiverin wid age
As he gibes a call
Come en git yo lemonade - - - - ! !
Ice col de bes ob all!

En Sallie Brown en Anna Fry
Dey allus has a stan
Wid chicken cake en pie
De fines in de lan

Chicken fried so nice en brown
It sho looks good to me
En when de Circus cums to town
I'se happy as kin be

I stans en watch em fall in line
To start de gran parade
Animals ob ebery kine
While de Circus ban it played

De Elephant was fus to come
Followed by de ape
De monkey in a great big cage
Standin at de gate

De hosses dey did march in line
Ponies dey did too
De Zebra like a barber sign
En den de kangaroo

All did seem to step in line
Marchin to de front
But de camel took his own good time
As he followed wid his hump

Ob all de cuts en monkey shines
Is made by dat ole clown
Dey sho do git de peoples dimes
When de Circus cums to town

STROLLING IN THE MOONLIGHT

We went strolling in the moonlight
Many many years ago
Yes how well do I remember
All the beauty all the glow —

Of that soft moonlight still beaming
Lighting up the hills afar
Moon Oh moon your gentle streaming
Hides the glitter of each star

Oft times I can see the picture
Clear as tho' it were to day
Bringing back the happy past time
Of those years so far away

Visions come and visions linger
As the pictures come and go
Of that far off country hill-side
'Neath the old moon's mellow glow

Moon Oh moon! your soft light glowing
    Brings back mem'ries of the past
With your light thrown on the hill-side
    Where e'en shadows come and pass

Years have passed we still are strolling
    'Neath the mellow Summer moon
Bringing back the happy mem'ries
    Singing old familiar tunes

Thinking of the many old friends
    As we march yea! to an fro
Where is now the merry party
    We remembered long ago

They are scattered o'er the world wide
    Some still marching to an fro
'Neath the glimmer of the moonlight
    As in days of long ago

WHEN YOU ARE NEAR

When you are near the whole world turns to song
    When you are near no day is drear or long
The sun comes out the winter turns to Spring
    Blossoms sprout and birds begin to sing

When you are near all nature seems to change
    When you are near her winter togs all re-arrange
The dull and track worn carpet turns to green
    And pink buds peeping here and there are seen

When you are near the clouds are pink and gold
    And unseen beauty quickly does unfold
When you are near the stars all peep and twinkle
        at the sight
    The moon gives warning with her silver light

When you are near the birds begin to sing
    And warble out their little song "Tis Spring"
When you are near the clouds all fade away
    And make this dark old earth one brilliant day

When you are near all malace and all hate
    Are blocked by roads of cheer which lead to fate
And mirth and joy and love are all aglow
    When you are near the whole earth seems to know

THE WATER MELON MAN

Water Melon! jis as ripe
    Suits de fines appetite
Meat so mellow! meat so red
    makes a fellow shake his head

Water melons! come en buy!
    Ef a slice you will but try
You'll have a dyin fit
    You can't help yo-self a bit

You aint seed no melons fine
    Like dese ones on Tony's vine
Blackes seed en redes meat
    Takes a fellah off his feet

Water melons! what you say?
    Jis aint got de price to pay
See you den dis time nex yeah
    Dese aint credit melons here

Not de way I wuked dem vines
    To mek dese melons all dis fine
I aint gibin dem away
    Les I git some kin ob pay

Wuk dem melons all de day
    Til dey git so big en ripe
Den wid out a sign ob pay
    Sets up all de live long night

Les some good fer nuffin chap
    What has a melon appetite
Fines de patch takes off his cap
    En eats de melons all dat's ripe

I dun wuk too long I say
    On dem water melon vines
Dey dont go wid out some pay
    Is what's bin on my mind

JIM'S THO'TS

I jim am sot to thinkin
    Ob dis worl we's libin in
Ob de turmoil en de troubles
    How it's cler brimful ob sin

De folks dont go to churches
    Like dey did in days gone by
Der minds is clean cler out ob place
    I sits en wonders why

THANKSGIVING DAY

This day Oh God we give to Thee
    Who gave us life and love and made us free
To Thee who keepest us thro thick and thin
    That we might live with Thee and dwell within

This day Oh God a day of praise and thanks
Not given for frivolity or pranks
But that we might free ourselves of depths of love
By pouring out our thanks to Thee above

Oh God we know not where to start
But do acknowledge with a contrite heart
We have not lived so close with daily prayer
As should we live—we who're in Thy care

But Thou yes art a merciful forgiving God
Who knoweth all our tho'ts and ev'ry inch of earth we trod
We beg for-give-ness for in Thee we do confide
Thou dost for-give that we might in Thy love abide

VACATION DAYS

Vacation days are over
But memory is sweet
The honey-sucks and clover
were fragrant at our feet
The honey bees were humming
Gath'ring sweetness from the vine
While Jim and I were strummin
Pop'lar tunes of olden time

I remember mother singing
Many songs of long ago
"Silver Threads" and "Swanee River"
"Loves Sweet Song" and "Old Black Joe"
How the mem'ry haunts me ever
As I see her smiling face
Understanding sweet and clever
Ah! there's none can take her place

FORSAKEN CHILD

A child was standing on the street
His home was drear and cold
No shoes to cover naked feet
"You must not beg" he's told

Other children passed him by
With shoes and hat and clothes
A big tear dropped he wiped his eye
"I must not beg I knows"

He wanted so to be like them
To go to Sunday School
He had no hat no shoes no clothes
The day was biting cool

But he was happy there to stand
And see the others go
Some day I'll grow to be a man
Then I'll have things I know

A TALK WITH DAD

Dad I'd like to speak to you
Just a hasty word or two
I see you now give Ma the wink
But I'm not joking as you think

You've been mighty good to me
List'ning to my ev'ry plea
When in fact I'm kinda bad
But you're just a dandy Dad

I'm disobedient at school
    Breaking all the teacher's rules
I've been wrong in ev'ry way
    Making zeros ev'ry day

Coming home you smile at me
    Then jis caus I feel so free
I tell you all the things I've done
    Then you start like this "My Son—

Daddy wants an honest man
    One who does the best he can
One who never breaks the rule
    In church at home or in the school

Daddy always wants to see
    His son as happy as can be
But trying too as best he can
    To be a good and honest man

So Dad I think what you have done
    That I might have a world of fun
I've had scooters I've had skates
    Boxing gloves to try my traits

I've had sleds and base ball bats
    Billy goats ponies dogs and cats
It seems that wishes made each day
    You have granted in some way

You've done ev'rything for me
    You've been faithful kind and true
And when I think of all Ah gee!
    It's my time now to do for you

I'm starting out to day dear Dad
    To work and do my best
I'll prove the sturdy lad
    Who'll show he'll stand the test

I'm trudging to the road of fame
    No day I'll ever stop
Nor even tell my name
    Until I've reached the top —

Where great men of to day have gone
    Men who've scaled the heights
And glitter in this waiting world
    As bright and shining lights

What men have done Dad—men can do
    The world needs men good men and true
I'm now Fifteen yea! just a lad
    But you'll be proud of me dear Dad

AMERICA

America to thee we sing!
    Our land so free our land so brave
Our tributes yea! to thee we bring
    We'll fight America to save!

America thou cradled me
    When but a babe at birth
I'll never know nor see
    A dearer land on earth

No skies to me are e'er so blue
    No stars are e'er so bright
No land can ever be so true
    As this our land of light

We pray that we may ever stand
    'Neath skies of true ethereal blue
To honor this our native land
    America! Our land so true

We pray that we shall ever be
While leaning on our God above
A nation honest brave and free
'Neath His protection care and love

America! thy flag so true
Shall ever wave red white and blue
We'll never let her trail the dust
For in our flag we hope and trust!

MEMORIES

[The author was invited to speak at Virginia State College on President's Day using as a subject, "Virginia State College As I Knew It As A Student" she closed her speech with this poem.]

Dedicated to Dr. John Manuel Gandy, President of Virginia State College (Now Pres. Emeritus)

Far beneath the hardened surface
Of the velvet campus lay
Many foot-prints of alumnae
'Neath the strata of the clay
Foot-prints made by those who wandered
O'er the campus to an fro
Making path-ways for the future
Path-ways they were wont to know

Those were days, yes happy bygones
Days we never can forget
E'en tho we've strayed far from them
Mem'ries linger with us yet
Days when merry peals of laughter
Rang out softly on the air
Oft we listen for the echo
In the ether yet somewhere

Somewhere happy tho'ts do linger
    Somewhere uttered speech has flown
Somewhere in the far off somewhere
    Voices linger yet unknown
Voices from this dear old Campus
    Voices of the long ago
In the happy sea of somewhere
    Voices you would want to know

Even now I oft times wonder
    In the evenings calm and still
Should we hear some brave instructors
    From the past years on the "Hill"
Would we recognize the voices
    And rejoice to hear the tone
Or would they float un-recognized
    Back to some-where all alone

I can see the school assembled
    Yes the school of long ago
I can hear the voices mingle
    Students marching to and fro
From the Chapel to the class rooms
    Where with eager minds and zest
Students study to make records
    That they might withstand the test

I can see the brave instructors
    Shaping-moulding-brain and brawn
Working for the future leader
    'Til sun-set again at dawn
I can hear the voices singing
    In the chapel "Sweet and Low"
Where is now the merry party
    Of that long yes long ago

Some have gone to far off regions
Some have waited yet to know—
And meet others by the fire-side
With it's soft and cherry glow
Some have braved the hardened winters
Faced the Summers calm and cool
Praying as they journey onward
For their leader and their school

For their dear old Alma mater
May her colors gold and blue
Always wave for higher standards
Ever faithful ever true
Never cringing—never failing
Never losing in her fame
Pray to God she keeps her record
For their's glory in a name

LIFE OF A FLOWER

You're rocked to sleep by the howling wind
And covered with blankets of snow
You calmly rest 'til the birdies sing
And then you'll awake you know

Your long long sleep gives you rest and life
To awake 'mid beauteous song
You have no dream of the battling strife
Of the world as she struggles along

Your coverlet of downy white
Transforms to a living green
And you awake from the long long night
To your day where you are queen

Queen of the earth until the leaves
Turn to yellow and gold
And rippling waves and gurgling seas
Their tales of love unfold

Queen of the earth so long as the dead
Are planted beneath the sod
With chants thro' the hours they lay 'neath the flowers
With their souls returned to God

SMILES

Which would you rather wear going to town
A new hat gingham dress a smile or a frown
A new hat perhaps few people would see
And none would so recognize but you or me

Gingham dress 'bout the same for many more seen
Would take off the smartness the color or sheen
A frown would cause others to soon turn their heads
In another direction with great fear and dread

But a smile'd be remembered by all whom you met
They'd say "Twas a face I can never for-get
If I'd meet her again it matters not where
I'd know that sweet smile and most pleasant air

She'd make you for-get you'd worked hard all day
That money was scarce you'd received little pay
You'd e'en lose the hunger you had coming to town
If all faces wore smiles instead of dread frowns

You'd skip down the street with a satisfied air
Going home or to town it matters not where
You'd think life worth living yes life worth the while
If each day you'd meet that girl with the smile"

TO AN OLD TREE

[Reveries of one born in slavery who spent his childhood days under an old tree playing while mother worked in the Big House.]

Many years have passed old tree
    Since I sat beneath thy boughs
Great things in fancy I could see
    And make my childish vows
That some day I'd be grown
    And since you sheltered me
You'd never be a lone
    And unprotected tree

Many years have passed old tree
    Since I have had a chance
Thy massive form to see
    Or even give a glance
As in the days of old
    When often in great glee
I'd pluck thy leaves of red and gold
    And cuddle under thee

Many years have passed in which
    In mem'ry I could see
The velvet lawn the ditch
    And thee my dear old tree
I'd see my childish self
    With mud pies all content
Resting 'neath thy shelt'ring arms
    And thus my hours were spent

In constant daily reverie
    I'd fall asleep and dream of thee
Thy beauty and thy fragrance sweet
    With blossoms falling at my feet
No place was e'er so sweet to me
    No quiet yea! so calm
Like that thou gavest me
    When sheltered 'neath thy arms

And tho' I'm stricken now with age
I stand and look at thee
Tears blot the lines on Life's old page
In memory of thee
And should I die I'd be content
So happy yea! so free!
To sleep where child-hood days were spent
'Neath thy balmy shade dear tree!

THOUGHTS OF A SOLDIER

America And You

I would not venture now to write
To tax my brain from morn 'til night
I would not seek to lose the time
For any pompous fame or shrine
But I would go Yea! out my way
Would seek to work both night and day
Make any sacrifice 'tis true
For dear America and You

America! that land divine
America! our home our shrine
'Neath shining stars and skies so bright
America for thee we fight!
We could not leave our mothers out
Each terms us as her "brave boy scout"
And mother dear you know 'tis true
We love America and you!

MY FAITH

Oh gracious God my Maker who knoweth ev'ry care
To Thee I come dear Father and humbly bow in prayer
I thank Thee God for everything that Thou hast done for me
And thus I humbly bow Oh Lord to offer praise to Thee

We know that Thou art good we know that Thou dost care
We know that Thou art merciful and Thou dost answer prayer
We know that sins abound in lands both near and far
We pray that guilty souls will seek that guiding star

That star which leads to Thee Oh God and shines so bright and clear
That none may lose the way though the night be dark and drear
That star which led men years ago who sought thine only son
And found Him through that brilliant light that Thy will might be done

We know that in Thy wisdom Thou dost plan the way
And thus with faith in Thee Oh God we humbly bow and pray
That Thou mightest touch the hearts of those who need more faith in Thee
That all the world may live in peace we beg with this our plea

OUR COUNTRY'S CALL

[Dedicated to the relatives of those who lost their lives in World War I.]

Our Country's call! our boys went marching on
To time of drum to tune of song
'Mid many a hidden tear many a broken heart
The old ship drew to pier our boys with friends must part

Our Country's call! our boys went sailing on
To Time of drum to tune of song
To dare to do to die away
Their Country's call they must obey

Our Country's call 'mid heat of summer sun
Our boys went marching on to beat of drum
They sang and marched and called "To arms ye braves!"
Stalwart steady sons their lives they gave

And now in Flanders Field so far away
Our hearts go searching 'mid the foreign clay
To kneel beside those forms so dear
And let them know that we are near

In Flanders Field there lying side by side
The rich the poor alike have died
With hearts alike they died so brave and true
Alike each gave his life for me for you

In Flanders Field where stalwart sons went down
And won each for him-self a warrior's crown
Are braves with not a marker at their heads
Whose forms are numbered with the "Unknown dead"

In Flanders Field the poppies side by side
Were witnesses to many a soul who died
And now to day they too with bowed down head
Alike give homage to their honored dead

Oh Flanders Field and let us ever pray
　　That soon will come the wanted day
When men of this earth must defy
　　That shot and shell should say when men must die

Oh Flanders Field Oh poppies red
　　Give homage to your honored dead
And let us ever pray again
　　That peace on earth shall ever reign

HALLOW E'EN

Come heah chile I's skeered to deaf
　　Dont you see I'se out of breaf
Sumpin funny in de air
　　Spooks is 'pearin ebery-where
I jis stepped out-side de house
　　Tippin quiet as a mouse
When dey popped up all aroun
　　I 'mos fell den to de groun

You jis can't go out eny-where
　　Case dey's flyin in de air
Spose dey snatch you off de groun
　　No! I aint gwine to town
Spirrets heah spirrets dere
　　I jis see em ebery-where
Can't you see em look! look! look!
　　Look out dar you see dat spook?

Now what do you jis think it is
　　What you think it aint it tiz
Dey's spirrets I done tole you dat
　　Whar you been en whar's you at?
Ah! dis heah day is Hallow E'en
　　De day dat spooks is allus seen
Eben yo own spirret's out
　　Wan'drin roun en all about

Look! dey jis skeers me so
    I heah em knockin at my doe
Dey's at my winder sho's you born
    Yellin out en flingin corn
I'se gwine drive em all away
    En I say I dont mean no play
Git out spirrets! flee! flee! flee!
    No mo Hollow E'en fer me

RIDDLE

What is it? so very white
    A handful is so very light
It always thrills you when it's new
    It's light and sometimes heavy too
It's very high then very low
    It follows you where e'er you go
That's when it comes into your town
    You sometimes welcome it around. **(Answer Snow)**

ANGELINA WEDS

Dar was 'citement in de village
    En all de country 'round
When de notice it was read out
    By Parson Reuben Brown—
"Dat on next Wednesday mornin
    Edmon Rufus Johnson White
Will be boun in matrimony
    To Miss Angelina Knight

All is vited to be present
Gent'men all mus war full dress
Ladies wid yo tucks en ruffles
Try to look yo bery bes"
Dar needn't be no odder viting
Case de news it farly flew
En when Wednesday morning cum I tell you
Dem folks knowd jis what to do

All de mules en all de hosses
Dey was hitched en placed in line
Gals wid fellows in de ox-cart
Gwine to see Miss Angeline
Sich anodder fuss en coatin
Mules a stallin on de road
Hosses too dey got to balkin
Case dey had sich heaby load

De hour fixed was Seben Thirty
En dey started in a rush
But de teams had all got stalded
Case de roads was in a mush
De bride en groom dey was behin
Ed der ole hoss did farly fly
'Til dey kotch up wid de odders
Den dey axed to let dem by

But dar was no room to pass
Case de teams was two abreas
Mule teams hoss teams en de ox teams
Side by side wid all de res
Den de folks all in de ox cart
Dey did jump out one by one
Ole Jim Buster was de driver
He said "Sumpin mus be done—

Case de hour is fas proaching
    When de bride en groom mus wed
We'll hab to move dese hosses
    Cum en hep us Uncle Ned"
Uncle Ned he cums a hoppin
    Wid his high silk beaver hat
En his big leg pants a floppin
    Stumped his toe en fell right flat

Sich anodder lookin mess
    En he to gib de bride away
Standin mud from head to foot
    Eyes en mouf all full ob clay
"You had no business axin me
    You scoundrel see what you's done
Ruined me en all dese clos
    Dat I borrowed from Jim Gun

En all dis nice silk beaver hat
    It am all done ruined too
I kin nebah pay fer dat
    What on earf is I to do"
While he stan dar sayin dat
    Up jumped ole man Jimmy Cole
Him en ole man Eli Black
    Wid a heaby cedar pole

Placed it under dem two mules
    Prized dem out de big mud hole
Den yo heah de folks a yellin
    "Gib three cheers for Jimmy Cole!"
Den dey gib dem mules a cut
    Chillun dey did sholy fly
Eb'ry team was in de road
    Dem two mules did pass dem by

Soon dey rived right to de chuch
    Preacher he's already dar
Wid his boots en socks off restin
    Case he'd walked so bery far
De chuch it was all decerated
    Wid apple blossoms pink en white
Pine tops hangin to de center
    Mornin glories fresh en bright

Sunflowers wid der heads a bowin
    Johnny-jump-ups by der side
All a bowin en a smilin
    In full honor ob de bride
Dogwoods too did gib der honor
    Ox-eye daisies snowy white
All a blossomin in honor
    Of Miss Angelina Knight

De bride she woe white satin
    Wid a veil dat totch de flo
En a long train to her dress
    Reachin cler bac to de doe
She woe white satin slippers too
    Little gals dey hel her trail
She cum down de aisle a trippin
    Doe she's walkin on some nails

De ladies marched down one aisle
    De gent'men down de odder
While strollin long behin
    Cum Angelina's mudder
She a walkin wid a cane
    A kerchief on her heahd
A long stem pipe was in her mouf
    As down de aisle she sped

De preacher was a little late
De Reverend Richard Root
His feet had swole up so
He couldn't war his boots
En he cum down de aisle
De bride en groom to meet
A bowin en a smilin
In his stockin feet

En Uncle Ned was standin dar
To gib de bride away
You cud skercely see his face
Fer all de mud n clay
You sholy wud bin boun to laf
Case he wid all his pride
Standin dar in all dat mud
To gib away de bride

De preacher axed Miss Angeline
"Ef she'd take dis lubin man
En cherish him thro' troubles
Doe dey be as grains of sand
En ef you tinks you lubes him
Fer better or fer wuss
De answer is I do
Doe yo' life might be a cuss"

Miss Angeline she gibes a smile
En twis her head jis so
"I do but Mr. Preacher
Please dont ax no mo"
He tuns den to de groom
Says he "Well brudder White
Kin you kere fer dis heah lady
Thro de gloomy days en bright

Kin you meet her wid a smile
Doe youse angry as a bar
Ef you kin my deares brudder
De answer is I swar"
Wid perspiration drippin
Mr. White he bowed his head
In solemn wuds he said "I swar
Now hand her to me Ned"

Ned let a loose her arm
As she kotch hol Brudder White
De Preacher said "I nounce you
As her husban she yo' wife"
Den dey 'ceived de gratulations
En marched on up de aisle
Each gent'man wid his lady
Dey a struttin in sich style

Rigs outside de doe a waitin
Hosses trying not to stan
Mules a kind er actin gaily
Oxen dey a raisin sand
All was gibin ob der honors
Showing forth der great delight
In carryin off de bridal party
Of Edmon Rufus Johnson White

OUR PRAYER (Prayer for Peace)

[Used in the Year Book of the Woman's Study Club of Parkersburg and many copies sent over seas during World War II to boys of all races.]

Oh God we thank Thee for this day
For every blessing every care
And thus at eventide we pray
We offer this our fervent prayer

We thank Thee for the sunshine and the rain
For food for raiment and for gain
Such as Thou wouldst give us as our share
To help us live and cherish and forbear

Oh God give us again a peaceful land
We pray Thee give us minds to understand
And do the things that Thou wouldst have us do
To make us constant tried and true

We pray Thee for the fathers and the sons afar
And beg of Thee to be their guiding star
And bring them safely home again
With peace for all the world we beg—Amen

DEDICATION DAY

Dedicated to the memory of the late Dr. W. H. Moses

[Having been asked by the pastor the day previous, the author sat up until the wee hours, wrote these verses and read them to a large audience the following afternoon at Mt. Zion Baptist Church, Staunton, Va.]

What means this vast assemblage here
Of people great and grand
Who've come to us from afar and near
At the heed of one's commands

Why come ye to Mt. Zion's walls
Ye folks in grand array
"We've heeded to the pastor's call
'Tis Dedication Day"

List! hear ye not those songs
Which pour forth streams of love
It seems that some Angelic throng
Has sent them from above

Why are these souls with music stirred
What means all this I pray
Can it be you haven't heard
'Tis Dedication Day

The work of a hand is finished
The toil of a tay is done
One's labor is diminished
Yet a great work to be done

We stand 'mid beauty and splendor
And gaze on these sacred walls
While our hearts many thanks do tender
To Him who dost heed our calls

You've struggled yea! toiled unceasing
To complete a glorious work
Each day new efforts increasing
Daring not shrink nor shirk

Part of your toils are at an end
And part yea just begun
As your feeble efforts blend
In love to the Holy One

And now you have assembled here
'Mid efforts good and great
With happy hearts minds full of cheer
A gift to dedicate

To dedicate means to give to God
And may He who inspires us to live
And trod each day earth's lowly sod
Instill in us power to give

And as we our minds in holiness lift
We offer to Him above
A sacred yea! a noble gift
In honor of His love

For 'twas He who gave us power
    To erect this building grand
A monument to tower
    A glory to this land

Let all unite in these songs
    Yea your feeble voices lift
And help this mighty throng
    To dedicate this gift

And thank your God above
    For the true hearted leader he sent
He's led seven years in love
    Calling sinners to repent

He's toiled for Mt. Zion's Daughters and Sons
    That they might a true people be
That they live in love to the Holy One
    Has been his prayer and plea

'Tis Moses He sent to lead you
    That you heed His gentle command
He'll lead you safely thro'
    'Til you've reached the promised Land

A man inspired by God
    He a noble work has done
He'll reap his just reward
    When the harvest time has come

And to Mt. Zion's daughters and sons
    I pray that your life may be
An emblem of the Holy One
    From strife and malice free

And may the good Saviour above
    Bless this congregation great
As they in prayers and songs of love
    This building dedicate

And to all who have helped in the cause
You've won for yourself renown
I pray you abide in His laws
He'll add many stars to your crown

[The pastor, the late Dr. Wm. Moses, spent his last years in New York City where he pastored until his health prevented. Eager to do he wrote a number of books while confined to his bed.]

THE ROSE

Take not this rose from me
If thou'd not be guilty of theft
Rob me not of this beauty flower
If thou'rt not of reason bereft

This simple little rose I prize
Yea! not for it's name
But for it's every day use
Whis has bro't it world wide fame

Take not this rose from me
For it may not aid you much
But it gives me magic power
And too would rob me of such

Ah! dear little rose thou hast bro't much joy
To the hearts of many I know
Thou hast bro't smiles to the sweet-heart
When handed by a beau

Thou hast bro't joy and sunshine
To many a gloomy heart
Ah! blessed little rose
I cannot from thee part

Take not this rose from me
    Oh ye little flower!
The gracious God above
    Gives you wondrous power

He makes the whole world smile
    When on thy face they gaze
Bewildered by thy beauty
    They offer up great praise

Thou bringest joy to the sick
    To have thy presence there
Thou spreadest joy and sunshine
    Alike yea! every where

And dear little flower
    E'en however small
We rue the coming of the day
    To see thy petals fall

To see thy petals one by one
    Drop wiltered to the ground
Tells us too thy work is done
    Thou'st already won thy crown

Dear little rose thou'rt blushing now
    To hear me call thee dear
But with thy attractive beauty
    I'd love thee always near

I'd love to see thy blushing face
    Always before my eyes
I'd then forget the cloudy day
    And too see clearer skies

Ah clearer skies! for then the clouds
    Would gladly give their space
To let the blessed sunshine
    On thy smiling face

Dear little rose thou'rt drooping now
Thou art getting weak
Would'st thou have one drop of water
To cool thy burning cheek

Or would'st thou rather droop
And slowly die away
Until the coming Spring
Thy resurrection day

When thou in all thy beauty
Wilt shine forth ever new
To perform thy lasting duty
Ever faithful true

Yea! to perform thy lasting duty
To the sick and to the dead
Dear rose that thou art loyal
Hast been nobly said

Take not this rose from me
From it I will not part
To me 'tis ever dear
I'll press it to my heart

The withered leaves I'll keep
That I may have them near
For the mem'ry of the precious rose
I'll hold yea! ever dear

AUNT CLOE'S TRIP TO SEE MISS LIZA KYLE

I'se been libin in de country
Fer lo dese many years
Country life to me am dear
Wid no worry en no fears

But a frien had kindly axed me
To de city fer a while
Dat I might joy de city life
De pleasure en de style

Ob style I nebah tho't befo
En I wondered what was bes'
Since to de city I mus go
Whar folks all stood de tes'

Well I pondered en I wondered
How I mus dress in style
To go into de city
To see Miss Liza Kyle

So I writ to her a letter
"Dear Liza says I den
Dese few lines I writes to you
As I takes in han my pen

I aint so well to day
En I hopes you is de same
I has de rheumatiz so bad
Dat makes me kinder lame

I'll try to be in readiness
To leabe here Tuesday late
But Lize I wants to know de styles
Case when I nears yo gate—

I wont be called so countrified
Not by a hundered miles
When you see Cloe right at yo doe
She's gwine to be in style

So splain to me jis how to dress
So anything I lac'
I'll fix en make mysef look good
Case I wont be no ways bac'

I specs to heah from you right soon
    In a week or mo'
Wid lots ob lube en kisses
    I'm lubingly, Ant Cloe"

Well a day or two had passed
    When I got from her a letter
I'se feelin kinder scrumptious den
    Case my rheumatiz was better

En I felt jis right to go to wuk
    To fix mysef in style
To go into de city
    To see Miss Liza Kyle

"Dear Aunt Cloe, de lines read
    I was glad to get your letter
And truly hope by this
    You're feeling something better

Yes fix yourself in style
    I'll meet you Tuesday late
For the folks wont understand
    Unless you're up-to-date

You must wear a hobble skirt
    Your hair in puffs must be
With a band of ribbon round your head
    Where a bow you'll fix you see

Your shoe heels must be very high
    And make yourself look small
Be careful too just how you walk
    Or else you'll have a fall

You'll have to take short steps
    In your hobble skirt you see
But that's the latest thing
    And in style you must be

Your hat must be extremely large
With a feather quill behind
And then you'll be a model sure
Aunt Cloe you'll just look fine

I enclose a picture here
Cut from a fashion book
To show exactly how—
The hobble skirt will look

Now imitate the picture
The skirt looks rather tight
But lace your stoutness down
And then you'll be alright

"Well Fodder what a picture
Dat skirt looks awful tight
En fer me to war a ting like dat
I know I'd look a sight"

I goes to seamstress nex day
Wid dress goods under arm
To hab my hobble made
So I cud leabe de farm

A handsome piece of red I took
Wid green to make de border
En axed de seamstress please
To make my skirt in order

"Jis like dis picture heah
Case I mus be in style
To go into de city
To see Miss Liza Kyle"

De picture called fer four yards
But didn't say de size
Ob de woman in de picture
En I was den surprised

When I took two yards ob each
Two ob green en two ob red
De seamstress shook her head
It aint enuf she said

Well do de bes you kin I said
I got four yards in all
Dat's all de picture called fer
En I aint near dat tall

Dat's all de samples dat dey had
In colors dat was bright
En I wants to look a little gay
When I gits dar Tuesday night

Well I goes to git my dress nex day
En de seamstress she did tell
'Twas de fus one she had done in style
En tho't she'd done so well

"I jis did have enuf" she said
So I made de front ob green
En de bac I made ob red
Whar it wouldn't be much seen"

I axed her den to hep me dress
En git mysef in style
To go into de city
To see Miss Liza Kyle

I guess de puffs is used fer bangs
Case I haint seed dem befo
So I pins dem on de front my head
En behin I puts a bow

De puffs felt heaby on my head
But I knowd I'se in style
To go into de city
To see Miss Liza Kyle

I den puts on de hobble
    En Oh! but it was tight
Sich a squeezin I did do
    To get my skirt on right

I was den so sorry
    I didn't put my hat on fus
Case I was skeered to move
    For fear my skirt wud bus

I takes de train fer New York
    Wid satchel in my han
En de car it was so crowded
    En dar I had to stan

De folks dey looked me up en down
    But I knowd I'se in style
To go into de city
    To see Miss Liza Kyle

De Ductor axed me whar I'se gwine
    Ef I'se on de proper car
I tole him none ob his bizness
    Jis so I paid my far

Soon we landed in de city
    De city ob New York
En de folks dey stood in swarms
    As we landed on de walk

I seed Miss Liza she steps bac
    En den she starts to run
I says "Hole on dar—
    None ob dat city fun

I specs you doesn't know me
    In all dis city style
Dis is Ole Ant Cloe
    Does you hear me Liza Kyle"

I calls out again
 Den she starts out walkin fas'
En I was right behin her
 But I tell you 'twas a task

Case my hat cum cler down on my nec'
 My puffs was in my eyes
My shoe heels pitched me up so high
 I tho't I'se in de skies

En ebery step I'd make
 My skirt wud pull me bac'
'Til I took de scissors out de grip
 En ripped it down de bac'

I pulled dem high heel shoes off
 En den I sho did run
To ketch ole Liza Kyle
 But I tell yo 'twarn't no fun

She wid dem city friens
 Didn't want to own
Precious ole Ant Cloe
 But I followed her right home

Wid my hobble skirt cut down de bac
 My high heel shoes in han
I followed her right in de doe
 En she was raisin san

Mutterin out some hobo
 Had made a big mistake
En I was settin dar so warm
 I tho't dat I wud bake

She sent de sarvents in
 Said dey "Dar's some mistake
Lady, you'se missed de number
 We's skeered we's mos' disgraced"

I flung my shoes right in der face
No leasman in de lan—
Kin git me out ob here
Right here I takes my stan

Ef dis am de greeting dat you git
When you cums in style
I'll war ole clos de nex time
To see Ole Liza Kyle

CHRISTMAS TIME

When are the children all happy and gay
When do they ne'er grow tired of play
When do their mouths seem like bells in their chime
It is the merry Christmas time

When do the little boys all get good
And bring in the coal and cut all the wood
And ev'ry command of their parents mind
'Tis just a week before Christmas time

That is the time when all the work
Is done without a grumble or shirk
The little boys then ne'er turn or twist
When mother says "Son come here and do this"

Let the word be said he's at her command
Not once does he frown nor attempt to stand
But goes at her bidding all happy and gay
He knows it will soon be Christmas Day

And then Old Santa thro' all the snow
Will come to those who've been good you know
Down the chimney he'll come and will not stop
'Til ev'ry stocking is filled to the top

When his task is o'er he takes his stand
Gazing at little ones off in Dreamland
Who in that land all happy and gay
Their minds all fixed on Christmas day

And in a few hours with merry hearts
Little ones out of their warm beds dart
All happy and gay hearts full of cheer
To see what's been bro't by Santa dear

How happy now each little mind
When ev'ry stocking full they find
With presents scattered on the floor
Now could they ever wish for more

No no but for many a year
Christmas time to them will be dear
And e'en in their prayers they make a pause
To ask many blessings on Santa Claus

JIM'S BABY SITTING JOB

Christmas time was drawin nigh
En jobs was hard to get
Dar was presents yit to buy
But wid no luck I met
I started out to hunt a job
'Mid all de Christmas glitter
En lookin thro de Want Ads
I read dis "Baby Sitter"

Mrs Jones on Harding Street
Number Sixty-eight
Wants a Baby Sitter

Who kin stay out late
I goes en dresses up
White shirt en black neck tie
De bestest suit I got
Wid shoes a shinin high

I looks into de glass
Well Jim I do de-clar
You looks good enuf
To set up any whar
En what I calls a swell job
Dressed in my Sundays bes
Jis to set in cushioned cheers
En watch de baby res

I started out fer Harding Street
De number Sixty-eight
I was walkin bery fas
To keep from being late
I run de dor bell bery hard
De lady let me in
All out ob bref I axed my-sef
Is dis de place fer Jim

I cum in answer to your ad
(My heahd was in a whirl)
"We do not want a man nor lad
But a good and trusty girl"
Lady I'se out ob wuk
En Christmas time is nigh
Not a cent fer Old St. Nick
Wont you let me try?

"Can you bathe a baby
Can you feed a child
Can you put a babe to sleep
Is your temper mild?"

Dont mek me answer dis
    Jis go en let me try
Jobs is hard to git
    En eberyting is high

Well, we'll be back at Twelve
    Perhaps as late as One
Good luck to you my man
    Have the job well done
Now Gertie goes to bed at Eight
    She has her night clothes on
Give her a glass of milk
    Make it a little warm

Neddie wont retire so soon
    He's been asleep all day
After he gets his milk
    Perhaps he'll want to play
He takes milk from a bottle
    Sterilize all Six
Give him just one to night
    In which you fix this mix—

Three ounces of water to which you add
    Of Carnation milk just four
He may fret a little
    Dont give him any more
While the milk is getting warm
    You may sweep the kitchen floor
Wash the dishes in the sink
    And wipe the spots off the door

After you put the kiddies to bed
    You may run the sweeper in the hall
Some one may ring the bell
    On pretense of making a call
That's all you need do

Until Ned and I return
Except you may watch the oven
And dont let the lamb roast burn

Come kiddies kiss mother good night
Give Daddy a little hug
Mind everything Jimmy Brown tells you
And dont spill milk on my rug
I sterilizes de bottles
En measures de milk fer Ned
Gives Gertie her glass of milk
En puts her in de bed

But Neddie seemed to think 'twas day
No sleep was in his eyes
All he tho't ob den was play
He's jis a little wise
I gibs him his bottle ob milk
En puts him in de bed
He slung dat bottle straight at me
En struck me in de heahd

Milk all on de rug
Glass all on de floe
While he sets dar a cryin
En yellin out fer moe
I cleans all de milk
From dat preshus rug fer sho
En picked up all de glass
When she walks in de doe

I gibs him anudder bottle
While she hung her coat en hat
He tends dat he is sleep
I'm thankful too fer dat
All drenched in spots of milk

My Sunday bestest coat
A great gash in my heahd
A big lump in my throat

She handed me Two Dollars
I felt like I cud hit her
Nebbah moe wud I go
As a "Baby Sitter"
My heahd was hurtin so
I found de Docter fus
En had him dress my wounds
Or else my heahd mite bus

Three Dollars he did charge
I handed out my Two
En said to wife when I got home
I charged de res to you
I wuked hard fer dat money
It makes my Christmas sad
I lost it fo I got it
De money I tho't I had

Baby Sitter too
All night I wuked en scrubbed
Washin dishes sweepin flos
Cleanin ob de rug
Den had my heahd mos knocked off
It's bandaged up so tight
I'll nebbah git anudder job
Dey'll think Ise had a fight

I wurried so it's Christmas
En jis to think my honey
Here all cut en bandaged up
Wid out a cent of money
It's ruined my repartashin
It makes me feel so bitter
To think how I los all my jobs
To be a "Baby Sitter"

TO A FLOWER

Ah! little flower you peep at me
As tho' you think I cannot see
The jutting of your tiny head
Easing from your little bed

You teach a lesson so to me
That my mind too could be so free
If I'd let God command the throne
And not me try command my own

You live at ease with no complaint
E'en giant trees bring no restraint
When with their massive limbs and boughs
They cannot hide your face some-how

You reign so on your little throne
By God's command and not your own
You shine above all earthly power
And you are queen my little flower

If sunshine comes you do but smile
If rain stays back a little while
You simply wait it's late return
E'en tho' your face does wilt and burn

You are so patient yea! so calm
That none would wish to do you harm
You vie in beauty with the age
And write your own line on Life's page

JUST PRAY

If your troubles seem so heavy
You can't smile nor e'en be gay
Let them drop the smile will come then
Look up to the Lord and pray

Always pray and then you have it
    Then I know you'll always smile
Frowns dont ever mix with praying
    Just as prayer dont mix with guile

If thy days seem ever dreary
    If a task has not been done
If of toiling you grow weary
    'Neath a broiling summer sun

Matters not just how you're traveling
    Walking-riding thro' the air
All will work out as you want it
    Take it to the Lord in prayer

As you walk along the road-side
    No need thinking of your cares
Just keep substantial as your guide
    Those oft re-peated prayers

THE HOO-DOO MAN'S DISGRACE

[This story was given to the author from real life but in putting it in poetry she used fictitious names for persons and places.]

Dar was curious times in Georgetown
    When de folks met face to face
To listen to de story
    Ob de Hoo-doo Man's Disgrace

For days dar'd been great citement
    'Mong de ole folks ob de town
Cernin diff'rent pains en ailments
    Ob de ones who's stricken down

"Dese here folks is tricked"
Ant Mandy Skinner swore
As she called to see de patients
In her roun from doe to doe

"Yes dey sho' is conjured
Case all has curious spells
En all de Medicin dat you gib
Will nebah make em well

En to let dese folks all die
'Twill be a ragin sin
So you jis well cide right now
En call de Doctor in

Dr Henry Edmon Tyler Fox
Dat libes Four miles away
Is a fus class Conjur Doctor
So all de people say

En ef you calls him in
Fo' anodder Sunday night
I bet dese curious ailments
Will be cured alright"

Ant Mandy she was talkin
To Brudder Johnny Lynn
Who tho't to jis say Conjur
Was a powerful sin

Says he "I nebah beliebed in sich
But I'll zolv to try
Dis ole conjur doctor
Rader dan to die"

So he calls his son Joe Billy
To saddle up ole Bess
En go en git de doctor
To try de conjur tes

Joe Billy starts out in a race
    To fin de conjur man
He went so fas he lef no trace
    Ob foot-prints in de san

En soon he's to de house
    Ob de famous Doctor Fox
De fus 'ting Joe did recognize
    He nebah woe no socks

A tall en lanky man
    Wid bar feet dey right flat
Dese pants yo call high-waters
    En a rusty ole felt hat—

Wid de top of it cut off
    Whar his wooly hair cum thro'
Make him a funny sight
    Ob a typical hoo-doo

En a sho hoo-doo he was
    Case ob all de roots en pills
Doctor Fox he had ob ebery kind
    Dat sho might cure or kill

"I'll sho be dar by daylight"
    He turns en says to Bill
As he gins to pick up roots
    His satchel fer to fill

"I'll go fus to de grave yard
    En dar I has to look
En search dar 'til I fin
    A lef hind rabbit foot

En wid dis rabbit foot
    En anodder est 'you see
I'll soon fin out de place
    Whar de trickery mout be

"You see sometimes dey lay fer folks
En puts it in de groun'
Den sometimes fer a change
Befo yo doe 'tis foun

En yo poe pap's sad condishun
Will sho grow wus en wus
'Til I fin de bery spot
Whar de conjurer went to fus

I'll hab to take de conjur tes'
En turn it ebry way
Fus to de East Den to de West
To see jis whar it lay

So dont be wurried 'tall my boy
Cheer up cheer my lad
I'll sho be dar by day light
To cure yo poe ole dad"

Joe Billy started den fer home
De message fer to tell
Dat soon de conjur man wud come
To make poe daddy well

De ole man in good spirits
Sot near de window den
En zolved he'd nebah shet his eyes
'Til he seed his conjur frien

Sleep gins to ober-come him
But he'd nod den take a look
'Til soon he recognized a form
Says he La! dar's a spook

He watched de so called spook
En called to his son Joe
Jis den de spook gin diggin
Wid sumpin like a hoe

Den takes a little package
En puts it in de groun
Kivers it wid dirt
Den tramps it roun en roun

De ole man sot en watched
'Til de spook it went away
Soon he nods agin
'Twas 'bout de peep ob day

He heahs a knoc' den at de doe
En Joe de doe unlocks
En face to face he meets
De famous Doctor Fox

He cums en feels de pulse
Ob Joe's poe daddy den
Says he "My frien I's jis in time
You's almos at de end

Yo life is in my hans
En fer Fifteen Dollars cash
I'll move dis conjuration
En save you in a dash

Dat you is tricked my man
Is de truf ef I mus tell
En dis heah rabbit foot
Will sho ward off de spell

Ef you'll set right by de window
Whar you kin look and see
I'll take dis tes' en fin'
Whar de trickery mout be"

He goes outside de doe
En wid his so called tes'
He turns to see which way it pints
To de East or to de West

Says he "Right to de East
      You see de dose it lay
I'll dig too 'til I fin' it
      Yes fo' anudder day"

He digs en digs 'til soon
      He ketches by a string
En pulls ob sumpin heaby
      En gibs ob it a sling

A big red ball of cotton
      En a bottle to it tied
"Ef dis heah 'ting had not be foun
      My frien you sho wud died"

Ant Mandy she jis clapped her hans
      En says "I tole you so
I knowd dat he cud cure you"
      En den she calls fer Joe

To go en tell de friens
      En neighbors all aroun
Ob de famous Doctor Fox
      En de trickery he foun

Soon de hous was full
      De yard en kitchen too
To look at Doctor Fox
      En see what he cud do

De lame de halt de blin'
      All standin at de doe
To ax ob Doctor Fox
      To gib up dem a sho

"I'd like to say a wud"
      Den put in Brudder Lynn
En all did gaze wid glarin eyes
      As to talk he did begin

"Now dis heah Doctor Fox
    Am nuffin but a bluff
Wid all his lies en talk
    About dis conjur stuff

I sot en watched dis bery imp
    About de peep ob day
A diggin in my yard
    De conjur fer to lay

En now he digs it up
    En tells de woeful tale
Dat sum ones laid fer me
    To gib his roots a sale

Now famous Doctor Fox
    I'll gib ob you a tes'
You see dis gun now turn
    Fus to de East or West

Look not behin or else
    De bullets tell de tale
Ob de famous roots en herbs
    Dat nebah got a sale

Doctor Fox he lef wid rapid pace
    He nebah looked behin'
To see de congregashun
    Ob de lame de halt de blin'

His coat tail stood out in de breeze
    His foot-prints in de san'
De leabes did wave on Dog-wood trees
    "Good bye to Hoo-doo man"

He lef ole Georgetown sho
    Wid a mighty rapid pace
But de folks dar all remember
    De Hoo-doo man's disgrace

THE TWINS

Come Daddy come
    Dere's some mistake I fear
I looked in Mudder's room
    Two babies is in dere

Dey bof is in de little bed
    Where I did always sleep
I tipped up softly to dem
    En tried to take a peep

I wonder ef she knows it
    Fer some po' Mudder now
I spec is cryin awful hard
    Fer 'tother one I'll vow

En some ole ugly 'Oman
    Has stealed it I jis bet
En bro't it to my Mudder
    Some money fer to get

But bof look jis alike
    Come Daddy come en see
Der hair is jis like Mudder's
    En eyes bof jis like me

What did you say my Daddy
    Dat bof longs at dis hous
En dat I mus be quiet
    Quiet as a mouse

So de babies dey kin sleep
    En not worry my po' mudder
I wish dey hadn't bro't jis one
    Much less to think anodder

CAN'T HAVE A BEAU

I'm vexed yea! truly vexed
      Why shouldn't I be so
To know I'm sweet sixteen
      And then can't have a beau

Can't have a beau!
      To me there is no joy
When I can't speak or laugh
      Or think about a boy

Aunt Emeline at Eighteen
      Married Uncle Si —
They courted too for three years
      Suppose it had been I?

Grandma Green at Thirteen
      Had married too I think
Furthermore there's Bob
      And little Annie Brink

They married very young
      Yes they are happy yet
I'm sure they have no cause
      For worry or regret

But it seems that I
      Must never speak to boys
To me the world is blank
      No pleasure ah! no joys

I dare not give a smile
      To William or to Joe
But what some one replies
      Your mother ought to know

And I too sweet Sixteen
I know I'm plenty old
But all the mouthy neighbors
Say mother must be told

I know what I'll do
Yes just for real spite
I wonder if they'll think
I've done exactly right

I'll never notice any boy
But act as tho' afraid
And live tho' destitute of joy
An old and cranky maid

WHEN THE HEART GROWS FONDER

Absence makes the heart grow fonder
One writer so hath said
Another says stay by me longer
If you're certain we must wed

For when you cease to see me dear
You'll soon forget me then
For miles and leagues I fear
Make differencs my friend

Absence makes the heart grow fonder
When all your money's spent
'Tis then to her your mem'ries wander
For a letter—one you sent—

Asking her to be so kind
And lend me car fare dear
For you know that love is blind
I wish that you were near

SUPERSTITIONS

I aint superstitious
    But dis I sho do know
Dat ef a rooster walks up
    En crows right in yo' doe
Dar's sho some one a comin'
    Say jis what you might
Dar'll be a stranger at yo' hous'
    Fo' de comin' ob de night

I aint superstitious
    But dis I know is true
Say what you will
    En do what you will do
Ef yo' lef' han' itches
    You may tink it funny
But you sho soon gwine er git
    A little sum ob money

I aint superstitious
    'Tis ignance I'll vow
But sho 's you're born
    Dis is tru' somehow
Dat ef you starts a place
    En has to turn bac'
En fergits to make a cross
    En spit right in yo' track

Some bad luck sho will follow
    Dis ting sho is tru'
Ef you dont beliebe me
    I tell you what to do
Jis go some whar fer fun
    En den turn bac' to see
Some bad luck sho will follow
    'Tis true as it kin be

I aint superstitious
    But I tell you what I've seen
Ef you eats at a table
    Whar dar's jis thirteen
You min' what I say
    As sho's dar's a sky
One ob dat Thirteen
    Will be sho to die

I aint superstitious
    But here's 'anodder fac'
En dis ting sho is tru'
    No matter whar you's at
Dat ef you starts a place
    En a black cat crosses you
'Tis sho en sartin bad luck
    No matter what you do

I can't be superstitious
    En sho I airt to blame
But ef you cum in one do' ob de hous'
    En dont go out de same
You min' it sho is bad luck
    You kin turn dis way en dat
But bad luck sho will follow
    No matter whar you's at

I aint superstitious
    But some tings I do know
Ef you sweeps yo' hous' up arter dark
    'Tis bad luck fer you sho
En please dont spill no salt
    It jis as sho is true
Dat sumpin's gwine to happen
    Min' what I say too

I aint superstitious
    But I tell you fus en las'

It sho is awful luck
    To break a lookin glass
Bad luck for seven yeahs
    Is de title read
Dat sho is one ting dat I fears
    One ting dat I dread

I aint superstitious
    But dis aint no lie
Ef a bird flies in de hous'
    Dar's some one gwine to die
'Tis jis as tru' as it kin be
    En when you see de bird
Some one's gwine to leabe dat house
    Case die am de word

I aint superstitious
    But let yo' lef' eye quiver
Trouble sho will follow
    You jis well gin to shiver
En let yo' lef' foot itch
    'Tis jis as tru' fer sho
You jis well pack yo' satchel
    Case on strange lan' yo' mus' go

I aint superstitious
    But dis I sho do know
In de ebening arter dark
    Ef you heahs a rooster crow
Hasty news am cumin
    'Tis tru' as it kin be
En yo' jis well war a long face
    En set en wait to see

I aint superstitious
    It's ignance 'Tis a fac'

En it jis sho's too
Dat fer 'telligence you lac'
But when settin' at de table
La sakes! dont sneeze
It's a sho sign ob death
Say what you please

I aint superstitious
En ebery body knows
Dat I aint superstitious
Eny whar I goes
But y'all sho kin tell
En read between de lines
I aint superstitious
But I do beliebe in signs

WHEN DADDY COMES FROM WUK

Cum heah Mandy what's you chewin
Take dat bread right out yo mouf
Do you know what youse doin
You'se de worry ob dis hous

Put dat bread right on de shef dar
Case 'tis much as we kin do
To gib you bread at meal time
'Til hard times is fru

En Ike you shet dat safe doe
Take dat spoon right out dem beans
Member well you gits no mo
Yall's de wus chaps eber seen

Yo Daddy'd be distracted
Ef he know'd jis how yall eat
Case it takes mos all his earnings
Jis to keep you brats in meat

Now member well you ebery one
No bread between yo meals you eat
Beans nor taters no not one
Cabbage nor bacon meat

En la sakes! here comes little John
Mudder's baby boy
Wid my ham bone under arm
Lickin it wid joy

Gib it to Mudder honey
Come let's wash yo face
En Jane you set de table
Fix 'tings all in place

Yo Daddy'll soon be in de doe
He'll be hungry too
Hurry Jane dont be so slow!
Ike min' dar what you do

You chillun wash yo faces
Put on dem aprons new
Be kereful now dont tar dem
What eber else you do

Gib me my linsey dress dar
Does you heah my lad
Yo mammy mus be lookin good
When she meets yo dad

Jane take de rabbit off de stove
De hominy en taters
En git dat smalles chiny dish
Fer de stewed tomaters

Leabe dat gravy dish alone!
Mincing in it on a sly
La sakes! Mussy me!
Who eat dat punkin pie?

You boys stop dat fightin
Sich noise I nebah heahd
Put de stools up to de table
Not another word!

All de eatins minced in
Dat's de kin ob luck
I seems to hab wid you kids
When Daddy cums from wuk

WHEN MA AND PA WERE COURTING

When Ma and Pa were courting many many years ago
Grand-pa watched the clock and walked yea to an fro
Grand-ma with her knitting losing stitches one by one
Forgetting if she'd purled or knit not knowing what she'd done

When Ma and Pa were courting one sat here one there
She a chewing on a kerchief he a thumping on a chair
Ma's sister peeping thro' the key-hole grand-pa walking up and down
Grandma still a losing stitches Jim a wishin he's in town

Jim of course was Pa you know and Anna-belle was Ma
He tho't she was the sweetest girl he'd ever seen by far
And Anna-belle tho't Jim the swellest dude in town
But Grand-pa couldn't think for walkin up and down

Then he'd yawn so loud I know that Jim could hear
Then Anna-belle embarrassed would say "Good night my dear"
But Jim still sat astounded not knowing how to start
To bid adieu to Anna-belle the darling of his heart

Grand-ma still a losing stitches and nodding of her head
Because she was so sleepy and should have been in bed
Grand-pa yawns "Tis almos Ten" Then Jim arose to go
And that's just how Ma courted 'bout forty years ago

OLD MAID'S SOLILOQUY

I'se been upon de carpet
Fo' lo dese many days
De men folks seem to sneer me
In der kin' ob way
But I dont min' der foolin
Case I sho is jis as fine
As any Kershaw punkin
A hangin' on de vine

I looks at dem sometimes
But hols my head up high
Case I is fer above dem
As de moon is in de sky
Dey sho do tink dey's so much
But I sho is jis as fine
As eny sweet potato
Dat's growd up from de vine

Dey needn't tink I'se liken dem
Case my match is hard to fin'
I dont want de water-millyun
Dat's lef' upon de vine
Case I aint no spring chicken

Dis am solid talk
En I dont want anyting
Dat's foun' upon de walk

Case ef I'd wanted anything
I'd hitched up yeahs ago
En had my sher ob trouble
But my min' tol' me no
I'd rader be a single maid
Wanderin' bout de town
Wid skercely way to earn my bread
En face all made ob frowns

Den hitched up to some num-skull
Wid skercely sense to die
I know I cudn't kill him
Dar'd be no use to try
So dont let ole maids bother you
I'll fin' a match some day
Or else I'll sho 'main single
You heah me what I say!

YEARS

Since the beginning man has stood
A devoted loving brother-hood
Leading the path-way to the right
Giving aid in the glorious fight

For God hath given aid to man
To help him carry out his plan
To shape a world in godliness
That every man might stand the test

For God so loved the world
    That he gave His begotten Son
That men of the world be saved
    That His will might be done

Now man has made a wondrous stride
    Because in God he does confide
He built great cities thro' the land
    Churches and schools on every hand

He's whispered to the lovely soil
    And brought forth coal and gas and oil
And thro' his struggling fight each hour
    Continues with unbounded power

Past years he labored and he walked
    But now he's riding as he talks
And through his striving hard each hour
    He brought out motivated power

He found on that he can rely
    So now decides that he must fly
God works wonders in His plan
    Thro' all His works and love for man

And since the world is in a plight
    And man decides that he must fight
He's flying here he's flying there
    With every caution every care

Thro' out the world in every land
    From England's Shore to Africa's Strand
Our boys are scattered there
    And as they shoulder arms to fight
To battle for their country's right
    We offer up for them a prayer

A prayer that God may be their guide
    May ever keep close to their side
Giving strength and faith each day
    That they may ne'er forget to pray

Oh God and let them ever pray
    That soon will come the wanted day
When men of this earth must defy
    That shot and shell should say when men must die

THE SOLDIER'S ADIEU

Farewell dear heart
    It grieves me this to say
But ere you read these lines
    I shall be far away

Yea! far beyond
    Where ocean cries bemoan
The soldier boy
    Afar from friends and home

Farewell dear heart
    'Tis sad to bid adieu
To one whose love
    Has been so stanch and true

And as I pen these lines
    My heart doth beat
And gentle whispers seem
    To say retreat

But Nay! my Country's call
    I must obey
Altho' I'll miss thee dear
    While far away

Yet pray! dear heart
    Yes sweetheart pray
For him whom thou dost love
    So far away

Pray that though
    'Mis shot and shell
Thy soldier boy be spared
    And now—farewell!

TUMBLED DOWN SHACK

Oh tumbled down shack I remember thee well
    Thou didst stand on the top of the hill
Many weird tales in thy walls did we tell
    'Til our frames with horror did thrill

Thy great massive frame with pillars of white
    Thy lawn of velvety green
Stood as a monument to the fair night
    When all within were in dream

Oh tumbled down shack thy once painted walls
    Of gold of white and of blue
Seem far in the night to issue their calls
    To friends far away and to you

To all who assembled in years of the past
    When thou wert in thy prime
At thy festive board—Oh could they but last
    Ye days of the olden time

Oh tumbled down shack for years thou didst stand
    As the queen of surrounding hills
Thy great social set have made their disband
    But remnants of thee remain still

What are thy thoughts while lying so still
Crumbling dust to dust
Thy power hast gone thou hast no will
Thou'rt going as all of us must

Oh tumbled down shack with earth to earth
Thou art fallen dust to dust
Within thy frame many thoughts gave birth
To greater things I trust

In mem'ry books thou art standing still
With a cherished hope that'll always fill
The hearts of those who remembered thee
In thy stand 'neath the shade of the old oak tree

Oh tumbled down shack may thy scattered dust
Planted by winds here and there
Place 'neath the earth a sacred trust
For all who once lingered there

SOMETIMES

Sometimes the days seem dark and dreary
We wonder what is life
Sometimes of work we soon grow weary
All pleasures seem but strife

Sometimes of aiming we grow tired
And finally give up all
Leaving the mind once inspired
Heedless to a call

Sometimes we give no tho't to those
Who in some way we might aid
Sometimes others pains and woes
Are at our mercies laid

Sometimes if we'd stop to think
 And count the good deeds we do
To help those on poverty's brink
 We'd find them to be few

Sometimes a good act we might render
 By saying some kind words
To those whose hearts so tender
 By kindness has ne'er been stirred

Sometimes 'twould help us to resolve
 That each day while we live
Some difficult problem we will solve
 Or aid to others give

And thus instead of pondering
 And making all efforts strife
Instead of always wondering
 To find out what is life

By our actions by the deeds we do
 Each day while we live
Let them be many or let them be few
 We make life what it is

MOTHER'S LITTLE WOMAN

[Dedicated to little Waltye Adelaide Johnson]

I'm my mother's little woman
 My Daddy's little girl
They thought I was the sweetest
 Of any in the world

But now the scene has changed
 Since brother came along
Everything he does is right
 And sister does the wrong

DADDY'S WOES

I've worked 'neath heat of Summer sun
'Till going down of same
I've gasped for breath when day was done
And said "What's in a name"?

I've sat down in my easy chair
And crossed my legs to read
When mother calls out peevishly
And then begins to plead

"Oh Daddy! call Eugenia
And little Jimmy too
If I must bother with these kids
I never will get through

You helped me wash the dishes
But that was not enough
Mother has it all to do
I tell you it is tough

I picked the paper up again
With a babe upon each knee
Little Jimmy almost two
Eugenia turning three

When goodness me! and gracious land!
I hear an awful noise
The door goes bang! and then a slam
It is those awful boys

When who should enter but the twins
Bob and Billy Knight
I knew when they came in
They'd both been in a fight

I called their mother to the scene
    We heard their tales of woe
Johnnie had struck Bobbie
    And Billie he struck Joe

We called them in and dressed their wounds
    And put them both to bed
Such always are the daily rounds
    When Daddy could have read

THE NEGRO SOLDIER

I volunteered to answer to my Country's call
    Where ever I am needed I must go
I'll give my blood and even should I fall
    'Tis that my Country may be safe I know

I volunteered to fly o'er land and sea
    Vast lands and oceans yea afar
I volunteered to fight for you for me
    With faith in God my only guiding star

I volunteered to man great ships of war
    And sail the oceans deep and cold
I volunteered to stay within the law
    And yet I must be brave and bold

I volunteered to fight this war 'til won
    To give my best our allies too to aid
I volunteered to see it all well done
    E'en though thro' sweat and blood we wade

THE LEAP YEAR PARTY

Was you at de hall las night
    To de Leap Year Party
I reckon dat I was
    But didn't I eat hearty

I wouldn't missed gwine dar
    Fo sumpin pretty fine
Dem folks was sholy lookin good
    En had a sumptious time

En eb'ry which a way you went
    About de day befo
Some un was standin at yo fence
    Or knockin at yo doe

Axin dese heah questions
    Is you gwine out to night
What color is you gwine to war
    Yaller blue or white

Is you gwine er twis yo hwar up high
    Or let it cum down low
Is you gwine er walk dar
    Or how'se you gwine er go

En ob all de questions
    I nebar heahd befo
As dey met me wif upon de street
    En eben at my doe

'Til I jis took to thinkin
    As I walked aroun
Dat dis wud be de grandes ting
    Dat eber cum to town

Case ole en young was fixen
    En primpin up to date
Leabin all de wuk undone
    Fo fear dat dey'd be late

En when I got into dat hall
    Goodness what a sight!
De same as pictures on a wall
    De folks did look dat night

Cud'n tell ole folks from de young
    Case all was lookin gay
Chattin to der fellers
    In a stylish kin o' way

Yo bettah had bin kerful too
    Dar'd bin one de bigges fights
Had yo called eny body ole folks
    On dat Leap Year Party night

Eben to de ole men
    Who'd always had der canes
To keep from fallin in de street
    Or slippin in der rain

Had flung dem all away dat night
    En cum in struttin too
Wid long tail Jim-swingers on
    En I said "Who but you"

It wud had tickled you so much
    'Til you on yo knees wud fall
Cud yo jis hab seed dem folks
    A settin in dat hall

Like sardines in a box
    Dem folks was sholy packed
Hardly room to draw yo breaf
    'leabe me 'tis a fac'

De music it was playin too
Like ragtime at a ball
De folks cud hardly hol dey feet
But de Parson viewed dem all

En dey was skeered to move dem
Or make a silent tread
So dey kep time wid de music
By de bowin ob der heads

When eatin time did cum
Dey all was at de table
Puttin way de grub
Fas' as dey was able

Gibin no tho't to dem aroun
En not a wud dey said
Stuffin dey moufs wid chicken
Tater salad ham en bread

De odder folks wid hungry looks
Sot waitin fer dar turn
Hopin dar'd be sumpin lef
As dey gazed wid faces stern

As dey finished ob der eatin
Dey moved up from der places
En turnin dey did meet
A number ob smilin faces

Now 'twas der turn to eat
Sich a scrumagin dey had
En dem dat failed to git seats
Did turn wid faces sad

Dey soon got thro der eatin
Case de hour was growin ol'
Dey heahd de clock a strikin
En de mornin hour it tol'

Dey called out fer der coats
Wid faces gay en bright
En eber dey'll remember
Dat Leap Year Party night

OUR HOME DOWN ON THE FARM

We lived down on the farm
Mos nigh twenty years
Mem'ries of our dear ole barn
Brings joy 'mid showered tears

We had a house with three rooms
A kitchen en a stove
A couple beds a flat irn
En an ole ox Andy drove

We had two hosses en a cow
Eight children en three dogs
Ten chickens en a plow
Six pigs en three ole hogs

With ten of us in all
It made us scratch our heads
To figger out our rest at night
In two ole narrow beds

We placed the chillun one by one
Cross-wise in a row
When they had slept an hour or two
We put them on the flo

We kep a piller ready
So-s when they moved ther heads
We'd slip it gently under
To think theys still in bed

Our res was so un-sartin
    In two ole narrer beds
To keep a changin pillers
    Under eight chilluns heads

Near peep of day we changed agin
    En put them in the bed
En we tuk turns upon the flo
    With pillers under head

That life to us was dear
    That home down on the farm
The dogs the cows each ricket cher
    The bed en tumblin barn

The well so near the kitchen doe
    The pond the ole farm gate
En everything we know
    In mem'ry seems to wait

Each brings joys that never fade
    En tho' new things we larn
No life to us was ever made
    Like that down on the farm

DECISION

You can be anything you want to be
    Do anything you want to do
So long as God is first
    And to yourself you're true
Be a woman—be a man
    Strive always for the best
Ask God to help you with your plan
    And He will do the rest

THE DRUNKARD'S DREAM

Crime? murder did I hear you say
Yes I killed my wife!
Outside the door in blood she lay
The victim of a knife!

The victim of a heart that craved for crime
That craved for blood!
Who feared no foe in face of time
Nor retribution's flood

The victim of a soul so black
Black with earthly sin
Who feared no blood-hound on his track
Nor even death's cold grim!

Haunted yea! by wild desire
I plunge in depths of crime
My very soul it seems afire!
Yet am I sick or blind

Yes I killed my wife!
Yes I killed my child!
My child a girl of eight—
Yet am I crazed or wild?

My girl a beauty to behold
Those eyes I see them now
How with expressive look they told
Her love for me—I'll vow!

She was her father's heart
Each evening at the gate
I'll see my Nell—how can we part
But now it is too late

I pierced the daggers shining blade
Thro' the heart of my dear wife
Who's now a victim for the grave
And yet there was no strife—

Betwixt my wife and me
We always lived as dear
As any couple you might see
She full of love and cheer

But it seems some savage beast
Had cast his heart in mine
I could not rest in peace
With anger I was blind

I rushed inside the door
With the dagger's shining blade
For murder or for crime
In blood I wished to wade

I killed my wife, I killed my child
And for fear I might be found
I set the home a-blaze
And soon 'twas to the ground

My home, my wife, my child
In one heap of ashes lay
My heart! my treasure! Yea my all!
Swept within a day

And now I'm crazed I'm wild!
What spell was this I pray
That caused me kill my child
Oh help me God I pray!

My wife—and where is she
I did not kill her too
Oh God in mercy hear my plea
What must a sinner do

Without a home, without a wife
Without my child my all!
Battling thro' a world of strife
Wilt Thou hear my call?

Oh wife! Oh child! Oh do but speak
I never meant the crime
'Twas drink, 'twas cursed rum
Oh cursed rum I'm blind!

As I reached my hand the cold cold touch
Was that of a prison wall
The next the judge and jury
And then the prisoner's fall

The sentence fell cold and heavy
In words clearly cut and bare
"The prisoner found guilty of murder
His doom the electric chair"

Oh God! I'm choking I'm dying
Gasping for ev'ry breath
The result of rum—Oh how trying
How bitter and cruel is death!

As I lay there gasping for life
In a cold cold prison cell
Some one shook me and Oh! 'twas my wife!
And beside her my daughter Nell

Why haunt me like this!
I gave a scream
Wife pressed a kiss
"Dear you're in a dream

Thank God I cried!
You've saved my life
I was almost gone
My darling wife

Dying from thoughts of—
    To utter I dare
Meeting my fate
    In the cursed chair!

But thanks be to God!
    From this very day
I'll worship Thee only
    Oh help me I pray!

For Thou in this dream
    Hast shown me the strife
And the bitterness gleaned
    From a Drunkard's life

Thou in this dream
    Hast broken the spell
And saved my soul
    From a drunkard's hell!

BY GONES

[This poem is dedicated to the memory of those slaves whose lives were so inter-woven with their Master's family that even—tho they wanted to be free, they regretted leaving the only connection they knew in the world, the family.]

Let our tho'ts wander back to the days as of yore
    Where the cotton fields ever were white
The foot-prints still linger then weary and sore
    But made ever after so light

Let us list for the voices yet floating in air
    The voices of mothers long gone
From the old fields of cotton they whisper a prayer
    If you listen you'll hear too a song

The cabins are gone and we know very well
They too in some place have their story to tell
The old logs lay silent can't speak any more
But prayers songs and tears they've held by the score

They lay in deep tho't of the days past and gone
Of the secrets they held from mid-night 'til dawn
When meetings were held with song and with prayer
The mothers of yesterday yes they were there

Lightly tread back to the cotton fields white
Where the days and the years were so long
The sun too it seems never shone ere so bright
They were trudging to work too at dawn

Lightly Oh! lightly tread back and we see
Their spirits still hov'ring around
On the spot where they prayed to their God to be free
To them now 'tis hallowed ground

Our minds sweep in mem'ry way back to the past
The impress of foot-prints still there
In the old fields of cotton the mem'ry'll last
Of the souls who once lingered there

Souls worn and weary but faith in their God
A God who's always so near
Tread softly this earth now is hallowed sod
Each mem'ry is ever so dear

For joy gave it's birth in the cotton fields white
In the long long days of the past
The sun on that day never shone ere so bright
It's mem'ry ever will last

Forms bent with age went marching along
God had sent a message a song
'Mid tears of regret tears of delight
They bade a good-bye to the cotton fields white

Let our minds wander back where the sun shines so bright
Where mem'ries linger we know
To the old old fields of cotton so white
In the days of that long long ago

TODAY

To day is all thou hast
To work for friend of mine
Yesterday is past
To-morrow is not thine

To day thy best work must be done
If thou wouldst reach the goal
Feeble efforts ne'er have won
Vict'ry for a soul

To day the sky is clear
And thou canst see thy way
To-morrow may be drear
Of that we cannot say

Then if thou hast a task
Proceed with all thy might
To day is all thou hast
And then 'tis dark 'tis night

THE LOST TEDDY BEAR

Well Teddy I have found you
It's been one week to day
Since I missed you Teddy dear
While in the yard at play

I wandered far and wide
And knew not where to go
To find you Teddy dear
And Oh! I missed you so

I know some naughty boy
Stole you dear from me
And if I only knew
Who that boy could be—

I'd scold him yes I'd scold him
And I just bet he'd dare
To interfere again
With my Teddy Bear

And Oh you were so nice and clean
One would scarcely know
You were the same little Teddy
Lost one week ago

But still I welcome you my dear
And will wash you nice and clean
And try forget that you were lost
And believe it all a dream

So again I embrace you Teddy
For I love you just the same
And tho' you look so dirty
'Twas the boy—you aint to blame

I WISH I WAS A GROWN UP MAN

[Written for Walter W. Johnson, Jr., to recite when he was Four years old.]

I wish I was a grown up man
And then I'd get a chance
To wear those great high collars
Stiff shirts and nice long pants

I wish I was a grown up man
Not too big and fat
But just the size to look nice
In a beaver hat

I'd wear the nices vest and gloves
And patent leather shoes
And all the girls would fall in love
And I'd flirt with whom I choose

I wish I was a grown up man
I'd try the girls to please
I'd wear a long Jim-swinger coat
Just below my knees

I'd wear eye glasses too
And wouldn't I look good
I'd be the swellest dude
In this neighbor hood

Some day I'll be a man
And do just what I say
And give my heart to some nice girl
And then I'll go away

AS WE SOW WE SHALL REAP

As we go about the toils of life
And witness each day it's burdens and strife
Thinking not of the days of the future or past
Knowing not where in life our lots may be cast—

'Tis then in Life's broad and fertile field
In tho'tlessness to fate we yield
Not deeming it wise our minds to cast
On any works or deeds of the past

Still tho'tlessly we struggle along
    Amid Life's great and fearless throng
Thro' darkened caves o'er rugged steeps
    Thinking not that as we sow we reap

But later on when years have flown
    And of Life's cares we've weary grown
'Mid silence tho'ts in our weary minds creep
    That as we've sown we now do reap

We think of our heavy burdens and cares
    They seem to us more than we can bear
Our heart is faint we utter a groan
    Yet we're reaping what we have sown

If we could only blot out the past
    And e'en it's mem'ry in some sea cast
Oh could we but live our life again
    We'd see such burdens would not remain

But now our eyes grow dim with age
    We near the last line of Life's page
We'll seal it's contents with a groan—
    Reaping — reaping what we have sown

Before your eyes grow dim with age
    You who're on Life's busy stage
As each day you labor—do mindful keep
    That as you sow you'll surely reap

KRISMAS DINNAH

We's invited down to Brudder Browns
    On a Krismas Day
To an ole time Krismas dinnah
    So de imbertation say

De deacons en der wives war dar
De Parson en his wife
All dem folks did sho look good
You kin bet yo life!

De wimmen folks was dressed to de'f
Wid ruffles en wid laces
Har all hangin down in curls
En powder on der faces

Der dresses had sich great long trains
We stood bac wid de res
As dey marched into de Ception Hall
To keep from steppin on der dress

En de men folks wasn't fer behin
I'se heah to tell
Dey was dressed too in der bes'
Lookin kinda swell

Dey woe dese long Jim-swinger coats
Wid big leg pantaloons
High silk hats wid broad red bands
En rived dar promp at noon

Dey woe dem low cut ves
Wid great broad white neck tie
En each man woe an eye glass
Stickin on one eye

Ole man Edmon Jones was dar
Dressed jis like de res
It wud hab tickled you so much
To hab seed him look his bes

Him en Ole man Sly-back
Was an hour behin'
Dey was ole en walked so slow
Dey cudn't cum in time

Still when dinnah time did cum
Dem two was in de line
Marchin to de chune ob music
Keepin' ole folks time

Den dey stood up at de table
'Til de Blessin it was sed
At de tappin ob de bell
All did bow der heahds

Parson Reuben Jones was called on
To say de blessed wuds
En as he gin to cler his throat
His inmos' soul was stirred

"Heabenly Fodder look down on us
En dis earfly blessin'
We tanks De fer dis possum roas'
All brown wid Ash cake dressin

We tanks De fer dis sausage
En squirrel cooked wid beans
En all dis nice fried chicken
Dese onions en dese greens

En as we goes to eat it
Wilt Dou be our frien'
To keep us all from dying
We ax dis en Amen"

De wimmen folks was helped fus'
To all de kins ob meat
En den we men was helped
As we sot dar in our seats

Den we menced to eatin
Dat was a stuffin time
Case no one said a wud
To pass away de time—

Cept jis to ax fer eatens
Den in a quiet way
Dey wud cler der throats
En hab a wud to say

You talk about folks eatin
But nebah in my rouns
Has I eber eat up so much grub
As I did at Brudder Browns

En when dem folks did git up
Dat table was cleaned up right
Possum carcuss chicken bones
Was all dat's lef in sight

THOUGHTS

Had I the wings of a bird
I'd make it a constant duty
To fly far above the earth
And gaze on it's wondrous beauty

Had I the mind of a poet
I'd always try to write
Poems of thrilling beauty
To fill some mind with delight

I'd love to stroll in distant lands
Among the rocks and rills
And see the works of Nature's hands
And gaze on the distant hills

I'd love to listen to the birds
That sing their songs of praise
And make some poor souls happy
In their saddest days

It would be to my delight
    To stand at the river side
And gaze on the placid water
    As it slowly and playfully glides

I'd love to write of the beautiful
    I'd love to write of the brave
And read the minds of others
    And note their winning ways

I would not judge the beautiful
    By the beauty of their faces
By suppositions or the like
    Nor their pretended graces

It brings to my mind once again
    A maxim that I love
And one of the sayings as of old
    "Beauty is that Beauty does".

PA GETS HIMSELF A CAR

I never will for-get the day
    Tho' years may come and go
But none in Mem'ry's Garden
    With root so deep I know

'Twas when we lived just out of town
    A little country plot
A place I can't for-get
    And learned to love a lot

We had our hosses en our cows
    Our chickens en our hogs
Our apple en our Cherry trees
    En a few ole huntin dogs

So one day Pa decided
    We lived a little far
To keep on drivin hosses
    So gits him-sef a car

Fer weeks he's in town ev'ry day
    Sho's I'm alive
Leavin off his cuttin hay
    Learnin how to drive

One day we's settin on the porch
    Me and Ma en Bess en George
When we heard an awful shiftin
    En a powrful puffy noise

A car was comin round the curve
    At a powrful mighty speed
Cut on thro' the corn-field
    Cuttin up the weeds

Then on thro the tater patch
    Then thro the melons new
Melon seeds was sowed
    Fer bout a mile or two

I looked round at Ma
    She was out of breaf
Bess she fainted at the sight
    George most skeered to death

Ma sez who is that chap
    A drivin like he's mad
I gave a glance at George
    I know that he felt bad

Fer who was settin at that wheel
    En drivin of that car
But my Ma's own dear husban
    En our out-dashus Pa

Then stead of turning at the curve
    On the wagon drive
He jumped the raillin fence
    Sho's I'm alive

Ma was sho disgusted
    And a cutting glance did cast
Then with a silly grin Pa said
    "Well Ma I'm here at last!"

WHAT TASK MUST THE WOMAN FULFILL

As the sun finds it's way to the golden West
    And soon disappears from sight
Then the moon takes his place to watch o'er us
    Thro' the still and silent night
As we gaze on the stars above
    Our hearts with ecstacy fill
While we ask in tones of love
    What Task must the woman fulfill

Ah! woman in by-gone years
    Thou wert not recognized
Save as slave to thy helpmeet with fears
    'Neath the gloom of a cloudy sky
Thou knew no other place
    Save labor toil and yield
Thy record had no space
    For honor or for zeal

But Ah! the buried past
    May well forgotten be
The mem'ry still may last
    But the dreaded yoke is free

Yea! free and woman now
Stands in her strength alone
To battle for the right
And for her sins atone

Ere since the days of Christ
We've read of woman's boon
The last to seek His face
The first one at the tomb
From thence to future years
She'll hold an upward sway
She's laid aside her doubts and fears
Now woman has her way

What progress would there be to day
What honor or what fame
Could you in garb array
Without a woman's name
Yea! man may be the hero
But woman placed him there
She pushed him with her zeal
Her cheering words her care

What hero in the world to day
Could well have won the fame
Lest woman in her modest way
Had led him on to fame
'Tis she then who inspires him
And gives him zeal to work
She urges him with earnest prayers
From duty ne'er to shirk

Yea! woman with her prayers
Woman with her love
Has soothed so many cares
And wafted them above

Wafted them on wings of prayer
      To Him who dost heed our call
And notes each little needed care
      E'en to a sparrow's fall

We gaze on the clouds above us
      Sometimes they're tinted with gold
Sometimes they're dark and heavy
      And dread and gloom enfold
Tho' the clouds be dark and heavy
      And dread and gloom dispel
There's inside a silver lining
      Which a brighter story tells

Then our lives may have some dark days
      But there're brighter days to come
Which may enswallow the dark clouds
      And they leave us one by one
Man has been hovering o'er us
      As the dark and heavy cloud
But the silver lining bursts forth
      In the form of woman proud

She comes with words of cheer
      With rapture our very hearts thrill
As she asks of many here
      "What Task Must the Woman fulfill"
What must she find to do
      In a world so cheerful and bright
In a land where laborers are few
      Who're struggling to do the right

Man has won laurels of fame
      And kept them yea! for years
Hist'ry records his name
      And we laud his Mem'ry with cheers

Now woman comes upon the scene
Her chances may be few
But records soon will glean
What woman too can do

She stands with outstretched arms
Waits ere the morning dawns
To do some act of kindness
For the helpless or forlorn
She gazes in the darkness
Of the cities lowest dives
Where girls have gone to shame
Where men have wrecked their lives

Slowly she wends her way
'Til she's reached this lowly place
Where many lives are wrecked
In sorrow and disgrace
With a prayer she enters in
To lead the straying girl
From the depths of blackest sin
To an outside praying world

And on she goes thro' life
With ready waiting hands
To work thro' sin and strife
What e'er be the urgent demand
To lead the wanderer on
In paths of truth and right
And crush the sin and wrong
'Neath the wings of darkest night

Now her mind it slowly wanders
As she struggles on thro' life
Thro' the rugged highway
Onward up the hill of strife

Treading slowly treading
Marching to the road of fame
Woman with her earnest efforts
Each year in and out the same

What task must the woman fulfill
Wait not for the answer to come
Conscience speaks obey the will
Woman's vict'ry will be won
Let not the precious years go by
And find your record blank
Catch the moments ere they fly
With woman out of rank

Woman place thy record high
When the flag of honor's unfurled
Let woman's name against the sky
Glitter to the world
Glitter in letters of gold
Against the placid blue
Let Woman's fame be told
In letters bold and true

Let her name glow brighter brighter
May the letters ne'er grow dim
For He who makes the burdens lighter
Always keeps His lamps in trim
Woman may thy name be written
That thy deeds may ever shine
In the land of golden treasures
Where the vict'ry may be thine

THE NEGRO HAS A CHANCE

As my mind in fancy wanders
While we figure on life's stage

While in queries deep we ponder
    O'er the past years ripe with age
While sipping slowly from Life's cup
    And in tho'ts deepest trance
This question often rises up
    Has the Negro had a chance?

'Tis true they lived one life
    Thro' out the darkened age
When 'mid events full of strife
    They wrote upon Life's page
In darkest hours of the night
    Their souls would seem entranced
Wondering if some time in life
    The Negro'd have a chance

But now those days are gone
    And on Life's page are blank
And sons of ages newly born
    Are being placed in rank
Just as they file in line
    To make a slow advance
They read in front this sign
    "The Negro Has A Chance"

The doors are open wide
    That He may enter in
And time ripe to decide
    Where in life He will begin
And as He slowly turns Her page
    He gives a quickened glance
And sees in every avenue and age
    The Negro has a chance

With outstretched arms the college stands
    And with inviting voice
She gives the Negro Her demands
    To make befitting choice

Of the station He would choose in life
    To make himself advance
"Now we've cleared away the strife
    And the Negro has a chance

Our race needs fitted teachers
    Their knowledge to impart
And elevated preachers
    With the work of God at heart
Men whose noble work
    Will have power to enhance
Men who dare not shirk
    But bravely grasp the chance

Then heed ye to this call
    Which means for a race success
And what e'er may befall
    Bravely stands the test
Let not fickle minds
    Check your brave advance
When every event shows the signs
    That the Negro has a chance

The preacher needs your aid
    To help save Negro souls
For the price so dearly paid
    That they may reach the goal
He begs with earnest heart
    That you lend a helping hand
That in this work you take a part
    And heed the Lord's command

The Doctor gives a call
    That you come into his field
And as the sick and wounded fall
    To their weakened voice you yield

He sees your help he needs
    As o'er his field he gives a glance
And your steps he'll not impede
    But the Negro give a change

The lawyer opens up his book
    The leaves all gold with age
And as he gives a steady look
    And turns from page to page
He sees a page all blank
    And calls the Negro in
And tells him "Fall in rank
    In law you must begin"

The skilled mechanic works away
    As he performs his part
He toils away from day to day
    And well displays his art
He loves his work with all his soul
    And in it he confides
But soon before he's reached the goal
    The Negro's at his side

The merchant takes his stand
    With ready merchandise
He meets the world's demands
    And each day sells and buys
But soon upon the scene
    The Negro makes his way
So in the merchant's scheme
    He too must have a play

The carpenter now stands aside
    To give the right of way
As slowly in the Negro glides
    Now he must have his day

In carpentry he'll show his skill
We may see this at a glance
His soul with ecstacy does fill
As He sees his future chance

The tailor in his shop we find
And as he cuts and sews
He has his work upon his mind
For the art in it he knows
The Negro too has learned this art
And so with weary brain
He toils away with earnest heart
That a living He may gain

So all these stations must be filled
As we journey on thro' life
And we must struggle with a will
And aim to banish strife
And when we've reached the utmost round
We'll send up notes of praise
To Him our happy tho'ts resound
To Him these songs we'll raise

And Negro yea! of Afric's strand
Ye strong men make advance
We do of you make this demand
With vigor grasp your chance
Let not these happy moments pass
But make good of each one
And when you've reached the realms at last
And work on earth is done—

You'll soar 'mid scenes of beauty
You'll live in seas of love
When you've done your duty
To reach that land above

And Negro be not far behind
But on yea! on advance
Strive hard to reach that dearer clime
Yes make good of your chance

JIM'S WIFE BUYS A CAR

We driv our ole hoss ten years
On trips bof near en far
En I had begged wid tears
Dat Jim wud buy a car
But he clared out we's too poe
Dat cars was fer de rich
En too sez my Jim furder-moe
We'd soon be in de ditch

I listened to his talk each day
Fus one scuse den anodder
Fer dis en dat he had to pay
En what he bought my mudder
'Til I got tired ob it all
Says I, "look heah Jim Spar
We's got to rise be-fo we fall
We's gettin us a car"

He looked at me wid blank surprise
En den sez, "honey, honey
How's we gittin us a car
When we aint got no money"
We aint all dat poe
You's wukin ebery day
En one 'ting I do know
No wuk wid out some pay

So git yo-sef all ready Jim
De man is on de way

I tole him on las munday
    To bring de car to day
He gins to swell up den
    Who'se payin ob dis money
"Ise traded in de hoss
    En we will git it honey"

Soon de car was at de doe
    A bright en shinin blue
Wid trimmins dat was silver like
    It sho was pritty too
I gits in at de front
    On de driver's side
En Jim he looked so mad
    You'd tho't some one had died

De driver turned en axed
    Which was gwine to learn
Or wud we radder cide
    On lessons by de turn
Dont know bout de turn I said
    But I'll tek lessons fus
Den Jim he looked at me
    As doe he's bout to bus

De man he shows me how to stop
    Den how to start de car
Den Jim he busses in
    Wid "Look heah Jinny Spar
You aint killin me
    On larnin how to drive
I'se gittin out dis car
    While I'se still alive

I didn't tun my heahd
    But put on plenty gas
En ax me Mr. Spar

Ef I aint runnin fas
De han it pints at sixty-five
En runs jis lak 'Tis flyin
De man he tetched me fer to stop
He tho't dat Jim was dyin

I cud'n stop jis den
I'se runnin mos too fas
I'se almos at a turn
Where a man I had to pass
De green light it was on
En I was mekin time
En sho as you is born
'twas fifty cars in line

En out dem I struck twenty five
En made in each a dent
En do I'se still alive
I dont know whar Jim went
But I has cided once fer all
Show's my name's Jinny Spar
I finds dat we is way too poe
To ebah own a car

THE HERO OF AFRIC'S WILD

Bound in fetters and chains
They come from a country afar
Sons of Chieftains and Kings
Their priestly records mar

Clothed in slavery's garb
Doomed to a wretched life
Away from friends and home
To battle thro' blood and strife

We hear the piercing shrieks
    Echo from Afric's wild
Of natives frenzied and crazed
    Mournin for Afric's child

Mourning for sons of Kings
    And princes of wealthy estate
Brought from the land afar
    To bury in slavery's weight

Crushed 'neath bondage and fear
    They mourn their awful fate
Heirs of princes and kings
    Doomed to an awful fate

Yea! doomed to slavery's chain
    To live 'neath the awful spell
To suffer and bear the pangs
    Which none would be able to tell

To suffer—yea! that is small
    Amid the burden of hate
But think of Afric's fall
    And degradation great

Her kings stand back in disgust
    And curse the land where befell
The crime of slav'ry's lust
    Worse than the pangs of hell

Burdened 'neath slavery's hate
    A fervent prayer is heard
As the slave succumbs to his weight
    And utters on High a few words

"Master above wilt Thou hear this—
    A slave's poor pitiful cry
Wilt Thou grant us freedom
    Freedom ere we die

Wilt Thou listen to the cries
    Of husband mother and babe
And 'mid their suff'rings great
    Spare mercy to the slave

We know Thou wilt hear our cry
    Oh! Master hear us now
As humbly at Thy feet
    Before Thy throne we bow

Soon the clouds began to scatter
    And the dread and gloom dispel
And the slave with all his burdens
    Could a brighter story tell

List! we hear the news of freedom
    Echo yea! from land to land
Slaves rejoice 'mid tears of sorrow
    As they grasp each other's hand

Ah! thank God at last we're happy
    For He's heard our woeful cry
And in turn He gives us freedom
    Now we see a clearer sky

Then an aged Afric Chieftan
    Sorrowed to the very grave
That he of noble blood
    Had suffered as a slave

Bids his dear ones come around him
    To say a last good-bye
"Since our God did give us freedom
    I feel happy now to die

Happy yea! to leave the land
    Where my dear ones face to face
Have suffered spilt their blood
    And wore the brand of slave's disgrace

For way in Afric's sunny wild
Our fathers true and brave
Would lose each drop of blood
Before they'd be a slave

And let me die Oh! die so happy!
And tho' I've been a slave
Before my people get the message
I'll be happy in the grave"

SOMEBODY'S MOTHER

[Dedicated to my mother, The late Lucie Bannister **Pogue**]

The world in it's wild and maddened flight
Goes heedlessly along
Pays no thought to the darkest night
And heeds not a ceaseless throng

A wanderer poor and forsaken
May pass by one then another
But he's not noticed at all
Lest it be by somebody's mother

Somebody's mother tho' old and gray
And bent by life's lengthened years
Has helped the beggar so poor by the way
And gives him her prayers and her tears

The girl who falls by the wayside
And wrecks her dear sacred life
Who ceases to heed to her guide
Now repents in bitter strife

The world now laughs her to scorn
    Kicked and buffed by one then another
She begs for sympathy long
    None offers but somebody's mother

Somebody's mother holds out her hand
    To take this wanderer in
Battered and cuffed by a wreckless band
    With tattered garments of sin

The boy who has lived the most wreckless life
    And in shame wanders wildly home
Thro' the world he stumbles in darkness of night
    With a pillow of rock or stone

He begs from house to house
    Refused by one then another
But at last he's aided by one
    You may know 'twas somebody's mother

Somebody's mother with aching heart
    Feels for somebody's child
Who has no one to take his part
    And wanders so wreckless and wild

Somebody's mother with waiting hand
    Stands ready to help the poor
Whenever there's want in demand
    Just go to some mother's door

Yea! some mother's door—for none can feel
    And offer with greatness of heart
Like a dear and honored mother
    Who dearly performs her part

Yea mother! that sacred word
    Is as dear as the costliest pearl
To the son who wandered afar
    And the mother's only girl

Was there ever a word so sweet
    To sister husband or brother
That every demand could meet
    And in form so simple as mother

Yea none! for each letter is dear
    And sacred to many a heart
Others may give words of cheer
    But can't do a mother's part

THE UNKNOWN CHILD

[Dedicated to the memory of George Washington Carver]

No further could they take the struggling babe
    The weakling was not worth the while
They had no time to nurse nor try to save
    This offspring of a slave this weakened child

The child and mother on a winter's night
    Were taken in an awful raid
No one knew the mother's plight
    Nor e'en the price she paid

The child was found and sold again
    The dealer soon was on his way
The master deemed this man a friend
    A straggling horse was given him as pay

And thus a life starts out so young
    No mother for it's sickened whims or frets
But destined that in years to come
    To win such laurels none would soon forget

For God adopted as His own
    This child who to himself unknown
Did cast a picture in a world so great
    That rich and poor alike should know his fate

He walked and talked with God each day
    And begged as Solomon of old
Not for riches not for pay
    But wisdom Lord instead of gold

And as he roamed the forest wild
    And tramped the earthly sod
This one time cast off child
    Talked each day with God

He dug his fingers in the clay
    And praised the worth of it each day
And as he looked up to his God
    Gave thanks for this the earthy sod

He prowled into the things that grew
    And found out facts man never knew
This wand'rer of the forest wild
    This unknown one time cast off child

He dug into the reddened clay
    Which man has trampled day by day
Finding colors of varied hue
    And one the rivalled sought for blue

He found good in everything
    It seemed as tho' a magic spring—
Would gurgle up at his command
    To make things fertile by his hand

Tuskegee called him as her son
    "There is a great work to be done
Let not this as a vision fade
    Your people sorely need your aid"

It seemed to him a call from God
    That he might sift the earthly sod
And in that vastly peopled land
    Instruct and make folks understand

And thus he answered to the call
    His task was not an easy one
But Carver leaned upon his God
    And toiled from rise to set of sun

This weak and cast off unknown child
    Made his way thro' life
'Mid conflicts in a world of guile
    Unheeding petty strife

But God so willed that he should stand
    With fame unequalled in the land
With a heritage so great to wit
    That all the world shall benefit

So long as this old world shall stand
    So long as stars do shine
The name of Carver in this land
    Shall twinkle out divine

His name is in the cotton
    His name is in the corn
He made the peanut famous
    By toil from early dawn

The sweet potato shines forth
    To show what she can do
Since Carver made a test
    And brought forth values true

A monument he made which stands
    Erected to the skies
To show the work of noble hands
    With toil and sacrifice

The epitaph by his own hands
    Glows out every year
Is read by thousands through the land
    Who never saw his bier

So resting 'neath the southern soil
    This saint this noble sage
Leaves a heritage so great
    To sons of every age

THERE IS NO DEATH

[In memory of Mrs. E. T. Bond and the son of Dr. and Mrs. Quinland]

Read at the Memorial Service of the Woman's Auxiliary to The National Medical Association at Cleveland, Ohio in August 1942, having been written about two hours before the meeting on hearing of the death of one of their members and the son of another of their members whose sudden death by drowning was a shock to the members who had expected the attendance that day of the parents.

There is no death but just a soft a silent sleep
    When easing softly out their spirits creep—
From all the glamour of a busy world
    Where peace and love and sweetness of a life unfurl

There is no death but just a peaceful rest
    They would not be disturbed for they are blest
Away from all the bustle all the strife
    Where quietly they sleep "a peaceful happy life"

Oh! faithful wife Oh! darling son
    We cannot yet believe that this is done
Altho' your loved ones grieve—they cannot be consoled
    But God does not deceive and will His love unfold

He loves thee none the less when He takes thee away
    But God does bless and comfort and repay
He plants His flowers in His garden fair
    And none in beauty can with them compare

And when He does select He has the power
    And always plucks away the choicest flower
And thus from all the flowers rare
    He plucked a tender bud with care

Which soon by God's own gracious power
    Would have been a sturdy growing flower
Lifting up it's head o'er all the earth
    As did the Christ the lowly child of birth

There is no death Ah! no a slumber—that is all
    When God decides His loved ones so to call
Call them from a world of turmoil and of zest
    To where there's joy and peace and rest

THE LAD WITHOUT A NAME

[Dedicated to the memory of Booker T. Washington]

In a lowly one room cabin
    Lived a little Negro boy
Hampered by the chains of slav'ry
    Yet this did not him annoy

Often tho' he noticed mother
    While he played in childish glee
Praying with her hands uplifted
    "Master wilt thou make us free"

He was then too young to take in
Yea too young to understand
The awful curse of slav'ry
Which was spread thro'out the land

Never'less he watched his mother
Oh! the love that mother had
Caring for her little children
Poorly fed and poorly clad

She was struggling with great efforts
To supply her children's need
Bringing bits of after-leavings
That her children she might feed

When she came into the cabin
There they'd gather at her knee
The younger was the nameless lad
Since known as Booker T.

His mother called him Booker
Just because of books he's fond
He had no real name
This lad of slav'ry's bond

So now is spread thro'out the land
The hist'ry of the fame
Of him who started his career
As a lad without a name

Soon he hears the bells of freedom
Ring thro'out the entire land
He heard folks say that he was free
Yet little could he understand

So he started out into the world
And found he had no name
Then he added more to Booker
That he might have some claim

Booker had great thirst for knowledge
"There is something I must learn"
So decides to find a way
As for wisdom he did yearn

All ye children know the story
How he tramped the rugged road
Facing knowledge facing wisdom
Burdened 'neath the heavy load

For he had no means to meet it
Meet the monster he must face
But his great desire for learning
Did the hindrances erase

So sickened worn and weary
To Hampton he found his way
Thirsting for the understanding
Which he hoped to have some day

There he struggled for his learning
Which prepared him for his fate
And in after the yearning
Which did serve to make him great

He left his school with highest honors
That his people he might serve
And thereby give to them the knowledge
Which he hoped they might deserve

For years he struggled for his people
Toiling yea! thro'out the land
Making every sacrifice
That they might understand

So he built a towering statue
Monumental mammoth grand
Which will serve a lasting tribute
Wavering yea! thro'out the land

Serve as tribute to the mem'ry
Of him who gave his life
Probing out the greatest problem
Which has banished bitter strife

Greater work was ne'er accomplished
By a poor and nameless lad
Who won a noble reputation
Which should make his people glad

And now we know that we have lost him
Oh the bitter pangs we feel!
As we think about our hero
While around Thy shrine we kneel

May his statute ever tower
Bringing knowledge bringing fame
To the children who give honor
To the Lad without a name

May the lasting mem'ry ever
Cherished by his people be
That each letter may be sacred
In the name of Booker T.

And years to come will give the story
Write the hist'ry of the fame
Of him who started his career
As a lad without a name

* These are facts put into poetry after reading his life story.

LONG AGO

It seems from recollections of the old days past and gone
From what I've heard my mother say of days still further on

That this old world has made a change so vast that all
must know
Which makes it very diff'rent from the days of
long ago

In the days of long ago it seems that life was more at ease
That faces wore more smiles—and friends so liked
to please
In ev'ry task they under-took—to do it well and so—
It made life move so smoothly in the days of long ago

There were no folks back in those days whose envy and
whose hate
Devoured their better selves and made it worse
for fate
They seemed to wish each other well—and were so
pleased to know
When friends were so successful in the days of
long ago

The folks back in those days just seemed one happy band
So stanch and ever ready to lend a helping hand
To lift—to pull—that each might have an equal
chance to go
And this made life so happy in the days of long ago

POET LAUREATE

[Dedicated to the memory of James Weldon Johnson]

He was our poet laureate
He was our laurel king
Who reigned in visioned state
Whose heart did always sing

Of beauty and of love
    Of fairness and of powers
And now he sings above
    These are his glorious hours

Thy voice which had its over-flow
    Of that which gave us life
Its blessings too and thou didst know
    The balm to soothe out strife
We miss thee dear one here
    In this cold world of ours
We cannot hear thy soothing voice
    Which had its gifts and powers

Thou singest now above
    With that angelic throng
Of everlasting love
    And glorifying song
Of peace and everlasting faith
    Which our great God doth give
And thou our poet laureate
    In peace and love doth live

TUSKEGEE'S SORROW

Weep not Tuskegee tho' great be thy sorrow
    For him who didst fight and fall for thy cause
We know thou wilt miss him to day yes to-morrow—
    Thou'lt list for his voice for his steps thou'lt pause

Weep not Tuskegee for him who has left us
    Left us in sorrow and heart rending grief
His was a life of toil for his people
    Great was his life work and yet his life brief

Weep not Tuskegee tho' great be thy burden
  Burdens of thought yea! burdens of care
Fell from the shoulders of our greatest hero
  Now thou wilt have the burdens to bear

Weep not Tuskegee a nation is weeping
  Save back thy tears and console them in grief
While thy great hero is peacefully sleeping
  Thousands of grieved hearts pray for relief

Weep not Tuskegee for sorrow unspoken
  Is thine we know and will ever be
We know too well that thy heart is broken
  We beg thee to weep not for we weep for thee

Weep not Tuskegee for thy honored hero
  Is resting from labor resting from care
Peaceful his slumber with no thought of worry
  No thought of even a burden to bear

Weep not Tuskegee the gates now stand open
  The Angel who came so peacefully down
Bore him on high to his great home in Heaven
  Placed there upon him a star studded crown

Weep not Tuskegee but sing of thy hero
  Brave honored hero who fell for thy name
We'll laud his mem'ry forever with praises
  Praise for the hero our hero of fame

POET OF OUR RACE

[Dedicated to the memory of Paul Laurence Dunbar]

Oh poet of our race
  We reverence thy name

As thy hist'ry we retrace
Which enfolds thy wide spread fame

We loved thee yea! too well
But He didst love thee more
And called thee up with Him to dwell
On that Cèlestial shore

Thy sorrows here on earth
Yea more than thou couldst bear
Burdened thee from birth
E'en in thy visions fair

And thou adored of men
Whose bed might been of flowers
With mighty stroke of pen
Expressed thy sad sad hours

Thou hast been called above
Where all is peace and rest
To dwell in boundless love
Eternally and blest

And yet thou still dost linger near
For thy words as sweetest flowers
Do grow in beauty 'round us here
To cheer in saddest hours

Thy tho'ts with rapture seem to soar
So far yea far above
And shower a heavy down-pour
Of sparkling glittering love

Thou with stroke of mighty pen
Hast told of joy and mirth
And read the hearts and souls of men
As cradled from their birth

The language of the flowers
Thou hast read them all
And e'en the little brook
Responded to thy call

All nature hast communed
And lingered yea with thee
Their secrets were entombed
But thou hast made them free

Oh poet of our race
Thou dost soar above
No paths wilt thou retrace
But those of peace and love

Thy pilgrimage is done
Thy toils on earth are o'er
Thy victor's crown is won
Thou'lt rest forever more

OLD VIRGINIA HAM

Dar's things I likes and things I dont
Dar's things I'll do and things I wont
But the things that bring about defeat
Am the things I allus likes to eat

I has a right good appetite
I likes to eat bof day and night
But allus shuns the eaten spell
Ef I dont feel so bery well

The things I likes is poke en beans
Sweet potatoes cabbage en mustard greens
Sour kraut rabbit veal en lam
Brown fried chicken en home cured ham

Ham dried en smoked en smoked en dried
    Dat makes my stomic satisfied
You kin take yo chicken veal en lam
    Ef you give me ole Virginia ham

Some-times I thinks Ise over-fed
    To look at me you'd think Ise dead
But to revive me call out Sam!
    Ise bro't you some Virginia Ham

Jis at the word Ise on my feet
    Well en ready den to eat
Dun loss de sick spell cool en cam
    To sample dat Virginia ham

I like pig feet bery well
    Souse en spare ribs too am swell
Roas beef too wid good ole yams
    But dey dont tech Virginia ham

I likes back bone too en chime
    De nose en ears are bery fine
But dey wud put you in a jam
    Compared wid ole Virginia ham

Dar's sumpin else so hard to beat
    I allus likes so well to eat
Tis chitlins too wid cracklin bread
    A taste ob dem en you'se well fed

But listen friens dar's nuffin fine
    Dat's good en lastin all de time
Dat allus so well pleases Sam
    Like dat ole sweet Virginia ham

MEAL TIME

Liza! call dat chile
En make her was her face
En cum on to de table
En let Pap say de grace

You let de chillun hab der ways
En soon dey'll manage you
Ef you dont try to check em
Come on Bob en Sue!

Y'all set up to de table
'Twill take a ha'f a day
To git Y'all to yo meals
Cumin in dat way

Dont make sich noise wid dem stools!
Does you heah me Jane
If 'twarn't fer we ol folks
You chillun wud raise Cain

Set up straight dar Jimbo!
We all is ready Pap!
Stop dat whisperin Lisha
En pull of dat ar cap

Yo'all cud'n sho keep still
'Til Pap cud say de grace
I dunno what's gwine to cum
Ob dis young Cullud race

Sal! git de spoon en git mo hash
Dont spill it on de flo
Take up all de co'n cakes
I tink Pap wants some mo

Abe dont stuff yo mouf so full
    You sho kin git some mo
Be kerful wid dat butter-milk
    Dont spill it on de flo

En pass de cakes aroun
    Dont T'ink all 'bout yo-sef
Try to larn some manners
    You ugly little elf

You kids don eat enuf
    Git up from dat table
En clean dem dishes up
    As fas as you is able

Em, you sweep de kitchen good
    Be quick about it too
'Twill be time fer anudder meal
    Befo you chaps git thro'

WHAT'S DE USE OB WUKIN IN DE SUMMER TIME AT ALL

What's de use ob wukin in de summer time at all
    When de sun am bilin hot en de sweat begins to fall
What's de use of diggin in de field ob co'n en taters
    Plantin squash en beans en pickin ripe tomaters

What's de use ob pickin in de fields ob huckle berries
    Or pullin at de trees pickin off de cherries
What's de use ob wukin or plowin in de heat
    Eatin haf cooked meals en blisterin yo feet

What's de use ob habin houses in de summer time
'Tis plenty good out doors when de blessed sun do shine
When de fields is clothed wid green de meadow en de lane
You need no kine ob shelter cept in fallin ob de rain

'Tis mighty hard a wukin when de sun am beamin down
En not a spot of coolness to be seen aroun
When ebery way you turn de sun am shinin hot
En ebery inch ob flesh am a bu'nin spot

'Tis mighty hard a wukin in fields of up-turned ground
Fer miles en miles a plantin out ob hearin ob de town
A sowin ob de wheat or plantin ob de co'n
It sho is bitter meat en hard wuk sho's you born

'Tis fearful hard a stayin in de field de live-long day
When de hours am slowly passin en you hab so long to stay
En you wuk so bery hard when you stop you hardly know
De way to take fer home dat wont seem kin' o' slow

But arter tinkin ober all de change is got to cum
I specs I'll take de summer wid all de shinin sun
Case when de winter sets his foot upon dis naked earf
He brings about much sadness to tek the place of Mirth

Den de hard times cum a peepin en a movin in fer sho
Sho'in ob his grinnin teeth knockin at yo doe
'Tis den he tries to rob you ob you trunk en clo's
En soon you fin yo-sef a settin out ob do's

De chills dey soon cum ober you you fin no whar to go
As you wander long about de street en seek from doe to doe
No wuk to do no shelter not a crus ob bread to eat
No good warm clo's to sooth de chill no shoes fer naked feet

'Tis den I see de use ob wukin in de sun
It matters not how hot no day I'll ebah shun
'Tis den I see de need ob plantin wheat en co'n
En puttin up fer winter 'tis a fact as sho's you born

Dis den I know de need ob drappin co'n en taters
Plantin beets plantin beans en pickin ripe tomaters
'Tis den I see de good ol' need ob pickin huckle berries
En pullin down de limbs a gatherin ob de cherries

Fer all dis helps I tell yo' when de winter cums wid col'
En starts his roun ob starvin en freezin many souls
It keeps away ol' hunger when he cums wid starin face
En leabes you a sufferin en starvin in disgrace

En now I'll tell you one en all de summer time am hot
I'd sooner be a little warm den freezin 'bout in spots
I'd radder be out in de field when de sun am beamin down
En wuk de blisters on my hand as I make my weary
roun

I'll tek ole summer any time on my list fer sho—
Den fool wid winter in his wrath when he knocks
upon de doe
I'll tek de heat en sweat en plant de fields ob co'n
Radder'n face ole Winter's breaf in de coolness
ob de mo'n

No day will ebah 'pear so long no field so bu'nin hot
But what I'll plant de co'n en fill in ebery spot
No idle moments will I spar but days ob earnest toil
To sho—de blessed benefits ob wukin in de soil

Case summer time to me am dear en 'tis den I specs to wuk
En ef I has de time to spar 'Tis winter time I'll shirk
I'll try to 'scape his freezin days en ba'r me burdens free
Take Winter time en all his ways but summer time
fer me

CREATION

God made this wonderful world
With beauty and love in His plan
Day and night and the firmament
Earth and seas all for man

The sun moon and stars
With brightness to see
The birds of the air
The fish of the sea

Then every living thing and man
The sixth day brought along
God had finished up His work
And thus the world moved on

God saw His work that it was good
A gracious loving father stood
Exultant O'er His wondrous plan
The making of the earth and man

We turn to see the skies of blue
The brilliant sun with its golden hue
The mountains the rivers while exultant we stand
To wonder why God made so much for man

He carved out such beauty in rocks and rills
And made such landscapes with beautiful hills
An Ocean here a great river there
Planning it out with such beauty and care

He topped the earth with beautiful trees
Under-neath a carpet of green
With flowers of beauty that live and breathe
'Neath the sun's soft and glamoring sheen

He placed man as king upon a throne
To rule o'er a world he might call his own
He gave him might of strength and power
To rule thro' ev'ry trying hour
We wonder then at God's gracious plan
And why He did so much for man

'Twas all through love that this was done
God is the Father man the son
He gives protection love and care
Man petitions Him through prayer

And thus our loving Father stood
And saw His work that it was good
Triumphant o'er His wondrous plan
The making of the earth and man

VERSES FOR MOTHER

Mother of mine to look in your face
I'd reflect your beauty copy your grace
I'd do just the things my dear that you do
To make me so trustful so kind and so true
I'd sing of the clouds that pass in the night
Of the sun in the day to make the world bright
I'd harbor not tho'ts but those clean and true
The world would be better if more were like you

Mother of mine the days would be drear
The sky would lose some of its blue
The wide old world would be void of its cheer
Were it not my mother for you

When I was a tot you put me to bed
And whispered sweet words in my ear
Your songs were so sweet and the words you said
Remain with me still mother dear

THE GYPSY QUEEN'S REVENGE

Revenge! the word is sweet
'Tis pleasant to the ears
To have on him revenge
For suffering and tears

Revenge! ah cruel heart
Thou'st bro't me to the dust
Now thou must suffer pain
In me thy soul must trust

Thy heart must burn as mine has burnt
With bitter pain and woe
Thou'lt lick the dust as I have
I make this vow! yes go!

Ye wretched cruel curse
To take my child my son
And sentence him to prison
This cursed deed thou'st done

I begged thee pity spare
He's not the guilty one
But cruel wretch thou didst not care
But took mine only son

Mine only son! my child
As innocent and pure
A s a babe at its mother's breast
My child I did adore

I begged on bended knee
And never before have I
Begged with broken heart
'Til my throat was parched and dry

And thou yea cursed wretch!
For this cruel deed
Thou'lt suffer all thy days
Thou and all thy seed

Thy son shall reap the woeful seed
For this that thou hast done
Thou'lt see him linger in the dust
When the harvest time has come

Revenge! ah sweet it sounds
Aha! I see them come
Your daughter she shall suffer too
For this that thou hast done

I see them settled yea! in pomp
At a feast a table grand
The family happy yea! so gay
All things at their command

The Earl whom I'd begged for pity
Standing at the head—
With all his sons around him
While mine to me is dead

Yea dead! for way behind the prison walls
He's dead to joy and mirth
My son why suffer this
I rue the day of thy birth

I hasten to the great house
Where all is grand and gay
And in an upper chamber
An infant baby lay

The mother at the great feast
The nurse was not about
So I wrap him in a blanket
And soon we're out the house

Slowly I stealt thro' the darkness
'Til we reached the edge of the town
There I placed him in safe keeping
That I might continue my round

When I returned to the great house
The gaiety serene
Had changed to a picture of sadness
Sadness and sorrow extreme

The screams of the grief stricken mother
I'll hear 'til the day of my death
But no greater to me than my sorrow
When I begged with choking breath

Begged to save my child
My only child! my boy!
From the walls of a cold dark prison
My son my only joy

I had no heart when I lost my son
For it seemed my innermost depths
Left me to go with my precious one
To suffer in prison and death

I saw the Earl's daughter wriggle in pain
Mourning the loss of her child
While the father with gun threats to blow out his brain
As he walks in delirium wild

They suffer just half that I suffered
For none as the gypsy wild
Can suffer the pain that I have borne
In the loss of an only child

I have no heart no tender chord
For my heart has turned to stone
As I wander to seek revenge
Thro' this cold cold world alone

The Earl's son has died heart broken
    Over the loss of his child
While the mother behind walls is a maniac
    Wandering in phantoms wild

The Earl himself is helpless
    Paralyzed with grief
And my visits are so frequent
    That he finds no time for relief

For I stand and wail revenge! at him
    'Til he seems a mass of stone
Gasping it seems for every breath
    As he sits in his study alone

My face will ever haunt him
    'Til his life slowly ebbs away
And the breath leaps from his stolid frame
    On his last his dying day

Revenge aha! 'tis come
    The smiles but freeze on my face
As I see his sons falling one by one
    In utter shame and disgrace

I hear the cries wildly o'er the town
    That the great great Earl has died
I gladly give up my Gypsy crown
    I can die now satisfied

Full satisfied for revenge
    Has had a powerful sway
She leapt into that family
    And took them all away

While their child remains to suffer
As my child my son
For both are but children of the dust
And neither a guilt has done

COULD DREAMS REPEAT

Last night I dreamed I saw you dear
And Oh! the mem'ries sweet
They cling as though you still were near
Oh could dreams repeat
That we might live from day to day
In ecstacy sublime
By dreaming dreams of yesterday
Yes! 'til the end of time

WHAT'S MO TEMPTIN TO DE PALATE

What's mo temptin' to de palate
When youse wuked so hard all day
En cum in home at even-time
Wid out a wud to say—
And see a stewin in de stove
A possum crisp en brown
Wid great big sweet potaters
A layin' all aroun'

What's mo temptin to de palate
Den a chicken bilin hot
En plenty ob good dumplins
A bubblin' in de pot
To set right down to eat dem
En 'pease yo hungar dar
'Tis nuffin mo' enjoyin'
I sholy do declar

What's mo temptin to de palate
    Den a dish ob good baked beans
En what is still mo temptin
    Den a pot brimfull of greens
Jis biled down low wid bacon
    Almos 'til deys fried
En a plate ob good ole co'n cakes
    A layin' on de side

What's mo temptin' to de palate
    Den on Thanksgivin' Day
To hab a good ole tuckey
    Fixed some kin' o' way
Wid cranberry sauce en celery
    All settin' on de side
En eat jis 'til yo' appetite
    Is sho full satisfied

What's mo temptin to de palate
    Den in de Summer time
To bus' a water mellon
    Right off from de vine
En set right down to eat it
    In de coolin breeze
Wif nuffin to moles' you
    Settin 'neaf de apple trees

What's mo temptin to de palate
    Den poke chops also lam'
En what is still mo temptin
    Den good ol col' biled ham
Veal chops dey aint bad
    Put mutton chops in line
I tell you my ole appetite
    Fo' all dese t'ings do pine

What's mo temptin to de palate
    When you cum from wuk at night

To set down to de fire
A shinin' jis so bright
De ole 'Oman walks in—
Wid supper brilin hot
En a good ole cup ob coffee
Jis steamin from de pot

'Tis den I kin enjoy my-sef
En eat dar by de fiah
Case puttin' way good eatins
Is my hearts desiah
Dar's nuffin dat's so temptin'
Dat to me is a treat
Den settin' at a table
Wid plenty good to eat

OUR MISSIONARY

Dedicated to The Memory of the Late Dr. W. H. Sheppard Presbyterian Missionary, Who Spent Twenty Years in Africa

On on to the darkest continent
As the Adriatic sailed
In Eighteen hundred and ninety
Many sad good-byes were wailed

When two brave sons left their homes
Their kindred yea their blood
To wade in Africa's unknown and
An overwhelming flood

A Caucasian and a Negro
United heart and soul
Bound for Ethiopia's soil
Yea Africa's distant goal

As from the New York Shore
The Steamer slowly starts
Sheppard and Lapsley bade good bye
To sad but anxious hearts

On on as the steamer glides
'Mid the rippling water's whirl
On to the wild and savage land
The darkest in the world

Yet, in that darkened land
Were millions yea unfed
Who never had been told
Of Christ the living bread

But God had sent a message
To these two men so brave
To go to Ethiopia's land
And try these souls to save

Gladly they heeded his command
To go 'mid danger and strife
And work in that distant land
Yes at the cost of life

And so in Ethiopia's wild
These two men so brave
Prayed for Ethiopia's child
Struggling a soul to have

For weeks yes months they struggled
Working day and night
Until at last how happy!
There came a ray of light

One soul had come to Christ
One made to understand—
The blessed Savior's voice
And heed to His Command

These leaders true and brave
Prayed to Him on high a prayer
To thank Him for this blessing
And for His Tender care

But ere many months had passed
There came a sad sad day
A cloud o'er Africa's land was cast
For one had passed away

A leader now was gone
One whom they did love
Rev. Lapsley had been called
To that land above

His comrade also missed him
For he was left alone
To dwell in Ethiopia's Land
Afar from friends and home

A work he had left unfinished
Which he had resolved to do
But Sheppard decided by God's aid
To carry the work on through

So he started out one day
With Africa's savage band
Determined to make his way
To the Forbidden land*

Months they spent on the way
To carry a ray of light
To Heathen who knew no day
In a land where all was night

After toiling daily
With Ethiopia's sons
Many were brought to Christ
A Victor's crown was won

They built a house of worship
    And toiled day after day
Soon Ethiopia's sons
    Had learned the narrow way

They too began to preach
    And teach their fellowmen
And for these blessings great
    Their prayers did upward blend

And in this land so dark
    Where never had been light
The lame in Christ were made to walk
    The blind were given sight

To Sheppard they gave great praise
    He'd ventured on their soil
And Ethiopia's sons were raised
    Through years of earnest toil

For twenty years he struggled
    In Africa's darkened land
Giving them the light
    As they heeded his command

Way off in Africa's land
    Let us in fancy look
To see a heathen band
    Who'd never seen a book

Now preaching Christ and teaching
    With minds all free and bright
All hail to Thee Oh Sheppard
    Who carried them the light

A great work Thou didst do
    In this vast darkened land
Many laurels thou didst win
    From toiling with this band

A great work thou hast done
Thou didst do thy best
Now God has called thee to thy home
To dwell in peace and rest

*The forbidden land herewith mentioned has reference to a tribe of savages in the interior, known as Bakubas.

THE STORY OF LOVER'S LEAP

[At Greenbrier White Sulphur Springs, West Virginia, one of the famous resorts of the South, may be seen the historic Lover's Leap which gave the inspiration for this poem.]

To the state of West Virginia
During the Summer days bright
Countless numbers are wending their way
To the Old Greenbrier White

A famous resort of the South
Which for years has held her fame
And dame and sage of every age
Honor White Sulphur's name

'Tis here many lovers meet
And stroll on her carpet green
As the eve grows old tales of love unfold
And many just sweet sixteen

Happy moments they do spend
Yea! moments of delight
As hearts in union blend
They praise Greenbrier White

Now for the places of interest
Of one I'll venture to speak
Which seems by far most visited
Long known as Lover's Leap

Where two lovers once upon a time
Whose love was true and tried
Both with determined minds
Ne'er to be denied—

Climbed to this very high precipice
Looked o'er the rugged steep
Decided within a few moments
To make the fatal leap

Said they "Together we'll end our lives
Rather than to part"
Within their minds they did contrive
To make the fatal start

All was quiet and undisturbed
The hour was growing late
For a while they uttered not a word
As they tho't to meet their fate

Theirs was a love so true
Not for a day
Love that ever seems anew
That never dies away

This love began in child-hood days
As days so glided by
They felt that for each other
Gladly they would die

Perhaps many minds have wondered
Why on this eve so late
This maid and lad with hearts so sad
Decided to meet their fate

But the parents of this couple brave
Firmly did object
And tho't that both the lad and maid
Their wishes should respect

For a while o'er this they did bother
    Why think of the trials of life
Now comes the words of our Father
    "Forsake all and cleave to thy wife"

Did it not seem hard for them to live
    Alone thro' the trials of life
Could he on account of others give
    The dear one he wished to call wife

No "But together we'll strive to live
    Or together we'll strive to die
'Twill be a pleasure our lives to give
    And so with our wishes comply"

So 'twas fully decided
    And on one evening late
To the Leap they slowly glided
    The two to meet their fate

On on to the fatal spot
    The couple made their way
To bring to an end the plot
    Before another day

As they reached the craggy edge
    The couple hand in hand
Carried out their fatal pledge
    Their own their last demand

Side by side the couple lay
    Hearts that beat as one
Ceased upon that final day
    Their toils on earth now done

And e'er since that gloomy hour
    The story has not failed to keep
It seems that some magnetic power
    Holds sway o'er the famous "Leap"

Ne'er shall the hist'ry be forgot
By those who the story seek
But ever famous will be the spot
Well known as "Lover's Leap"

WEST VIRGINIA

'Mid the hills of West Virginia
'Neath the mountain tops so high
Nature paints most charming beauty
Tinted flakes on azure sky
Gazing from the mountain tower
To the rivers far below
Trav'lers spend yea! many hours
Each day going to and fro
Some are writing some are thinking
Each day drawing up some plan
As they wander stop to ponder
Why God made so much for man

THOUGHTS

Had I the wings of a bird
I'd make it a constant duty
To fly far above the earth
And gaze on it's wondrous beauty

Had I the mind of a poet
I'd always try to write
Poems of thrilling beauty
To fill some mind with delight

I'd love to stroll in distant lands
Among the rocks and rills
And see the works of nature's hands
And gaze on the distant hills

I'd love to listen to the birds
That sing their songs of praise
And make some poor souls happy
In their saddest days

It would be to my delight
To stand at the river side
And gaze on the placid water
As it slowly and playfully glides

I'd love to write of the beautiful
I'd love to write of the brave
And read the minds of others
And note their winning ways

I would not judge the beautiful
By the beauty of their faces
By suppositions or the like
Or their pretended graces

It brings to my mind once again
A maxim that I love
And one of the sayings as of old
Beauty is that beauty does

A DREAM

I had a dream one winter's night
It filled my soul with pure delight
Ne'er ran my tho'ts in strains so sweet
I'm filled with rapture to repeat

Oh could I dream that dream again
'Twould be a song a sweet refrain
Oh could I wake to find it true
'Twould then my happy tho'ts renew

Dreams sweet dreams of the past
Which o'er our lives bright shadows cast
Yet sometimes in their course they change
And pleasure clouds they disarrange

What disappointments we do meet
In dreaming dreams yea! dreams so sweet
Joy and happiness flow in streams
We wake to find it but a dream

What is this mysterious way
In which we think we spend a day
Awaking ourselves amid delight
Finding 'tis not day but night

'Tis a fancy which o'er us does creep
When in that state of rest called sleep
The light of imagination which does beam
And form what we always term a dream

A dream is a miniature life
Often lived in a single night
When pleasant this tho't oft does gleam
Oh could we live just as we dream

FLOWERS FOR TOM

[Being a radio fan of Tom Breneman's, the author held him i high esteem, because of his attitude to those in need and the man kind deeds he did to make them happy. The many kind deeds he di to make others happy brought the inspiration for this letter which sh wrote to Tom and in turn received from him an appreciative card o thanks.]

I'm sending you these flowers Tom
In place of those you give
Remember they're not orchids
But flowers to help you live

Be sure to take in doses
Just as I prescribe
They may puff you up a bit
But you'll stay much alive

Read the prescription once
Then absorb and rub in well
'Twill make you throw your shoulders back
And also strut a spell
Your eyes will glisten like a gem
Small doses will be plenty
You'll be unlike all other men
And pass for under twenty

These pills are made of roses
To give you length of years
The capsules are of lilies
Filled with applause and cheers
The liquid is a tonic
Made from all the flowers—
That blossom in the spring time
To cheer in gloomy hours

A teaspoonful just once a day
Will drive all cares and gloom away
No vitamin you'll need than that
To whom all men will doff their hats
To you we say this homage give
With wishes that you long may live—
To spread your blessings as you may
In giving happiness each day

VIRGINIA

[This poem was set to music by the author and used in one of her pageants "Lifting As We Climb" which was written for The Virginia State Federation of Colored Womens Clubs and rendered at the meeting of this body at Covington, Virginia, in 1937. The women of the Federation were so well pleased that they asked the author to arrange to bring the girl participants to Hampton Institute in 1938 to appear before the National Federation of Colored Womens Clubs. The trip was arranged and the pageant was presented before a vast audience on the campus of Hampton Institute representing most of the states of the union.]

Virginia Virginia thy hills of verdant green
    Virginia Virginia thy valleys are serene
We climb thy mountain peaks so high
    We gaze with rapture on the sky
And clouds they disappear we feel thy presence near
    Virginia Virginia Virginia

Virginia Virginia thy clouds tinted with gold
    Virginia Virginia when heavy gloom infold
We pray that they may clear away
    And then will come a brighter day
The clouds of white and gold their stories do unfold
    Virginia Virginia Virginia

CHRISTMAS LETTER TO THE BOYS AND THE GIRLS OVER THERE (WORLD WAR II)

[During World War II, the author purchased paper with a heading of a Christmas tree, Santa Claus and boys in Navy uniforms and also the same picture with boys in Army uniform and upon this paper she had a Christmas letter published to the boys and girls "over there". These letters were sold through the Woman's Study Club for a scholarship fund and some of the money was used to send Bibles to boys in the Army, no nationality designated. Many letters were sold.]

This letter I write with the greatest of care
    To all of our boys and our girls over there
On this Christmas morn as the fires softly glow
    We gaze in the embers and think of you so

The turkey, the cake, the plum pudding's amiss
Since you're not here to enjoy all of this
You're working so hard and we know this so well
We want you to know that we think you are swell
Where ever you are in the lands far away
On this Christmas morning for you we will pray
'Mid flicker of candles as fires softly burn
We're praying and waiting for your return
Now merry Christmas! to each in the lands "over there"
Happy thoughts to those whose Christmas you share
God bless them too and give them much cheer
With freedom and happiness for many a year

IN MEMORY OF REV. C.B.W. GORDON, SR.

[In September 1941 Rev. C.B.W. Gordon, Sr., of Petersburg, Va., passed away in the home of his son, Rev. C.B.W. Gordon, Jr., the pastor of Zion Baptist Church, Parkersburg, W. Va. About an hour before the funeral was to be held at Zion Baptist Church, the author wrote these verses and sent them to the house, getting into the hands of his son just before leaving for the church. They were read during the funeral service by one of the officials of the church.]

Just a little message
Calling from the Land above
To a gentle loving shepherd
Message full of peace and love
Just a message to remind him
How he'd toiled and struggled hard
Working daily for his Master
Bringing others home to God

Just a whisper from the Heavens
Begging him to stop and rest
Years of service he had given
He had toiled to stand the test
He had listened to the murmurs
Of the poor the sick the blind
He had brought the Saviour's message
And the comforts he could find

Years he'd struggled for his Master
From dawn 'til set of evening sun
Never tiring—never weary
'Til His Master said "Well done"
He had filled his gracious mission
He had stood the rigid test
Now he hears the Master calling
Begging him to stop and rest

Just a calling from his Master
Just an urgent call of love
Just a peaceful whisper
From the restful Land above
Thou hast done thy faithful bidding
Thou hast worked 'til set of sun
Come thou faithful to the Master
He has said to thee "Well done"

DAYS MUST COME YEARS MUST GO

Days must pass days must come
From peep of morn 'til setting sun
Night time comes for peace and rest
When morning comes—man at his best
Must make his start with rapid pace
If he would keep up in the race—
With great men of this world and small
For none must stop e'en tho' he fall

Years must come and years must go
What they will bring no man can know
Until as out the clear blue skies—
Events spring up in great surprise
Yet some folks say there's nothing new
For God made man to dare and do
And since our God created man
He makes known to none His plan

THOUGHTS FOR IDLE HOURS

BY

MAGGIE POGUE JOHNSON

AUTHOR OF

"VIRGINIA DREAMS"

DEDICATED

TO

MY MOTHER

SOMEBODY'S MOTHER

The world in its wild and maddened flight
Goes heedlessly along,
Pays no thought to the darkest night,
And heeds not a ceaseless throng.

A wanderer poor and forsaken
May pass by one then another,
But he's not noticed at all,
Lest it be by somebody's mother.

Somebody's mother, tho' old and gray,
And bent by life's lengthened years,
Has helped the beggar, so poor, by the way,
And gives him her prayers and her tears.

The girl who falls by the wayside,
And wrecks her dear sacred life,
Who ceases to heed to her guide,
Repents in bitter strife.

The world now laughs her to scorn,
Kicked and buffed by one then another,
She begs for sympathy long—
None offers but somebody's mother.

Somebody's mother holds out her hand,
To take this wanderer in,
Battered and cuffed by a reckless band,
With tattered garments of sin.

The boy who has lived the most reckless life,
And in shame wanders wildly home;
Thro' the world he stumbles in darkness of night,
With a pillow of rock or stone.

He begs from house to house,
He's refused by one then another,
But at last he's aided by one—
You may know 't was somebody's mother.

Somebody's mother with aching heart,
Feels for somebody's child,
Who has no one to take his part,
And wanders so reckless and wild.

Somebody's mother, with waiting hand,
Stands ready to help the poor,
Whenever there's want in demand,
Just go to some mother's door.

Yea! some mother's door—for none can feel,
And offer with greatness of heart,
Like a dear and honored mother,
Who dearly performs her part.

Yea! mother—that sacred word,
Is as dear as the costliest pearl
To the son who has wandered afar—
And the mother's only girl.

Was there ever a word so sweet
To sister, husband or brother,
That every demand could meet,
And in form so simple as mother?

Yea! None—for each letter is dear
And sacred to many a heart,
For others may give words of cheer,
But can't do a mother's part.

THE ROSE

Take not this rose from me,
If thou'd not be guilty of theft;
Rob me not of this beauty flower,
If thou'rt not of reason bereft.

This simple little rose I prize,
Yea! not for its name,
But for its everyday use,
Which has brought it world-wide fame.

Take not this rose from me,
For it may not aid you much,
But it gives me magic power,
And, too, would rob me of such.

Ah! dear little rose, thou hast brought much joy,
To the hearts of many I know;
Thou hast brought smiles to the sweetheart,
When handed by a beau.

Thou hast brought joy and sunshine
To many a gloomy heart,
Ah! blessed little rose—
I cannot from thee part.

Take not this rose from me—
Oh, ye little flower!
The gracious God above
Gives you wondrous power.

He makes the whole world smile,
When on thy face they gaze,
Bewildered by thy beauty,
They offer up great praise.

Thou bringest joy to the sick,
To have thy presence there;
Thou spreadest joy and sunshine,
Alike, yea, everywhere.

And, dear little flower,
E'en however small,
We rue the coming of the day
To see thy petals fall.

To see thy petals one by one
Fall withered to the ground,
Tells us, too, thy work is done,
Thou'st already won thy crown.

Dear little rose, thou art blushing now
To hear me call thee dear,
But with thy attractive beauty
I'd love thee always near.

I'd love to see thy blushing face
Always before my eyes,
I'd then forget the cloudy day,
And, too, see clearer skies.

Ah! clearer skies, for then the clouds
Would gladly give their space
To let the blessed sun shine
On thy smiling face.

Dear little rose, thou'rt drooping now,
Thou art getting weak;
Would'st thou have one drop of water
To cool thy burning cheek—

Or would'st thou rather droop
And slowly die away,
Until the coming Spring—
Thy resurrection day?

When thou in all thy beauty
Wilt shine forth ever new,
To perform thy lasting duty,
Ever faithful—true.

Yea! to perform thy lasting duty
To the sick and to the dead;
Dear rose, that thou art loyal
Hast been nobly said.

Take not this rose from me,
From it I will not part,
To me 't is ever dear,
I'll press it to my heart.

The withered leaves I'll keep,
That I may have them near—
For the memory of the precious rose
I'll hold, yea! ever dear.

TUSKEGEE'S SORROW

(Dedicated to the Memory of Dr. Booker T. Washington)

Weep not, Tuskegee, tho' great be thy sorrow
For him who didst fight and fall for thy cause;
We know thou wilt miss him to-day—yea! to-morrow,
Thou'lt list for his voice, for his steps thou'lt pause.

Weep not, Tuskegee, for him who has left us,
Left us in sorrow and heart-rending grief;
His was a life of toil for his people,
Great was his life work and yet his life brief.

Weep not, Tuskegee, tho' great be thy burden,
Burdens of thought, yea! burdens of care
Fell from the shoulders of thy greatest hero,
Now thou wilt have the burdens to bear.

Weep not, Tuskegee—a nation is weeping,
Save back thy tears and console them in grief;
While thy great hero is peacefully sleeping,
Thousands of grieved hearts pray for relief.

Weep not, Tuskegee, for sorrow unspoken
Is thine, we know, and will ever be,
We know too well that thy heart is broken,
We beg thee to weep not for we weep for thee.

Weep not, Tuskegee, for thy honored hero
Is resting from labor, resting from care;
Peaceful his slumber with no thought of worry,
No thought of even a burden to bear.

Weep not, Tuskegee, the gates now stand open,
The Angel who came so peacefully down
Bore him on high to his great home in heaven,
Placed there upon him a star-studded crown.

Weep not, Tuskegee, but sing of thy hero,
Brave, honored hero who fell for thy name;
We'll laud his mem'ry forever with praises,
Praise for the hero, our hero of fame.

THE SOLDIER'S ADIEU

Farewell, dear heart,
It grieves me this to say—
But ere you read these lines,
I shall be far away.

Yea, far beyond
Where ocean cries bemoan,
The soldier boy,
Afar from friends and home.

Farewell, dear heart,
'T is sad to bid adieu
To one whose love
Has been so stanch and true.

And as I pen these lines,
My heart doth beat,
And gentle whispers seem
To say retreat.

But nay! my country's call
I must obey,
Altho' I miss thee, dear,
While far away.

Yet pray, dear heart,
Yes, sweetheart, pray
For him whom thou dost love,
So far away.

Pray that though
'Mid shot and shell,
Thy soldier boy be spared—
And now, Farewell.

THE DRUNKARD'S DREAM

Crime? murder, did I hear you say?
Yes, I killed my wife!
Outside the door in blood she lay,
The victim of a knife.

The victim of a heart that craved for crime,
That craved for blood,
Who feared no foe in face of time,
Nor retribution's flood.

The victim of a soul so black—
Black with earthly sin,
Who feared no bloodhound on his track,
Nor even death's cold grim!

Haunted, yea! by wild desire,
I plunge in depths of crime,
My very soul it seems afire,
Yet, am I sick or blind?

Yes, I killed my wife,
Yes, I killed my child—
My child, a girl of eight—
Yet am I crazed or wild?

My girl, a beauty to behold,
Those eyes, I see them now,
How with expressive look they told
Her love for me, I'll vow.

She was her father's heart,
Each evening at the gate,
I'll see my Nell, how can we part?
But now it is too late!

I pierced a dagger's shining blade
    Thro' the heart of my dear wife,
Who's now a victim for the grave,
    And yet there was no strife

Betwixt my wife and me;
    We always lived as dear
As any couple you might see,
    She full of love and cheer.

But it seems some savage beast
    Had cast his heart in mine,
I could not rest in peace,
    With anger I was blind!

I rushed inside the door,
    With the dagger's shining blade,
For murder or for crime,
    In blood I wished to wade!

I killed my wife, I killed my child,
    And for fear I might be found,
I set my home a-blaze,
    And soon 't was to the ground.

My home, my wife, my child—
    In one heap of ashes lay,
My heart, my treasure, yea! my all,
    Swept within a day.

And now I'm crazed, I'm wild;
    What spell was this, I pray,
That caused me kill my child?
    Oh, help me, God, I pray!

My wife, and where is she?
I did not kill her, too!
Oh, God, in mercy hear my plea—
What must a sinner do?

Without a home, without a wife,
Without my child, my all,
Battling thro' a world of strife,
Wilt Thou hear my call?

Oh, wife! Oh, child! Oh, do but speak—
I never meant the crime!
'T was drink, 't was cursed rum—
Oh, cursed rum, I'm blind!

As I reached my hand, the cold, cold touch
Was that of a prison wall;
The next the Judge and Jury,
And then the prisoner's fall.

The sentence fell cold and heavy,
In words clearly cut and bare:
"The prisoner found guilty of murder—
His doom the Electric Chair."

Oh! God, I'm choking, I'm dying,
Gasping for every breath,
The result of rum—Oh, how trying,
How bitter and cruel is death!

As I lay there gasping for life,
In a cold, cold prison cell,
Some one shook me and Oh! 't was my wife,
And beside her my daughter Nell!

Why haunt me like this! I gave,
I gave a scream—
Wife pressed a kiss—
"Dear, you're in a dream!"

"Thank God!" I cried, "you've saved my life!
I was almost gone, my darling wife,
Dying from thoughts of—to utter I dare—
Meeting my fate in the cursed chair.

"But thanks be to God! from this very day,
I'll worship Thee only, Oh! help me, I pray;
For Thou in this dream hast shown me the strife
And the bitterness gleaned from a drunkard's life.

"Thou in this dream
Hast broken the spell,
And saved my soul
From a drunkard's hell."

♰ ♰

THE HERO OF AFRIC'S WILD

Bound in fetters and chains,
They come from a country afar,
Sons of chieftains and kings,
Their priestly records mar.

Clothed in slavery's garb,
Doomed to a wretched life,
Away from friends and home,
To battle thro' blood and strife.

We hear the piercing shrieks
 Echo from Afric's wild,
Of natives frenzied and crazed,
 Mourning for Afric's child.

Mourning for sons of kings,
 And princes of wealthy estate,
Brought from the land afar
 To bury in slavery's weight.

Crushed 'neath bondage and fear,
 They mourn their awful fate,
Heirs of princes and kings
 Doomed to an awful fate.

Yea! doomed to slavery's chain,
 To live 'neath the awful spell,
To suffer and bear the pangs
 Which none would be able to tell.

To suffer—yea, that is small!
 Amid the burden of hate,
But think of Afric's fall
 And degradation great.

Her kings stand back in disgust,
 And curse the land where befell
The crime of slavery's lust,
 Worse than the pangs of hell.

Burdened 'neath slavery's hate,
 A fervent prayer is heard,
As the slave succumbs to his weight,
 And utters on high a few words.

"Master above, wilt Thou hear this,
A slave's poor pitiful cry,
Wilt Thou grant us freedom—
Freedom ere we die?

"Wilt Thou listen to the cries
Of husband, mother and babe,
And 'mid their sufferings great,
Spare mercy to the slave?

"We know Thou wilt hear our cry,
Oh! Master, hear us now,
As humbly at Thy feet
Before Thy throne we bow."

Soon the clouds began to scatter,
And the dread and gloom dispel,
And the slave with all his burdens
Could a brighter story tell.

List! we hear the news of freedom,
Echoed, yea! from land to land;
Slaves rejoice 'mid tears of sorrow,
As they grasp each other's hand.

Ah, thank God! at last we're happy,
For He's heard our woful cry,
And in turn He gives us freedom;
Now we see a clearer sky.

Then an aged Afric chieftain,
Sorrowed to the very grave,
That he of noble blood
Had suffered as a slave,

Bids his dear ones come around him,
To say a last good-bye.
"Since our God did give us freedom,
I feel happy now to die.

"Happy, yea! to leave the land
Where my dear ones face to face
Have suffered, spilt their blood,
And wore the brand of slave's disgrace.

"For way in Afric's sunny wild
Our fathers, true and brave,
Would lose each drop of blood
Before they'd be a slave.

"And let me die, Oh! die so happy!
And tho' I've been a slave,
Before my people get the message,
I'll be happy in the grave."

AUNT CLOE'S TRIP TO SEE MISS LIZA KYLE

I'se been libin in de country
Fer lo, dese many years,
Country life to me am dear,
Wid no worry en no fears.

But a frien had kindly axed me
To de city fer a while,
Dat I might joy de city life,
De pleasure en de style.

Ob style I neber tho't befo,
En I wondered what was bes,
Since to de city I mus go,
Whar folks all stood de tes.

Well, I pondered en I wondered,
How I mus dress in style,
To go into de city
To see Miss Liza Kyle.

So I writ to her a letter,
"Dear Liza," says I den,
"Dese few lines I writes to you,
As I takes in han my pen.

"I aint so well to-day,
En I hopes you is de same;
I has de rheumatiz so bad,
Dat makes me kinder lame.

"I'll try to be in readiness
To leabe here Tuesday late,
But, Lize, I wants to know de styles,
Case when I nears yo gate,

"I wont be called so countrified,
Not by a hundred miles;
When you see Cloe right at yo doe,
She's gwine to be in style.

"So splain to me jis how to dress,
So anyting I lac
I'll fix en make myself look good,
Case I won't be no ways back.

"I specs to heah from you right soon.
In a week er mo;
Wid lots ob lub en kisses,
I'm lubingly, Aunt Cloe."

Well, a day or two had passed,
When I got from her a letter;
I'se feelin kinder scrumptious den,
Case my rheumatiz was better.

En I felt jis right to go to wuk,
To fix myself in style,
To go into de city
To see Miss Liza Kyle.

"Dear Aunt Cloe," de lines read,
"I was glad to get your letter,
And truly hope by this
You're feeling something better.

"Yes, fix yourself in style,
I'll meet you Tuesday late,
For the folks won't understand
Unless you're up to date.

"You must wear a hobble skirt,
Your hair in puffs must be,
With a band of ribbon round your head,
Where a bow you'll fix, you see.

"Your shoe heels must be very high,
And make yourself look small;
Be careful, too, just how you walk,
Or else you'll have a fall.

"You'll have to take short steps
In your hobble skirt, you see,
But that's the latest thing,
And in style you must be.

"Your hat must be extremely large,
With a feather quill behind,
And then you'll be a model sure,
Aunt Cloe, you'll just look fine.

"I enclose a picture here,
Cut from a fashion book,
To show exactly how
The hobble skirt will look.

"Now imitate the picture,
The skirt looks rather tight,
But lace your stoutness down,
And then you'll be all right."

Well, Fodder, what a picture,
Dat skirt looks awful tight,
En fer me to war a ting like dat,
I know I'd look a sight.

I goes to seamstress next day,
Wid dress goods under arm,
To hab my hobble made
So I cud leabe de farm.

A hansome piece ob red I took,
Wid green to make de border,
En axed de seamstress please
To make my skirt in order.

Jis like dis picture here,
Case I mus be in style,
To go into de city,
To see Miss Liza Kyle.

De picture called fer four yards,
But didn't say de size
Ob de woman in de picture,
En I was den surprised,

When I took two yards ob each,
Two ob green en two ob red,
De seamstress shook her head,
It ain't enuf she said.

Well, do de bes you kin, I said,
I got four yards in all,
Dat's all de picture called for,
En I aint near dat tall.

Dats all de samples dat dey had
In colors dat was bright,
En I wants to look a little gay
When I git dar Tuesday night.

Well, I goes to git my dress next day,
En de seamstress she did tell,
'T was de fus one she had done in style,
En tho't she'd done so well.

I jis did hab enuf she said,
So I made de front ob green,
En de back I made ob red
Whar it wouldn't be much seen.

I axed her den to help me dress,
    En git myself in style
To go into de city,
    To see Miss Liza Kyle.

I guess de puffs is used fer bangs,
    Case I haint seed dem befo,
So I pins dem on de front my head,
    En behin I puts a bow.

De puffs felt heaby on my head,
    But I knowd I was in style,
To go into de city,
    To see Miss Liza Kyle.

I den puts on de hobble,
    En Oh! but it was tight;
Sich a squeezin I did do
    To git my skirt on right.

I was den so sorry
    I didn't put my hat on fus,
Case I was skeered to move
    For fear my skirt wud bus.

I takes de train fer New York,
    Wid satchel in my han,
En de car it was so crowded,
    En dar I had to stan.

De folks dey looked me up en down,
    But I knowed I was in style,
To go into de city,
    To see Miss Liza Kyle.

De ductor axed me whar I'se gwine,
Ef I'se on de proper car,
I tol him none ob his bizness,
Jis so I paid my far.

Soon we landed in de city,
De city ob New York,
En de folks dey stood in swarms
As we landed on de walk.

I seed Miss Liza, she steps back,
En den she starts to run,
I says, "Hol on dar,
None ob dat city fun.

"I specs you doesn't know me
In all dis city style,
But dis is Ole Aunt Cloe,
Does you hear me, Liza Kyle?"

I calls out agin,
Den she starts out walkin' fast,
En I was right behin her,
But I tell you, 't was a task.

Case my hat come cler down on my neck,
My puffs was in my eyes,
My shoe heels pitched me up so high
I thought I'se in de skies.

En ebery step I'd make
My skirt wud pull me back,
Till I got de scissors out de grip
En ripped it down de back.

I pulled dem high-heel shoes off,
En den I sho did run
To ketch Ole Liza Kyle,
But I tell you 't warn't no fun.

She wid dem city friens,
Didn't want to own
Precious Ole Aunt Cloe,
But I followed her right home.

Wid my hobble skirt cut down de back,
My high-heel shoes in han,
I followed her right in de doe,
En she was raisin san,

Mutterin out, some hobo
Had made a big mistake,
En I was settin dar so warm,
I thought dat I wud bake.

She sent de sarvants in,
Said dey, "Dar's some mistake,
Lady, you'se missed de number,
We's skeered we's most disgraced."

I flung my shoes right in der face,
"No police in de lan
Kin git me out ob here,
Right here I takes my stan.

"Ef dis am de greetin dat you git,
When you come in style,
I'll war ole clos de nex time
To see Ole Liza Kyle."

PARTING WORDS

'T is sad to say good-bye,
To part with best of friends;
The tear, the soul's deep sigh
With recollection blend

To make one e'en more sad,
And deepest feeling rent,
Till thoughts of happiness grow mad
O'er hours of pleasure spent.

'T is sad to part with friends,
If friends they be indeed,
When souls unite to blend
In friendship which we need.

'T is sad, tho' howe'er sad,
The soul its depth is touched
With love that makes us glad,
Of friends we love so much.

And tho' we say good-bye
To friends, yea! best of friends,
May He who watches keep thee nigh,
And His protection lend,

Lest we should soon forget
His sacred ruling power,
His love, His tender care,
Which guides each day and hour.

For Thou with jealous thought
Art watching o'er us all,
Lest we should stumble on our way,
And by the wayside fall.

Tho' friends, yea! friends must part,
    Our thoughts we bring to Thee,
For Thou canst heal the wounded heart,
    And make us glad and free.

The world grows dark and cold,
    The warmth it seems has gone,
We part with words untold,
    And dearest thoughts unborn.

Yea! the darkness He'll unfold,
    And place a shining light,
That the world may ne'er again grow cold,
    But stay forever bright.

For tho' some days be dark,
    He can make them bright,
He'll clear the skies with a single spark,
    E'en the darkest night.

And now the darkness leaves,
    The stars forever shine;
Tho' hearts with sadness bleed,
    We're Thine, forever Thine.

⚜ ⚜

WHEN THE HEART GROWS FONDER

Absence makes the heart grow fonder,
    One writer so hath said;
Another says stay by me longer,
    If you're certain we must wed.

For when you cease to see me, dear,
You'll soon forget me then,
For miles and leagues I fear,
Make differences, my friend.

Absence makes the heart grow fonder,
When all your money's spent,
'Tis then to her, your memories wander,
For a letter—one you sent.

Asking her to be so kind,—
And lend me car fare, dear,
For you know that love is blind,
I wish that you were near.

COULD DREAMS REPEAT

Last night I dreamed I saw you, dear,
And oh! the memories sweet,
They cling as tho' you still were near,
O! could dreams but repeat.

That we might live from day to day,
In ecstacy sublime,
By dreaming dreams of yesterday,
Yea! 'til the end of time.

THE TWINS

Come, daddy come,
Dere's some mistake I fear,
I looked in mudders room,
Two babies is in dere.

Dey bof is in de little bed,
  Where I did always sleep,
I tipped up softly to dem,
  En tried to take a peep.

I wonder of she knows it,
  Fer some poor mudder now,
I spec is cryin awful hard,
  Fer tother one I'll vow.

En some ole ugly oman
  Has stealed it I jis bet,
En brung it to my mudder,
  Some money fer to get.

But bof look jis alike,
  Come daddy, come en see,
Der hair is jis like mudder's
  En eyes bof jis like me.

What did you say, my daddy,
  Dat bof longs at dis house
En dat I mus be quiet,
  Quiet as a mouse—

So de babies dey kin sleep,
  En not worry my po' mudder?
I wish dey hadn't bro't jis one,
  Much less to think anodder.

THE GYPSY QUEEN'S REVENGE

Revenge! the word is sweet,
'Tis pleasant to the ears,—
To have on him revenge,
For suffering and tears.

Revenge! ah, cruel heart!
Thou'st bro't me to the dust,
Now thou must suffer pain,
In me thy soul must trust.

Thy heart must burn as mine has burnt,
With bitter pain and woe,
Thou'lt lick the dust as I have,
I make this vow! yes, go!

Ye wretched, cruel curse,
To take my child, my son,
And sentence him to prison,
This cursed deed thou'st done.

I begged thee pity spare,
He's not the guilty one,
But cruel wretch thou didst not care,
But took mine only son.

Mine only son! my child,
As innocent and pure
As a babe at it's mother's breast,
My child I did adore.

I begged on bended knee,
And never before have I
Begged with broken heart,
'Til my throat was parched and dry.

And thou, yea, cursed wretch!
For this cruel deed,
Thou'lt suffer all thy days,
Thou and all thy seed.

Thy son shall reap the woeful seed,
For this that thou hast done,
Thou'lt see him linger in the dust,
When the harvest time has come.

Revenge, ah! sweet it sounds,
Aha! I see them come,
Your daughter she shall suffer too,
For this that thou hast done.

I see them settled, yea! in pomp,
At a feast, a table grand,
The family happy, yea! so gay,
All things at their command.

The Earl whom I'd begged for pity,
Standing at the head—
With all his sons around him,
While mine to me is dead.

Yea, dead! for way behind the prison walls
He's dead to joy and mirth,
My son why suffer this,
I rue thy day of birth.

I hasten to the great house,
Where all is grand and gay,
And in an upper chamber,
An infant baby lay.

The mother at the great feast,
The nurse was not about,
So I wrap him in a blanket,
And soon we're out the house.

Slowly I stealt thro' the darkness,
'Til we reached the edge of the town,
There I placed him in safe keeping,
That I might continue my round.

When I returned to the great house,
The gaiety serene,
Had turned to a picture of sadness,
Sadness and sorrow extreme.

The screams of the grief stricken mother,
I'll hear 'til the day of my death,
But no greater to me than my sorrow,
When I begged with choking breath.

Begged to save my child,
My only child! my boy!
From the walls of a cold, dark prison,
My son, my only joy.

I had no heart when I lost my son,
For it seemed my innermost depths,
Left me to go with my precious one,
To suffer in prison and death.

I saw the Earl's daughter wriggle in pain,
Mourning the loss of her child,
While the father with gun threats to blow
out his brain,
As he walks in delirium wild.

They suffer just half that I suffered,
For none as the gypsy wild,
Can suffer the pain that I have borne,
In the loss of an only child.

I have no heart, no tender cord,
For my heart has turned to stone,
As I wander to seek revenge,
Thro' this cold, cold world alone.

The Earl's son has died heart broken—
Over the loss of his child,
While the mother behind walls is a manaic,
Wandering in phantoms wild.

The Earl himself is helpless,
Paralyzed with grief,
And my visits are so frequent,
That he finds no time for relief.

For I stand and wail revenge at him,
'Til he seems a mass of stone,
Gasping it seems for every breath,
As he sits in his study alone.

My face will ever haunt him,
'Til his life slowly ebbs away,
And the breath leaps from his stolid frame,
On his last, his dying day.

Revenge, aha! 'tis come,
The smiles but freeze on my face,
As I see his sons falling one by one,
In utter shame and disgrace.

I hear the cries wildly o'er the town,
That the great, great Earl has died.
I gladly give up my gypsy crown,
I can die now satisfied.

Full satisfied for revenge,
Has had a powerful sway,
She's leapt into that family,
And took them all away.

While their child remains to suffer—
As my child, my son,
For both are but children of the dust,
And neither a guilt has done.

THE HOO-DOO MAN'S DISGRACE

Dar was curious times in George-town,
When de folks met face to face,
To listen to de story—
Ob de Hoo-doo man's disgrace.

For days dar'd bin great citement,
'Mong de ole folks ob de town,
Cernin different pains en aìlments
Ob de ones who's stricken down.

Dese here folks is tricked,
Ant Mandy Skinner swore—
As she called to see de patients
In her roun from doe to doe.

Yes, dey sho is conjured,
Case all has curious spells,
En all de medicine dat you gib,
Will nebah make em well.

En to let dese folks all die,
'Twill be a ragin sin—
So you jis well cide right now,
En call de Doctor in.

Dr. Henry Edmond Tyler Fox,
Dat libes four miles away,
Is a fus class Conjur Doctor,
So all de people say.

En ef you calls him in,
Fo anodder Sunday night,
I bet dese curious ailments—
Will be cured alright.

Ant Mandy she was talkin,
To Brudder Johnny Lynn,
Who tho't to jis say conjur,
Was a powerful sin.

Says, he "I neber beliebed in sich,
But I'll solve to try,
Dis ole Conjur Doctor,
Rader den to die."

So he calls his son Joe Billy,
To saddle up ole Bess,
En go en git de Doctor,
To try de Conjur test.

Joe Billy starts out in a race,
To fin de conjur man,
He went so fas he lef no trace
Of foot-prints in de san.

En soon he's to de house
Ob de famous Doctor Fox,
De fus ting Joe did recognize,
He nebah woe no socks.

A tall en lanky man
Wid bar-feet, dey right flat,
Dese pants yo call high waters,
En a rusty ole felt hat—

Wid de top of it cut off,
Whar his wooley hair come thro,'
Mad him a funny sight,
Ob a typical hoo-doo.

En a sho hoo-doo he was,
Case ob all de roots en pills,
Doctor Fox he had ob ebery kind,
Dat sho might cure or kill.

I'll sho be dar by day-light,
He turns en says to Bill,
As he gins to pick up roots,
His satchel fer to fill.

I'll fus go to de grabe-yard,
En dar I has to look,
En search dar 'til I find,
A lef hind rabbit foot.

En wid dis rabbit foot,
En anodder test you see,—
I'll soon fin out de place,
Whar de trickery mout be.

You see some times dey lay fer folks,
En puts it in de groun,
Den some times fer a change,
Befo your doe 'tis foun.

En yo poor pap's sad condition,
Will sho grow wus en wus,
'Til I find de bery spot,
Whar de conjurer went to fus.

I'll hab to take de conjur test,
En turn it ebery way,
Fus to de East den de West
To see jis whar it lay.

So don't be worried tall, my boy,
Cheer up cheer up my lad,
I'll sho be dar by day-light,
To cure your poor ole dad.

Joe Billy started den fer home,
De message fer to tell,
Dat soon de Conjur man wud come,
To make poor daddy well.

De ole man in good spirits,
Sot near de window den
En solved he'd nebah shet his eyes,
'Til he seed his conjur frien.

Sleep gin to obercome him,
But he'd nod den take a look,
'Til soon he recognized a form,
Says he, la! dar's a spook.

He watched de so called spook,
En called to his son Joe,
Jis den de spook gin diggin,
Wid sompin like a hoe.

Den takes a little package,
En puts it in de groun.
Kivers it wid dirt,
Den tramps it roun en roun.

De ole man sot en watched,
'Til de spook it went away,
Soon he nods agin,
'Twas about de peep ob day.

He heahs a knock den at de doe,
En Joe de doe unlocks,
En face to face he meets,
De famous Doctor Fox.

He comes en feels de pulse,
Ob Joe's poor Daddy den,
Says he, my frien, I's jis in time,
You's almos at de end.

Yo life is in my hans,
En fer fifteen dollars cash,
I'll move dis conjuration,
En save you in a dash.

Dat you is tricked, my man,
Is de truf ef I mus tell,
En dis heah rabbit foot,
Will sho ward off de spell.

"Ef you'll set right by de window,
Whar you kin look en see,
I'll take dis test en find,
Whar de trickery mout be."

He goes out side de doe,
En wid his so called test,
He turns to see which way it pints,
To de East or to de West.

Says he, "Right to de East,
You see de dose it lay,
I'll dig, too, 'til I find it,
Yes, fo anodder day."

He digs en digs 'til soon,
He ketches by a string,
En pulls ob sompin heaby,
En gibs ob it a sling.

A big red ball ob cotton,
En a bottle to it tied,
"Ef dis here ting had not bin foun,
My frien you sho would died."

Ant Mandy she jis clapped her hans,
En says, "I tole you so,
I knowd dat he could cure you,"
En den she calls fer Joe,

En tells him go en tell de friens,
En neighbors all aroun,
Ob de famous Doctor Fox,
En de trickery he foun.

Soon de hous was full,
De yard en kitchen too,
To look at Doctor Fox,
En see what he could do.

De lame, de halt, de blind,
All standin at de doe,
To ax ob Doctor Fox,
To gib ob dem a sho.

"I'd like to say a wud,"
Den put in Brudder Lynn,
En all did gaze wid glarin eyes,
As to talk he did begin.

"Now, dis here Doctor Fox
Is nuffin but a bluff,
Wid all his lies en talk,
About dis conjur stuff.

"I sot en watched dat bery imp,
About de peep ob day,
A diggin in my yard,
De conjur fer to lay.

"En now he digs it up,
  En tells de woeful tale,
Dat some one's laid fer me,
  To gib his roots a sale.

"Now, famous Doctor Fox,
  I'll gib ob you a test,
You see dis gun, now turn,
  Fus to de East or West.

"Look not behin or else,
  De bullets tell de tale,
Ob de famout roots en herbs,
  Dat neber got a sale.

Doctor Fox he lef wid rapid pace,
  He neber looked behind,
To see de congregation,
  Ob de lame, de halt, de blind.

His coat tail stood out in de breeze,
  His foot prints in de san,
De leabes did wave on dog wood trees,
  Good-bye to Hoo-doo man.

He lef ole George-town sho—
  In a mighty rapid pace,
But de folks all do remember,
  De Hoo-doo Man's disgrace.

WHAT TASK MUST THE WOMAN FULFILL

As the sun finds it's way to the golden West,
 And soon disappears from sight—
Then the moon takes his place to watch o'er us
 Thro' the still and silent night;
As we gaze on the stars above,
 Our hearts with ecstasy thrill,
While we ask in tones of love—
 "What task must the woman fulfill?"

Yea! woman in by-gone years,
 Thou wert not recognized,
Save as to slave to thy help-meet with fears
 Neath the gloom of cloudy skies;
Thou knew no other place,
 Save to labor, toil and yield,
Thy record had no place,
 For honor or for zeal.

But Ah! the buried past,
 May well forgotten be;
Her mem'ry still may last—
 But the dreaded yoke is free;
Yea free! and woman now
 Stands in her strength alone
To battle for the right,
 And for her sins atone.

Ere since the days of Christ
 We've read of woman's boon;
The last to seek His face—
 The first one at the tomb;

From thence to future years
She'll hold an upward sway,
She's laid aside her doubts and fears,
Now woman has her way.

What progress would there be to-day,
What honor or what fame
Could you in garb array,
Without a woman's name?
Yea! man may be the hero—
But woman placed him there,
She pushed him with her zeal,
Her cheering words, her care.

What hero in the world to-day,
Could well have won the name,
Lest woman in her modest way,
Had led him on to fame?
'Tis she then who inspires him,
And gives him zeal to work;
She urges him with earnest prayers,
From duty ne'er to shirk.

Yea! woman with her prayers—
Woman with her love—
Has soothed so many cares,
And wafted them above;
Wafted them on wings of prayer,
To Him who dost heed our call,
And notes each little needed care,
E'en to a sparrow's fall.

We gaze on the clouds above us,
  Sometimes they are tinted with gold,
Sometimes they are dark and heavy—
  And tales of gloom enfold;
Tho' the clouds be dark and heavy,
  And dread and gloom dispel,
There's inside a silver lining,
  Which a brighter story tells.

Then our lives may have some dark days,
  But there're brighter days to come,
Which may enswallow the dark clouds—
  And they leave us one by one;
Man has been hovering o'er us,
  As the dark and heavy clouds,
But the silver lining bursts forth
  In the form of woman proud.

She comes with words of cheer,
  With rapture our very hearts thrill
As she asks of many here—
  "What task must the woman fulfill?"
What must she find to do,
  In a world so cheerful and bright,
In the land where laborers are few,
  Who're struggling to do the right.

Man has won laurels of fame,
  And kept them yea! for years,
Hist'ry records his name,
  And we laud his mem'ry with cheers;

Now woman comes upon the scene,
Her chances may be few,
But records soon will glean—
What woman, too, can do.

She stands with outstretched arms,
Waits ere the morning dawns,
To do some act of kindness
For the helpless or forlorn;
She gazes in the darkness
Of the city's lowest dives,
Where girls have gone to shame,
Where men have wrecked their lives.

Slowly she wends her way,
'Til she's reached this lowly place,
Where many lives are wrecked
In sorrow and disgrace;
With a prayer she enters in
To lead the straying girl
From the depths of blackest sin,
To an out-side praying world.

And on she goes thro' life,
With ready waiting hands,
To work thro' sin and strife—
What e'er be the urgent demand,
To lead the wanderer on,
In paths of truth and right,
And crush the sin and wrong—
Neath the wings of darkest night.

Now her mind it slowly wanders,
As she struggles on thro' life,
Thro' the rugged high-way,
Onward up the hill of strife;
Treading, slowly treading,
Marching to the road of fame,
Woman, with her earnest efforts,
Each year in and out the same.

What task must the woman fulfill,
Wait not for the answer to come,
Conscience speaks, obey the will—
Woman's vict'ry will be won;
Let not the precious years go by,
And find your record blank,
Catch the moments ere they fly,
With woman out of rank.

Woman place thy record high,
When the flag of honor's unfurled,
Let woman's name against the sky
Glitter to the world;
Glitter in letters of gold,
Against the placid blue,
Let woman's fame be told
In letters bold and true.

Let her name be brighter, brighter,
May the letters ne'er grow dim,
For He who makes the burdens lighter
Always keeps his lamps in trim;

Woman may thy name be written,
That thy deeds may ever shine
In the land of golden treasures,
Where the vict'ry may be thine.

✣ ✣

CAN'T HAVE A BEAU

I'm vexed, yea! truly vexed,
Why shouldn't I be so,
To know I'm sweet sixteen
And then can't have a beau.

Can't have a beau!
To me there is no joy,
When I can't speak or laugh,
Or think about a boy.

Aunt Emeline at eighteen,
Married Uncle Si—
They courted, too, for three years,
Suppose it had been I?

Grandma Green at thirteen,
Had married, too, I think,
Further more there's Bob
And little Annie Brink—

They married very young,
Yes they are happy yet,
I'm sure they have no cause
For worry or regret.

But it seems that I
Must never speak to boys,
To me the world is blank,
No pleasure, ah! no joys.

I dare not give a smile
To William or to Joe,
But what some one replies,
Your mother ought to know.

And I, too, sweet sixteen,
I know I'm plenty old,
But all the mouthy neighbors
Say mother must be told.

I know what I'll do,
Yes, just for real spite,
I wonder if they'll think
I've done exactly right?

I'll never notice any boy,
But act as tho' afraid,
And live, tho' destitute of joy,
An old and cranky maid.

ANGELINA WEDS

Dar was citement in de village,
En all de country roun,
When de notice it was read out
By Parson Reuben Brown,

Dat on next Wednesday mornin,
    Edmond Rufus Johnson White
Will be boun in matrimony
    To Miss Angelina Knight.

All is vited to be present;
    Gent'men all mus war full dress,
Ladies, wid yo tucks en ruffles
    Try to look yo bery best;
Dar needn't be no odder viting,
    Case de news it farly flew,
En when Wednesday mornin come, I tell you,
    Dem folks knowd jis what to do.

All de mules en all de hosses,
    Dey was hitched en placed in line;
Gals wid fellows in de ox-cart,
    Gwine to see Miss Angeline;
Sich anodder fuss en coatin,
    Mules a stallin in de road,
Hosses, too, dey got to balkin,
    Case dey had sich heaby load.

De hour fixed was seben thirty,
    En dey started in a rush,
But de teams had all got stalded
    Case de roads was in a mush;
De bride en groom dey was behin,
    En der ole hoss did farly fly,
Till dey kotch up wid de odders,
    Den dey axed to let dem by.

But dar was no room to pass,
    Case de teams was two abreas,

Mule teams, hoss teams en de ox teams,
Side by side wid all de res;
Den de folks all in de ox-cart,
Dey did jump out one by one,
Ole Jim Buster was de driver,
He said sumpin mus be done;

Case de hour is fas proaching
When de bride en groom mus wed,
We'll hab to move dese hosses—
Come en help us, Uncle Ned.
Uncle Ned he comes a hoppin,
Wid his high silk beaver hat,
En his big leg pants a floppin,
Stumped his toe en fell right flat.

Sich anodder lookin mess,
En he to gib de bride away,
Standin mud from head to foot,
Eyes en mouf all full ob clay;
You had no business axin me,
Yo scoundel, see what you has done!
Ruined me en all dese clos
Dat I borrowed from Jim Gun.

En all dis nice silk beaver hat,
It am all done ruined, too,
I kin neber pay fer dat—
What on earth is I to do?
While he stan dar sayin dat,
Up jumped Uncle Jimmy Cole,
Him en ole man Eli Black,
Wid a heaby cedar pole,

Placed it under dem two mules,
    Prized dem out de big mud hole;
Den you heah de folks a yellin,
    Gib three cheers fer Jimmy Cole!
Den dey gib dem mules a cut,
    Chillun, dey did sholy fly,
Ebery team was in de road
    Dem two mules did pass dem by.

Soon dey rived right to de chuch,
    Preacher he's already dar,
Wid his boots en socks off, restin,
    Case he'd walked so bery far;
De chuch it was all decerated
    Wid apple blossoms, pink en white,
Pine tops hangin to de center,
    Morning glories fresh en bright.

Sunflowers wid der heads er bowin,
    Johnie Jump-Ups by der side,
All a bowin en a smilin
    In full honor ob de bride;
Dogwoods, too, did gib der honor,
    Ox eye daisies, snowy white,
All a blossomin in honor
    Ob Miss Angelina Knight.

De bride she woe white satin,
    Wid a veil dat tech de flo,
En a long train to her dress
    Reachin cler back to de doe;
She woe white satin slippers, too,
    Little gals dey hel her trail—

She come down de aisle a trippin
Doe she's walkin on some nails.

De ladies marched down one aisle,
De gent'men down de odder,
While strollin long behin
Come Angelina's modder;
She a walkin wid a cane,
A kerchief on her head,
A long-stem pipe was in her mouth
As down de aisle she sped.

De preacher was a little late—
De Reverend Richard Root—
His feet had swole up so
He couldn't war his boots;
En he come down de aisle
De bride en groom to meet,
A bowin en a smilin,
In his stockin feet!

En Uncle Ned was standin dar
To gib de bride away,
You could scarcely see his face
Fer all de mud en clay;
You sholy wud bin boun to laf,
Case he wid all his pride,
Standin dar in all dat mud
To gib away de bride.

De preacher axed Miss Angeline
Ef she'd take dis lubin man,
En cherish him thro' troubles,
Doe dey be as grains ob san,

En ef you tinks you lubs him,
    Fer better or fer wuss,
De answer is, I do,
    Doe yo life might be a cuss.

Miss Angeline she gibs a smile,
    En twis her head jis so—
I do, but Mr. Preacher,
    Please don't ax no mo.
He tuns den to de groom,
    Says he, well, Brudder White,
Kin you care fer dis here lady
    Thro' de gloomy days en bright?

Kin you meet her wid a smile,
    Doe you'se angry as a bar?
Ef you kin, my deares brudder,
    De answer is, I swar;
Wid perspiration drippin,
    Mr. White he bowed his head,
In solemn wuds he said, "I swar,
    Now hand her to me, Ned."

Ned let a loose her arm,
    And she kotch hol Brudder White,
Den de preacher said, I nounce you
    As her husban, she yo wife;
Den dey ceived de gratulations,
    En marched on up de aisle,
Each gent-man wid his lady,
    Dey a struttin in sich style.

Rigs outside de doe a waitin,
    Hosses tryin not to stan;

Mules a kinder actin gaily,
    Oxen dey a raisin san;
All was gibin ob der honors,
    Showin forth der great delight
In carrying off de bridle party
    Ob Edmond Rufus Johnson White.

⚜ ⚜

THE LAD WITHOUT A NAME

(Dedicated to the Memory of Dr. Booker T. Washington)

In a lowly one-room cabin
    Lived a little Negro boy,
Hampered by the chains of slav'ry,
    Yet it did not him annoy.

Often tho' he noticed mother,
    While he played in childish glee,
Praying with her hands uplifted,
    "Master, wilt Thou make us free?"

He was then too young to take in,
    Yea! too young to understand
The awful curse of slav'ry,
    Which was spread thro'out the land.

Never'less he watched his mother,
    Oh! the love that mother had,
Caring for her little children,
    Poorly fed and poorly clad.

She was struggling with great efforts
To supply her children's need,
Bringing bits of after-leavings,
That her children she might feed.

When she came into the cabin,
There they'd gather at her knee,
The younger was the nameless lad,
Since known as Booker T.

His mother called him Booker,
Just because of books he's fond;
He had no real name,
This lad of slav'ry's bond.

So now is spread thro'out the land
The hist'ry of the fame
Of him who started his career
As a lad without a name.

Soon he hears the bells of freedom,
Ring thro'out the entire land,
He heard folks say that he was free,
Yet little could he understand.

So he started out into the world,
And found he had no name,
Then he added more to Booker,
That he might have some claim.

Booker had great thirst for knowledge,
"There is something I must learn,"
So decides to find a way,
As for wisdom he did yearn.

All ye children know the story,
How he tramped the rugged road,
Facing knowledge, facing wisdom,
Burdened 'neath the heavy load.

For he had no means to meet it,
Meet the monster he must face,
But his great desire for learning
Did the hindrances erase.

So, sickened, worn and weary,
To Hampton he found his way,
Thirsting for the understanding
Which he hoped to have some day.

There he struggled for his learning,
Which prepared him for his fate,
And in after years the yearning
Which did serve to make him great.

He left his school with highest honors,
That his people he might serve,
And thereby give to them the knowledge
Which he hoped they might deserve.

For years he struggled for his people,
Toiling, yea! thro'out the land,
Making every sacrifice
That they might understand.

So he built a towering statue,
Monumental, mammoth, grand,
Which will serve a lasting tribute,
Wavering, yea! thro'out the land.

Serve as tribute to the mem'ry
Of him who gave his life,
Probing out the greatest problem
Which has banished bitter strife.

Greater work was ne'er accomplished
By a poor and nameless lad,
Who won a noble reputation,
Which should make his people glad.

And now we know that we have lost him,
Oh, the bitter pangs we feel!
As we think about our hero,
While around Thy shrine we kneel.

May his statue ever tower,
Bringing knowledge, bringing fame,
To the children who give honor,
To the lad without a name.

May the lasting mem'ry ever
Cherished by his people be,
That each letter may be sacred,
In the name of Booker T.

And years to come will give the story,
Write the hist'ry of the fame,
Of him who started his career,
As the lad without a name.

THE STONE PRINTING & MFG. CO., ROANOKE, VA.

Original Poems and Essays

of

Bettiola Heloise Fortson

Preface

The contents of this book are true facts of the Negro race told in verse and prose. My purpose is to furnish some information concerning the Negro, which the white man has failed to print in his many text-books. Without the daily encouragement of my mother, Mrs. Mattie Forston Arnold, the task would not have been completed, and to her, above all others, I am greatly indebted. The research work gained by reading the Bible, and such authors as Baldwin, Hereens, Scholes, and Monroe Work helped to give information in the essay, "Contributions of the Negro Toward the Advancement of Civilization. I am also indebted to Rev. T. A. Smythe, Rev. H. J. Callis, and the Olivet Baptist Church, Chicago, Ill., for financial assistance, also to Rev. John W. Robinson for valuable suggestions and proof reading.

This work is submitted with the hope that it may assist in promoting a literary uplift of all who may have access to its pages.

THE AUTHORESS.

Introduction

The holy hush of an eventide; the bursting glory of an early dawn; sometimes, the rippling of a rill; the caroling of a bird; perhaps, it is the oppression of the poor, or man's inhumanity to man; maybe, it's the impassioned plea for the right, the bold defense of truth, graphic description of existing wrongs which have inspired poetic genius. Mental Pearls is but the soul-musings of a daughter of the Negro race. Read these verses and you are aware of the Negro heart which bleeds while it gathers strength for the future—the arena of the Negro's greatness. No one but a member of the race can interpret the soul-longings of that people: Miss Bettiola H. Fortson, born in Hopkinsville, Ky., Dec. 29, 1890, possesses gifts which must give her a place of distinction and renown. We most cheerfully commend Mental Pearls to the public in which we recognize the true facts of a loyal and patient people.

John W. Robinson,
Pastor of St. Mark Methodist Episcopal Church.
Chicago, Ill.

By Julius F. Taylor, Editor and Publisher

Bettiola Heloise Fortson was born in Hopkinsville, Ky., Christian County, December 29, 1890. She is the third daughter of Mr. and Mrs. James Fortson, well-known citizens of that city. Her early training took place in the public school of Hopkinsville, where her teachers found in her exceptional ability for retaining both poetry and prose writings of great length. At the age of twelve she was brought to Chicago, Ill., to live with her aunt, Mme. Toreado Mallory, who was a favorite soprano throughout Illinois, and who immediately placed her niece in the Keith school. But learning that the Douglas school was of a higher standard the following year, 1903, moved in that district. It was here, while in the eighth grade, she was appointed poet laureate of her class; this honor being given her for an excellent essay entitled "Our Teacher."

In May, 1905, she professed a hope in Christ at a revival held in the Bethel Sunday School. Owing to her aunt's going abroad she was sent to her mother the Christmas of 1905, who was residing in Evansville, Ind. In February, 1906, she entered the Clark High School of that city. In April of the same year she joined the Liberty Baptist Church and became a member of the choir and was ever giving programs for the benefit of that institution.

The fourth year in high school she composed a poem upon the surroundings of the school and named it "The Walls of C. H. S." During the years she spent in high school her marks were ever of a creditable showing but always leading in history and literature. In June, 1910, she graduated, completing a four-year Latin course. It was August of the same year when she came back to Chicago and learned the feather trade from Mme. Lambert. Afterwards went into millinery business of her own. At the same time she was constantly before the public as a dramatic reader and won favor from the Chicago critics while taking a leading role in the much-talked-of drama "Tallaboo." She has given recitals in and out of the city for almost every denomination, but it was not until October 28, 1913, did she present to the public a recital of all original numbers which won for her recognition in the poetical field.

She is an ardent suffragette and club worker, having served as president of the University Society of Chicago for one year and a half; second vice-president of the Alpha Suffrage Club, and city organizer of the Chicago Federation of Women's Clubs.

Mental Pearls

"Mother"

Who touches first our tiny lips
  Then gently lays our heads
To rest, upon the pillow slips?
          Mother.

Who rocks the cradle while we sleep?
  Who tucks the cover around our feet
And prays to God our souls to keep?
          Mother.

Who trains us from a little child
  To walk, talk and stand alone?
Who thinks her own worth while?
          Mother.

Who saw us pass to womanhood
  Facing problems of the world?
Who sat and cried and understood?
          Mother.

Who bore all of our grief
  When we were deep in trouble?
Who smiled and gave us relief?
          Mother.

Who knows our greatest fault
  But does not tell the world?
Who locks them in the vault?
          Mother.

Who grieves when we are dead
  Yet knows it's God's own will
As sorrow's tears are shed?
          Mother.

Brothers

This poem is dedicated to the Jones brothers of Mississippi who lost their lives defending the Negro Women's Virtue in that State, Oct., 1913. It has attracted much attention among many Northerners who advised the writer to publish the same.

In the State of Mississippi
  Where the cotton blossoms bloom;
Gives a story of a mulatto
  Who would soon become a groom.

For the Colored girl he courted
  Had said, "I'll be your bride";
But the master man of White
  Took her to his poisonous side.

And threatened if she even looked
  Upon men of her own race;
He wanted her for his use,
  Thus marked her pretty face.

Weeks passed and the serpent
  Stuck his fangs deeper in his prey;
And boasted of his Colored maid
  Whom he had took his way.

When Fred Jones heard of this,
  His blood boiled high with rage:
He asked his God to lend a hand
  To bring her from that awful cage.

To hear the name of one he loved
  Harassed, was too big a cup to drink;
So secretly with his brother planned
  To meet this monster upon the brink.

They vowed that they would rather die
  Than see virtue crushed to dust;
So they gathered all their weapons
  And started out to gain their lust.

But as they drew upon the scene
  The two lay side by side.
In deep slumber, they were dreaming
  Fancies of this world wide.

The sight made Jones grow furious
  Half blind he fired and struck the bed,
And 'ere the smoke had cleared away
  He saw both lying dead.

His brother caught him by the hand
  And said, "You know the cost
We pay here for such a sight;
  Come, make haste, before we're lost."

They waited for their doom
  In a far-off cotton mill;
While footsteps were approaching
  Behind the door each stood still.

The sheriff who led the mob
  Was distinctly heard to say:
"There's where the 'Niggers' are,
  They've got the price to pay."

But ere he had spoken
  He reeled half bent, then fell;
While from the knothole came smoke,
  Which rained down shot and shell.

Hours passed and every bullet
  Penned a paleface to the ground:
And when the bodies were all counted
  Sixty-five stone dead were found.

At last their ammunition gave out,
  Calmly they waited for the test;
With locked arms they stood together
  To be killed just like the rest.

The thirsty villains set on fire
  The mill that they were in;
The cotton burned until morning,
  O God! What an awful sin.

Next day, down in Mississippi,
  Where the cotton blossoms bloom,
Were found the ashes of the martyrs,
  The brother and the groom.

If you search the deeds of record
  Two names I'm sure you will trace;
Who died to protect the virtue
  For the women of their race.

In Old Kentucky

Dedicated to Mr. and Mrs. William Evans of Hopkinsville, Ky., whom the authoress lived with for several years.

Take me back to old Kentucky
  Where the tall blue grass grows;
In the state that's full of riches,
  And where everybody knows
How to treat you with respect,
  How to make the liquor red,
How to sell the fastest horses
  That ever stood beneath a shed.

Take me back to old Kentucky
  Where I spent my childhood days:
Playing ring a round my rosie
  While the boys stood all amaze;
Each waiting for his chance
  To be pulled within the ring,
And be chosen as the best
  While the others loud would sing.

I would like to see Bill Evans,
  Who kept his hacks uptown;
And who had so many apples
  That it made the neighbors frown.
For he owned the prettiest orchard
  There was in old Sharp's field;
That's why they all were jealous
  And at night the fruit would steal.

I can see old Pigeon creek
  Where it flows through Hopkinsville:
And the spot the lovers would seek
  Near the bend at Wood's mill;
I can see the old iron bridge
  Where they planned their wedding day,
As the moon crept o'er the ridge
  Of green hilltops far away.

Take me back to old Kentucky
  Near the hills of "Walnut Grove,"
Where we had our Sunday picnics
  And where Eddie and I would rove:
Looking for some new adventure
  As we stood on the Indian mound;
Face to face with life's old story
  While we gazed upon the ground.

I would like to have a drink
  Once more from Hoosier's spring,
Where the water flowed so cool,
  Where robin red breast would sing.
How I used to stand and dip
  From that hole deep in the ground:
How my head would touch the moss
  Every time I would stoop down.

Take me back to old Kentucky
  Once more to see the spot
Where my mother and my father
Told tales they've both forgot:
Sitting by the old fireplace
  While the logs were burning bright;
Until the town clock struck off ten
  Which meant time to say good night.

Take me back to old Kentucky
  To the place I love so well:
Where Aunt Agnes taught me manners
  And made my dresses up so swell;
And where all good things to eat
  Were placed before my eyes:
Chicken, doughnuts, and sweet potato pie,
  That's the place I idolize.

Quo Jure?

(BY WHAT RIGHT?)

You boast of your superiority
    And By What Right?
God made man of dust
And placed him here to teach
Every human being to trust
Or the goal they cannot reach.

You class me as being inferior
        And By What Right?
We breathe the self-same air,
We have a given sense of smell,
We, too, have some ways unfair,
And here we all must dwell.

You spurn and abuse my race
        And By What Right?
Don't you suppose the Lord made
My brains to think as well as thine?
Don't you suppose in me He laid
The best foundation He could find?

You place upon me a curse
        And By What Right?
My blood is just as red
As that which flows through your veins,
And for this country has been shed,
And caused many aching brains.

You insult His mighty cause
        And By What Right?
You, who are a Christian nation,
Who go to church from day to day,
Work for nothing but sensation
Which leads you on the downward way.

You place me upon the exterior
        And By What Right?
Yes, and drag men to degradation
And place the bar of prejudice in their face.
Have you forgotten creation
And how you came to be a race?

You laugh because I am black
        And By What Right?
I am here as God's own choice;
He made the color of my skin,
He gave me this my voice,
And to you made me akin.

You usurp His authority
        And By What Right?
You surely have forgot
That He died for us all,
Yes, even the worst lot,
And claims each alike with His call.

Dunbar

Look! at the height where Dunbar stood
  Upon yonder mountain side;
And see the small, the great and good
  Deeds, rise as the flowing tide.
Watch how he tottered up the hill
  Dragging the cares of his race:
And note! he never stood still
  But plunged on to a higher place.

Hear him call his fellow men,
  Come, although the way be marred,
We cannot help but win,
  For God has never barred
His children from a treasure
  That they could build upon;
For to Him it is a pleasure
  To see the work go on.

At last, His call is all in vain
  You gave him not your aid;
And he knew not your aim,
  So from God he was paid.
He heard his Master's voice
  And answered to His will,
And took for his own choice
  A home behind the hill.

He sleeps and yet he is not dead,
  His works go on and on
From generation to generation ever will be
    read,
  And to this race belong.
Although his life was short
  His name is wrapped in fame,
And needs no man's support
  But covers all the blame.

To Champion Jack Johnson

May I some day see that dark, noble face,
Which has caused words of envy or praise
And whose career has set the world amaze
To see so bold a hero of our race
Have his name where they're anxious to erase,
In order that the whites again may raise
To life, that Champion of former days
So as to gain his once original place.
But Oh! Sir Johnson, bear alone the blame
And win the fight if wisdom will provide
The strength to add all honor to your name.
Which some day may rise as the flowing tide
And place itself within the walls of fame
Where noble deeds well done are side by side.

Love's Plea

Bring back the love you took away
The love I cherished night and day:
Oh! give me back that treasure
Which was all mine for pleasure:
Why keep my days unhappy, dear?
When it's you whom I want near;
Oh! give me joy in life to-morrow
While my heart is in its sorrow.

CHORUS

Bring back the love that I called mine
That which was most divine;
Bring back those lips I fond did kiss,
So full of joy and bliss;
Oh! let me feel thy presence, dear,
It's you whom I want near;
Please let me hear you say to-day,
You'll bring back the love you took away.

Bring back the hours you took away
The hours I worshiped night and day;
Please say that you will never
Let our love come to sever:
Don't turn my thoughts forever down
And upon me, please, do not frown!
But give me chance in death to borrow
The kiss, which gave me this, my sorrow.

"Carve out your own career
 Pray don't wait to be led:
Then you won't feel the sneer
 Or have briny tears to shed."

A Man Among Men

Dedicated to Rev. E. J. Fisher, D.D., LL.D., late pastor of Olivet Baptist Church, Chicago, Ill.

Born down in the Cracker State,
Where Southerners are known to hate
Every Negro who has been born
Since the hour of Freedom's morn:
Locked within this awful den
Comes forth, a man among men.

For hours he studied to save
Black men whom they called knave
And at last found the light:
For God sent him to fight
And said that he would win
So went, this man among men.

Each day he dropped a seed
To save souls bad in need:
He prayed and sang a song
Then pointed out all their wrong
And told them it was sin;
Thus spoke, this man among men.

Why, he saved thousands of souls
And each day his roll unfolds
The names of those who came
And praised with him His name,
That they, too, might enter in.
Thus did, this man among men.

This man we've watched through life
Came up midst toil and strife;
And showed the world his sacrifice
To burn down guilt and vice
That a new life might begin;
Thus worked, this man among men.

You sneer because he is black
And say mentally there is lack
Of his will power to control,
But you forget the story old:
God cares not for the skin
But wants a man among men.

Listen, you will hear his cry,
"That God we can never defy."
So contented he pleaded the cause
And never stopped to pause—
That's why we hail him friend,
Crowned, as a man among men.
October 23rd, 1913.

A Generous Heart

Dedicated to Mme. C. J. Walker

Reared without the care of mother
  In days that were dark and drear;
But fought for strength and existence
  In a land that's filled with sneer.

Worked hard to establish a trade
  That others might know and see;
And recognize in the business world
  Black women as they should be.

Success has marked her future
  As she glides the pole of fame;
Bearing a banner gleaming bright
  With C. J. Walker in full name.

And the money which she earned
  Has been spent upon you and me;
For she freely gives the friendless
  That they, too, may hear and see.

Across the seas to dark Africa
  She has lent a helping hand
By establishing an industrial school
  To enlighten that far-off land.

Yes, she is schooling some poor boy
  Who may prove to be President;
Then with ease she can gladly rest
  And say that "life was well spent."

You may travel from East to West
  And think you've done your part,
But you will never come across
  One with such a generous heart.

The authoress, having met Madam Walker at the National Convention of Colored Women's Clubs, which convened at Wilberforce, Ohio, August, 1914, was greatly impressed with the Madam's life history which was told in a pamphlet given to the many assembled delegates, and was inspired to write the foregoing poem as a tribute to this great business woman with such a charming personality.

"Sympathy is the Cradle of Love"

You may wander forlorn,
With your heart all torn,
  You may keep your secrets for years,
But you will crave for one word,
From one who has heard,
  Your story while shedding tears.

REFRAIN

Sympathy is the pathway to loveland,
Sympathy is the want of every man,
Sympathy is the watchword to sunshine,
Sympathy is craved all the time;
Sympathy will lead to a heavenly goal,
Sympathy will brighten a burdened soul,
Just as sure as skies are above,
Sympathy is the cradle of love.

You may be composed,
And think no one knows,
  Of the trials and hardships you have had,
But you will want sympathy,
Or else you will be,
  Down-hearted and forever sad.

"Waste not your opportunities
  While in the best of health:
For pain may overtake you
  And crumble all your wealth."

Queen of Our Race

Dedicated to Mrs. Ida B. Wells-Barnett

Mrs. Ida B. Wells-Barnett, our prominent race and club leader, refused to be "Jim Crowed" in the Suffragette parade in Washington, D. C. Being a delegate from the Illinois Suffragette Movement, Mrs. Barnett protested against any such laws and was given her place with the Illinois Suffragettes. It was these facts that gave the inspiration to the writer for the following poem:

Side by side with the whites she walked,
Step after step the Southerners balked,
But Illinois, fond of order and grace,
Stuck to the black Queen of our race.

Mile after mile the throng moved on,
Soon there was heard a familiar song,
Right about face and give her space!
And its echo reached the Queen of our race.

To-day the grand old march is o'er,
There are many white women sore;
Because of their prejudice to trace
The dignity of the Queen of our race.

Still in their minds there is a thought,
And deep in their hearts a lesson taught:
Not to worry one's self about another's place;
Thus victory is won for the Queen of our race.

'Tis true, they're able at this age to bar—
But justice will soon send the doors ajar
And sit the black and whites face to face,
There will be seen the Queen of our race.

Page after page in history you'll read
Of one who was ready and able to lead,
Who set the nation on fire with her pace
And the Heroine will be the Queen of our
race.

Sighing For You

Could I but forget
Days when we first met:
When you smiled and said you loved me
And that we should always agree;
Though you pleaded in vain
I bade you come again;
Not knowing the anguish to be.

Chorus

Sighing, my heart is sighing
Each day for you;
I want you near me
To prove my love is true:
Yearning, my love is yearning
While here at home;
Though you are far from me
I am sighing for you alone.

Days may come and go
But you will not know
Of the pain you've caused my heart, dear,
Crushed with sorrow, grief, and fear;
Though you are far away
I will love you each day,
For I care not if me you sneer.

"Tuskegee's Band"

Have you heard that colored band,
The best that's in this land,
Tuskegee's famous boys
Who play those great big toys?

You can hear the shuffling feet
As they come marching down the street
Playing loud "Vansuppe's" strains,
Sending gladness to your brains.

You can feel yourself a-swaying
While the music they're playing
Takes the mind away from books
Makes one forget about his looks.

Why, Chicago's in a whirl,
Every banner does unfurl
As Tuskegee's boys stride by
Looking grand with heads lift high.

A push and scrouge for a seat,
Each one anxiously to greet
As they stand before the crowd
Waiting, while we halloo loud.

With baton, the leader starts
Pointing out the different parts,
While the music swells out grand
Harmonized by every man.

The flute, the cornet, the drum
Would make you think you're dumb,
And the old slide trombone
Was in a class all alone.

And the saxophones so clear
Give us tones we love to hear;
In the selection, "William Tell,"
Bagpipes certainly sound well.

Gee! those boys look good in white
Every time they come in sight,
And they sing so sweet and fine,
Give distinctly every line.

Why, Tuskegee should be proud
Of every one in that crowd,
The leader and his boys
Who play those great big toys.

That's My Guy

On being introduced to Mrs. John Guy, a North Side resident of Chicago, at a social function, the Poetess asked if she had not met a gentleman that evening having the same name. She answered yes, and pointing through the guests assembled, exclaimed, "That's My Guy." The expression was so full of humor that the Poetess penned the following poem in memory of the incident.

If he is handsome as can be
And has earned a college degree;
Then that's my guy.

If he's noticeable where he goes
And full of grace from head to toes;
Then that's my guy.

If he has studied medicine or law
And knows the game of life "seesaw";
Then that's my guy.

If he knows how to do hard work
And does not grumble or even shirk;
Then that's my guy.

If upon his face he wears a smile
To prove he likes my latest style;
Then that's my guy.

If at times he delights to smoke
Even though myself it does provoke;
Then that's my guy.

If sometimes he likes to flirt
Just so my feelings are not hurt;
Then that's my guy.

If he's musical and can play
Until it makes my body sway;
Then that's my guy.

If he knows how to hold a dime
To be used at some future time;
Then that's my guy.

If he is proud of his own name
And wishes mine to be the same:
Then that's my guy.

The House of God

How beautiful: the House of God
Where one can sit and hear the story
Of Him, who reigns in all his glory:
How beautiful.

How beautiful: the House of God
Where songs of praise ring through the air
Whose echoes ascend the golden stair:
How beautiful.

How beautiful: the House of God
Where man can worship Him, the crucified
The only one who gladly for us died:
How beautiful.

How beautiful: the House of God
Where one can softly whisper in His ear
Through prayer the things they do fear:
How beautiful.

How beautiful: the House of God
To stand within this sacred wall
And help the men who ofttimes fall:
How beautiful.

How beautiful: the House of God
Where death is welcomed as but a dream
As angels stoop to kiss the sunbeam:
How beautiful.

How beautiful: the House of God
Where joy and peace forever more
Are knocking at your closed door:
How beautiful.

St. Mark Methodist Episcopal Church
50th St. and Wabash Ave.
Chicago

While seated in the above beautiful edifice the inspiration came which caused the writing of the poem entitled "The House of God."

BETTIOLA H. FORTSON.

How beautiful: the House of God
Whose responsibility for those who are born
Will be judged upon the Resurrection morn:
How beautiful.

How beautiful: the House of God
When we no more shall be alone
But with Him, at the Heavenly Throne:
How beautiful.

Sonnet

This sonnet is one of the authoress' favorite poems. She has been quoted saying, "I believe I could write a book upon the character of Dr. Washington but, after all, the fourteen lines which I have composed would be my one thought."

Born in the depths of slavery's night,
For the uplift of humanity's cause;
Yet spared by providence to win the fight
Which makes other men stand and pause;
When they see the great educator of our race
High up on the weak ladder of fame,
Working hard to establish a place
To give the men of his race a name.
For this, Booker Washington, shine on as a
star,
And prove to these men equality
For time stands not so very far;
When justice shall weigh morality
And tell all the world to stop
And read with pride your name at the top.

Lest Ye Forget

You sailed to America to escape persecution,
Broke loose from your mother rule,
Came here to establish a great nation
That was to be no country's tool.

You came from the great land of torture
That you might worship your own way,
So you landed at Plymouth, then said,
"Peace, shall we have from this day."

You said, "All men were created equal,"
And that you wanted justice to be
The one thing for the good of all
And called this the land of the free.

How soon you forgot your own words;
Why, they rode upon the wings of the air,
For you took everything before your sight,
You cared not for others how unfair.

All the time while you were flourishing
You forgot the pain you once bore,
For money was what you were craving,
Each day trying to get more and more.

In 1609 you made a purchase
Of human flesh, through history I am told.
Men's hands and feet were bound with chains,
Then placed in stalls and marked "Sold."

Each day they were sold like cattle,
Ye, worse than the lowest of beast,
For you wanted their skillful labor,
Otherwise you cared not the least.

You who were once an oppressed people
  Went on from day to day still buying
The flesh of your brothers and sisters,
  Forgot about the time you were crying.

You took the mothers from their babes
  And thus destroyed their humble life;
You forced the women of my race
  To bear your child, which gave them strife.

And because God stopped your folly
  You regret and even curse the day
You brought the Negro as a slave
  From his native home across the way.

Now you have had your own way,
  Don't you think God would like the same?
Lest ye forget—go, fast and pray
  And ask forgiveness for your shame.

"Life vs. Strife"

What more is life?
When one can ponder o'er the pleasant hours
  Spent in the midst of a friend.
What more is life?

What more is strife?
When one doth lose all confidence in him
  Whom he did call his friend.
What more is strife?

The Walls of C. H. S.

Four years ago from the North I came
To enter in and fight for the fame
At high school down on old Clark Street
Where I had dreamed 'twould be a treat.
The Principal, quite frail, was first to see,
Who rolled his dark brown eyes upon me,
Then said, "For you I'll give a test,
To enter the walls of C. H. S."

The first room that I entered in
Made me look like a common pin,
When she who was stern as could be
Brought forth a new Latin book to me:
Things went on fine for near a week,
When all at once I failed to speak,
For I knew not the meaning of "est"
There in the walls of C. H. S.

The next in line for me to meet
Was the physiology teacher so neat,
Viewing me through his thick glasses slow
Said, "Young lady, I'll see what you know:
My customs you will find in a disguise
Do not let my discipline be a surprise;
For good behavior is all I request
Here in the walls of C. H. S."

The manual training teacher came next
Who hobbied upon her daily text,
That every girl should learn to cook
And at the same time how to look:
She saw our sewing neatly done
And never gave favors to any one,
So I was found doing my best
Within the walls of C. H. S.

A change was made, a new teacher came
Who taught us algebra, and won fame;
But had a time keeping us quiet
Because he was young, we had a riot:
So they sent him to another school
Where children knew the "Golden Rule,"
To tell the truth, I must confess—
Then we were lonesome at C. H. S.

That same year came a woman from Fisk,
Then all of the girls broke to her wrist:
And before her eyes were opened wide
All of the boys flocked to her side:
For she was loving and kind to all
Favoring neither fat, small, large or tall.
Yet her motto was strong as the rest
Of those who taught at C. H. S.

Our literature teacher was a great man,
He taught us etiquette, and was a fan:
In history he gave us more than delight
So I read books from morn until night:
For I wanted to make a very high mark
And be recorded as having the spark,
For he was always showing the guest
The good work we did at C. H. S.

The fourth year found us hard at work
And we did not even try to shirk,
For a new Principal was in our land
And his ways we did not understand:
He taught us physics from day to day,
Having propositions worked out his way;
So to keep from failing in his test
We worked like Trojans, at C. H. S.

"Whom Shall I Take"

A man wealthy in gold
Or the one who bares his soul?
    Whom shall I take?

The man who dresses swell
Or the one who digs in a well?
    Whom shall I take?

A man with a mansion by the sea
Or the one with a cottage full of glee?
    Whom shall I take?

"Found Out"

Why do you black your face
And imitate the Negro race?
If I classed myself so high
I wouldn't want you nigh.

I don't care how you tried
The secret you cannot hide:
I know why you black your face,
To rank in wit like my race.

As Told by One of the Sex

Come, sit and listen, Mary,
  To the story I have longed to tell
Since you were a little girl
  But the thought throws me into a spell.
When I think why you are motherless
  And of that dreadful night
That took your mother from you,
  All that was yours for light.

You see that weeping willow
  By the gate out on the farm,
That's the spot, that's the spot,
  O God, I meant to do no harm.
Quick! Quick! give me more air,
  My eyes grow dim from sight,
I feel myself growing weaker,
O! spare me to tell all right.

Your mother was an actress,
  Widely noted for her art—
She played in "Proper Gander,"
  And took the leading part;
Why, when she came upon the stage
  You would think there was a mob,
Until her voice had reached the crowd
  Which made the old and young sob.

Early one afternoon in June
  A stranger passed our door,
Asked shelter for the night,
  Said he was from the other shore;
So John, your father, took him in,
  And O, I shall never forget
How they played chess, then called Elnora
  And how coolly she the stranger met.

Next day John rode away to town
  And left the stranger here with us;
He talked about the pretty women
  And over Elnora made a fuss.
Then I grew jealous all because
  He paid no heed to me,
So I galloped over the commons
  And told John to come and see.

I lied and said he had fancied
  Elnora's dark brown eyes,
And that I saw him hug her,
  Saying her love he would idolize.
He took me at my word
  And we galloped back with speed
And ere we neared the open gate
  I realized the dirty deed.

Quick as a flash John got in the lead,
  Then turned and opened wide the door,
And without one word being spoken,
  Elnora lay dead upon the floor.
And ere that day had closed
  He, too laid down and died;
That's why I have kept you with me
  And the story tried to hide.

See! See! her long black hair
  And hear her child-like voice,
She is calling after me,
  Remorse—Remorse, I am her choice.
Do you understand all, Mary?
  For I am going to eternal rest
To answer for that murderous deed
  With the guilty stain upon my breast.
October, 1913.

His Will

Dedicated to the "Titanic" Survivors

Why stand there and weep
For the lost ones at sea?
When Providence willed it to be
That the rich should go
As well as the poor
Down in the ocean deep.

Why stand there and sigh?
Then a scream and a cry—
For those gone on high:
'Tis God's will, you see.
Performed upon you and me,
For Him, we all must die.

Don't stand there and keep
That burden upon your heart;
The soul from the body must depart:
For trials and wars will cease.
Soon or later all must be peace
For God puts us all to sleep.

Historical

The Part Played by Negro Soldiers in the Wars of the World

Drawing aside the portals of the Universe, and looking far back into the dim vista of time, we see the Negro soldiers on the battlefields taking part in the great wars of the world.

As early as 333 B. C., in the days of Alexander the Great, we find black men exerting high military command. Clitus a black soldier, and Alexander's foster brother, led the cavalry and saved the day at the terrible battle of Granicus, where his brother had been seriously wounded. Even in these days when Negroes were in the minority, in numbers, the patriotic spirit burned within their souls and thus made them heroes.

Hannibal the greatest military genius in history causes our very eyes to close from mental strain as we sit dazed reading his forced marches and the crossing of the Alps, in the year 218 B. C., during which time he suffered the loss of an eye from Ophthalmia, and yet with that great courage which placed him above his adversaries, he continued his march. Wonderful as his achievements were, we must marvel the more, when we take into account the grudging support he received from Carthage. The Romans feared and hated him. Horace reflected their sentiment in describing him as the "Dirus Hannibal." A man who for fifteen years could hold his ground in a hostile country against the veteran legions of Rome with her succession of able generals, must have been commander and tactician of supreme capacity. Ah! When Hannibal flashed his sword from its scabbard the boundaries of Rome oscillated on the map. He was the archangel of war.

Menelik, the ruler of Abyssinia, a descendant of King Solomon, belonging to the royal family of Shoa, showed military command. His army, led entirely by black men on the plains of Addis-Abeba annihilated an Italian army of thirty thousand men, taking one thousand prisoners of war. Gatewayo, the indomitable Zulu chief measured arms with the ablest English commanders and although his military resources were antiquated he was never conquered.

Henry Diaz, a full-blooded Negro in Brazil wrested his country from the iron grip of that stubborn masterful race, the Dutch, by organizing a black regiment officered entirely by men of his own race, and gives to us one of the most important chapters in the history of the Western Hemisphere. In the mutiny of the Brazilian Navy against the unfair treatment of the government, Joao Candido, a black man was chosen leader, and the mutineers gained the desired concession.

Negro officers as well as soldiers have always shared the perils and glories of the campaigns of Napoleon Bonaparte. David Thomas Dumas, division-general under Napoleon as well as General Alfred Dodds, to-day the idol of the French history. Over and over we see where the royal guard at the court of Imperial France has been mounted with black soldiers.

Haiti gives to us the most celebrated representative of the black race, Toussaint L'Ouverture, a man who turned the destiny of a country by the weight of his influence and of his sword, but after maintaining France's authority at Saint

Domingo by expelling the Spaniards and the English from the colony, his reward was to be bound like a criminal and sent into exile. Here he remained until death called him home where humiliations and sufferings are not known.

"By my overthrow the trunk of the tree of Negro Liberty at Saint Domingo is laid low—but only the trunk; it will shoot out again from the roots, for they are many and deep." These are the prophetic words of the great martyr, and in less than five months his prediction became verified for Dessalines known to his enemies as the "Monster Dessalines," united the blacks and mulattoes, and conquered his country and gave to Haiti its first black ruler.

Sylla, a Haitian, was never subdued. Alexander Petion, the founder of the black republic was the best artillery man of his time. Henry Christophe was one of the greatest liberators of the 19th century. Andrew Riegaud, the colored militiaman who fought at Savannah for the Independence of the United States a native of Cayes, was one of Haiti's strongest leaders. General La Plume and Amaurpas won fame at the Port Depeix but were brutally murdered by the French.

As we stop and view the lives of our ancient and foreign soldiers we greatly admire the heroism and unshaken courage, taking into consideration that most of them were men who before, yea even at that time were in the grossest state of ignorance, and still in the moment of rage and revenge they often refrained from acts of cruelty and torture.

Among those whose blood was first sacrificed for the cause of American liberty, was that of

Crispus Attucks who fell in the famous Boston Massacre, March 5, 1770. Two others, Samuel Gray and Jonas Caldwell were buried in one common grave with this epitaph on their monument:

"Long as Freedom's cause the wise contend,
Dear to your country shall your fame extend
While to the world the lettered stone shall tell
Where Caldwell, Attucks, Gray and Marverick
fell."

Prince Whipple captured General Prescott of the Royal Army, but Col. Barton received an elegant sword for this brave exploit which Prince achieved.

At the time Maj. Pitcairn was commander of the British forces at Bunker Hill, and victory seemed sure to the English and while he shouted "The day is ours," Peter Salem, a slave of Faringham, Massachusetts, with the leap of a tiger rushed forward and fired directly at the officer's breast and killed him.

Five thousand Negroes fought on the side of the colonies in the Revolution. The best drilled and disciplined regiment was that of Col. Green of Rhode Island, three fourths of which were Negroes. When Col. Green was surprised and murdered at Pt. Bridges, N. Y., May 4, 1780, a small bodyguard of these black soldiers were with him. Each could have fled and saved their lives but surrounding their colonel they defended him and not until the last man was cut to pieces was the colonel killed.

Who was more brave than that unknown colored artilleryman whom Judge Storey gives an account of. While stationed in charge of a cannon with a white soldier at Bunker Hill, he had one arm so badly wounded he could not use it but having that patriotic spirit he suggested to the white soldier that he change sides so as to use his other arm. This he did and while laboring under pain and loss of blood a shot came which killed him.

Jordan Freehan pinned Maj. Montgomery to the ground while he was being lifted upon the walls at Ft. Griswold. Samuel Charleon was in the battle of Monmouth and several others which gave to us heroes in the sight of both God and man. James Armstead acted as scout to LaFayette in the Virginia campaign.

When New London was taken by the British and the American troops retreated back to Ft. Groton, commander Ledyard was stabbed with the sword of a British officer. Lambo Lathan, a Negro slave stood near the American and scarcely had the British officer left this murderous deed when Layton run him through with his bayonet and although he was pierced by thirty-three bayonets his life was freely given in the defense of his country.

Side by side the sons of Africa with their countrymen of the white race fought, and among those conspicuous for their bravery were Salem Poor, Titus Cobern, Alexander Ames, Brazilian Lew and Cato Howe, and Charles Bowles.

Oliver Cromwell, a black veteran, served six years and nine months under Washington's command and was in the battles of Trenton, Princeton, Brandywine, Monmouth and Yorktown.

David Humpheys was captain of a company of fifty-seven Negroes in the State of Connecticut; Seymore Burr was in the siege of Catskill; Col. Lauren, spoken of by Hamilton as a man of zeal, intelligence and enterprise was placed at the head of a Negro army in 1779.

In those days when slavery bound every black individual from the cradle to the elders, the colored women were not idle. Mollie Pitcher, whose husband was killed in the battle of Monmouth, took his place at the cannon until the end of that battle. But history gives to us the record of a black heroine who faithfully discharged all the duties of a soldier for nearly a year and a half, Deborah Gannett, enlisted under the name of Robert Shurtleff, in the 4th Massachusetts Regiment and exhibited an extraordinary instance of female heroism. She was discharged with an honorable character, afterwards receiving a pension.

A Negro sailor was taken from the American Man-of-War, the Chesapeake, while she was being fired upon, at the Battle of New Orleans. Over four hundred Negroes took part. The idea of fortifying the city with cotton breast-works, recognized the world over as a stroke of genius, was the suggestion of a slave who was a native African who had learned this mode of defense from the Arabs.

In the navy of 1812 one-fifth of the marines were Negroes. John Johnson should be remembered with reverence as long as bravery is a virtue. Struck by a 24-pound shot which took away all the lower part of his body, and while lying on the deck several times exclaimed to his shipmates, "Fire away, my boys; nor haul a color down."

John Davis was struck in much the same way. He too, requested to be thrown overboard, saying he was only in the way of others. Major Jeffries, a regular, during the battle at Mobile, won fame under Andrew Jackson. Israel Titus and Samuel Jenkins fought under Braddock and Washington in the French and Indian war.

But the second part of this act, the Mexican War of 1846 takes place after which peace reigned for only a short time when we are face to face with the most important chapters in modern history, the Civil War.

Eighty-seven Negroes were enlisted, they participated in 213 battles and engagements and never allowed the Union colors to be dishonored by cowardice or treachery. Their brilliant achievements at Ft. Wagner, Olustee, Ft. Hudson and Milliken's Bend made them welcome into the Union. Captain Andrew Callious fell in the battle of Port Hudson.

"Colonel, I will bring back these colors to you in honor or report to God the reason why," were the words of the color sergeant. Bearing the flag in the front, a shell strikes the staff, and blows off half of the brave sergeant's head. He falls wrapped in the folds of his nation's flag, his brains scattered amid them, but still his strong grip holds the staff even in death till Corporal Heath takes it up and bears it to the front again, when he, too, is pierced by a musket ball.

The 54th Massachusetts regiment was the first regiment organized in the free states. Colonel Shaw was commander and played a prominent part at Ft. Wagner. Sergeant Carney, bleeding from one wound in the side and another in the thigh entered the hospital, crying, "Boys, the old flag never touched the ground."

We shall never forget the army of the Potomac in the bloody months of the contest where Negro soldiers fought bravely at Petersburg and Richmond. The battles of Deep Bottom and Hatchet's Run, won for them immortal glory. A Negro named Dabney established a "clothes line telegraph" in the Flammouth Camp of the Rappahannock. William Strains proved a hero at Belmont. While our intense interest has been aroused by these scenes our attention is turned to the Spanish-American War. The first Negro to fall was Elijah Tunnell in the harbor of Cardenas on the torpedo boat Winslow.

The 25th Infantry made a record for fighting at El Caney in Cuba and San Juan Hill. T. C. Butler of Company H. of the 25th was the first man to enter the blockhouse at El Caney and took possession of the Spanish flag. First Sergeant Andrew Smith and First Sergeants Mason, Russell, Wyatt, Huffman, were commissioned for their bravery.

The names of Captain A. M. Capron, Jr., and Sergeant Hamilton Fish, Jr., of the Rough Riders who were killed in the battle have been mortalized while that of Corporal Brown of the 10th Cavalry, who manned the Hitchkiss gun, which saved the lives of hundreds, is unknown to the public. "The smoked Yankees," as they were called showed splendid courage in these battles. Sergeant Berry was the first soldier who reached the blockhouse on San Juan Hill and raised the American flag in a hail of Spanish bullets.

San Diego gives to us the greatest Cuban soldier known, Antonio Maceo, who always held the Spanish at bay. The 25th Infantry has made an enviable record in Indian warfare in Cuba and in the Philippines.

Contributions of the Negro Race Toward the Advancement of Civilization

When God repeopled the earth with the generations of Noah, the Negro race sprang into existence through the offspring of Father Ham, to become a great factor in the advancement of civilization.

Long before the mythical Daedalus, or four thousand years before Christ, history relates the wonderful achievements of the ancient Egyptians; how they divided the time into years, months, and days, and of Khufu, who contributed the Pyramids so great in technique that even the world to-day is mystified over its method of construction; how Claudius Ptolemy, whose principles of Astronomy and Geography were the greatest the world has known, also of his branch of mathematics, never being excelled for 1,400 years, and what they gave to embalming and literature!

These accomplishments were given forth by African Negro descendants from Cush and Mizraim, so says our great historian, Scholes. Earlier than the thirtieth century before Christ, Negro descendants from Seba, Sabtah, Ludim, and Anamin were found compiling alphabets in the upper valley of the Nile. This was the primitive cause of the world's knowledge of commerce.

Nimrod and Ashur, both acknowledged ancestors of the Negro race, founded two of the greatest inland cities of the world, Nineveh and Babylon. Sheba, the grandson of Cush, founded a wealthy Kingdom which bore his name. The Moors of Morocco, who have been traced by Durham as being Negroes, send forth from that country the finest leather, so skillfully tanned that no country has equalled its manufacture.

These facts show what the Negroes of ancient Africa contributed to elevate Civilization when other nations of the world were unknown. Africa of to-day still carries the distinction of possessing knowledge of Arts and Sciences; look upon modern Liberia, the land where black men rule, and read its history. There you find the name of Joseph Jenkins Roberts, one of the founders and the first black president; Dr. Crummell, a graduate of Cambridge University, and one of the most celebrated theologians of the world; and Edward W. Blyden, diplomat and president of Liberia, who has given us the greatest works of Arabic history. Then trace the works of their poets. Notice the names of Capitien, who wrote Latin both in prose and verse; James Whitbread; Francis Harper; Chief Suana, and John Jacob Thomas, the great grammarian, author of the Creole Grammar, and when you have finished you will agree that Africa, the home of the Negro and his ancestors, has contributed wonderfully to the advancement of civilization.

In India, it is said that a hundred thousand black soldiers, under the command of Nizam, helped England to maintain that country from the Asiatic nations, thus receiving from the glories of the conquest advanced civilization. In the sixth century, Mohammedanism had begun to spread abroad, and it is during this time we find the name of Billal, an African, who was Mohammed's first crier.

Bagdad, a Turkish village that flourished in the ninth century under the rule of an African Kalif, Harom Al Raschid, was the home of the Oriental tales, "The Arabian Nights." Later an African named Abul Aswad reigned here and reduced to system the Arabic language.

The first Pygmy was brought from the White Nile to King Assa, 3300 years before Christ. Chao-Ju-Kua, a Chinese writer of the twelfth century, B. C., says that the Pygmies, a race of small, black people, descendants from Africa, but living in India, carried on maritime commerce with the Chinese. The same writer says that the Pygmies occupied parts of new Guinea and the Philippines, and were noted for their great knowledge of poisons and antidotes.

Crossing the Asiatic borders into the country of Europe we find in Spain the Moor, formerly from Africa, and who had subdued this country, introducing the manufacture of cotton, wool, sugar, and silk when Europe proper was in barbarism. Juan Latino, a Negro, a professor of Greek and Latin in the Catholic Cathedral in Granada, Spain, wrote Latin poems in the sixteenth century.

Italy sends from Rome Victor the First, who was made Pope about the Year of Our

Lord 185; he wrote many books on Catholicism.

Germany may claim Anthony Amo, who received the degree of Ph.D. from Wittenburg University, upon his merits for his thesis on "Government," and who was appointed as Councilor of the State Court of Berlin, but history traces him an African Negro, born in African Guinea.

The name of France cannot be spoken in English without the echoes sending forth the name of Alexander Dumas, Sr., who gave his great military skill as division general under Napoleon Bonaparte, and who departed this life leaving young Dumas, a son, following in his footsteps and who later became one of the greatest writers of Romance and Drama.

Since Paris has in recent years adopted Henry O. Tanner, the great painter, whose "Daniel in the Lion's Den" has never been excelled, and who is still master of numerous other paintings, we will here class him with the famous Negroes of France, for it matters not where he resides, the United States is his native home.

In the Highlands of Scotland, Dr. James Smith, a Negro graduate of the University of Glasgow, won the first prize out of five hundred competitors.

In England, Ignatius Sancho, an African-born slave, wrote many letters picturing the condition of his race, soon found as a contemporary the great English writer, Laurence Sterne. Coleridge Taylor, the celebrated Negro composer of England, gave to the world Longfellow's poem, "Hiawatha," in song. Battersea, England, elected its first Negro mayor by a vote of 30 to 29 during November, 1913.

Negroes were active in the earliest accounts of explorers in America. It is said that thirty assisted Balboa in building the first ship made on the Pacific Coast.

Estevanica, a Negro, sailed from Spain June 17, 1527, with the ill-fated expedition of De Norvez, and when the others returned he remained among the natives and became a medicine man. Later he discovered the Zuni Indians and the country of New Mexico.

In the West India Islands two of the world's greatest liberators known to history, are found, Toussaint L'Overture, the esteemed Haitian General, and the Great Dessalines; nine tenths of the population of Haiti are Negroes who are to-day carrying on extensive commerce.

Humboldt, the Great Scientist, says when he entered Caracas, Venezuela, he found no one in that community familiar with the summit of Mt. Silla but two Negroes: thus it was with their aid he was able to give to the world his great scientific discovery.

Since the freedom of the Negro in Brazil and the Guianas, they help carry on the rubber, coffee, and diamond industries to a great extent. South America has the distinction of having a Negro Archbishop in the Province of Amazonas, and an editor of the chief newspaper in Rio de Janeiro. But before we finish relating what South America has contributed to the advancement of civilization, let us mention the name of Henry Diaz, the full-blooded Negro, who organized a black regiment officered by men of his own race and who wrested his country from the Dutch.

Tracing the Negro's contributions toward the progress of civilization from his origin in Africa, to the various countries I have mentioned, you will find that in America from the time they were landed as slaves in 1619 up to the present date, they have contributed more than any other race living upon the face of the earth. Remember how in chains, they cultivated the great agricultural product, tobacco, which caused America to rank among the first countries of staple product. It is true that the American boasts of his rich soil, but there could be no products without the till of the laborer.

"The Negro" has fought every race's battle but his own.

Two of the greatest abolitionists the world has known were Samuel Ringold Ward and Frederick Douglas.

The Church of England was not complete until its pulpit had seated the black bishop Crowther Samuel Adjai.

In the medical profession Negro physicians have gained prominence. Dr. Daniel H. Williams won international fame when he successfully cut a man's heart open and sewed the same up again and the patient still lived.

Think of a race of people just celebrating their fifty years of freedom and owning three hundred million dollars' worth of real estate.

High up on the ladder of fame stands the great educator Booker T. Washington.

The National Baptist Convention, the Negro Business Men's Association, the African Methodist Conference, the Medical Association and the National Association of Colored Women's Clubs show that the Negroes of America are organizing their forces for coming competition.

Our historian, George Williams, has proved the value of the Negro soldier from the Revolutionary to the Spanish-American war.

The Negro sculptors are Edmonia Lewis and Meta Fuller with their statues, "The Death of Cleopatra" and "The Wretched," together with Bertina Lee of Trenton, N. J., who are ranked with the foremost sculptors of the world.

Added to the list of poets we have the names of Phyllis Wheatley, Paul Lawrence Dunbar and Fenton Johnson, who gave to the world the pleadings and heart throbs of a lyrical race in verse.

Negro musicians in America have been ranked among the first of the land—Will Marion Cook, James Reese, Harry T. Burleigh, Rosamond Johnson and Blind Tom, the greatest musical prodigy of the world.

The Negro singers have played no small part in the cultivation of American audiences. Sisseretta Jones, Flora Batson, Patti Brown and the greatest of them all, Mme. Azalia Hackley, have captivated many American minds and hearts.

Professor W. E. B. DuBois is the Negro's greatest modern author. His "Souls of Black Folk" and "Quest of the Silver Fleece" are beacon lights to civilization, as well as "The

House Behind the Cedars," of Charles W. Chestnutt.

Civilization has made the greatest progress through inventions. The first Negro scientist of the United States was Benjamin Banneker of Maryland, who constructed the first clock striking the hour and published an almanac from 1792 to 1906. The first patent issued to a Negro was in 1834, when Henry Blair took out a patent for a corn harvester. After twenty years of hard work Anderson Berd of Waco, Tex., invented a weight motor to be used in running machines. C. L. Baker of Savannah, Mo., invented a machine to heat without fuel.

In St. Louis, Mo., a Negro invented the "Billips Hydraulic Scrubbing Brush," which a $30.-000 company has been organized to manufacture. Elijah McCoy has taken out thirty patents for lubricating appliances. Sheamships of the Great Lakes and Canadian Northwestern railroads are using many of his patents. The inventions of adjustable mirrors, extension cornice, the porcelain onyx the razor strop, the paper bag machine and the rapid fire gun, shoe machinery and the automatic feed attachment for adding machines, hemp brake and steel tire, were all invented by Negroes. But the greatest inventor of to-day is Granville T. Woods of Ohio, who has invented many improvements in telegraphy and has sold many of them to the American Bell Telephone Company.

In the Aeroplane world have Negroes exerted great skill. Harding, of New York, won a prize in an aerial contest for obtaining the highest distance. Robert Mudy of Eureka, Ill., who is but twenty years of age, has erected a mono-hydro-plane, which, while sailing on water, will hold 6,000 tons. Aeroplanes have been made by William Swagert of California, and Charles Chappell of Brooklyn, both Negroes.

Two Negroes, Marshall N. Taylor and W. H. Lawson of Louisville, Ky., founded the Grand Order of the United Brothers of Friendship, August 1, 1861.

Woman Suffrage is an advancement to all civilization. In Chicago, Mrs. Ida B. Wells-Barnett holds the distinction of being President of the first Black Suffrage Club of Illinois. When we think of what political influences have done for the Negro, we are forced to mention the name of a Negro who held a high official position, B. K. Bouce.

Ask the question: What has the Negro contributed to the world for the advancement of civilization, and answer by saying "Life," for from the time that Crispus Attucks spilled the first blood at the beginning of the Revolutionary War to the present date, Negroes have been offered up as sacrifices for the advancement of civilization.

"Facts"

Of the Negro Race half has been told.
  Here upon earth where men are tools—
But the other half is covered with gold.
  By the Throne of Him who over all rules.

Some day the blank page of history
  Will be filled with your many deeds:
And to this world be a mystery,
  So don't stop scattering the seeds.

The doors to success have rusty locks
  And the keys have been thrown away;
That's why man watches time by clocks,
  Patiently waiting the crowning day.

When hinges screak and the screws fall
  And the locks from the doors shall break,
We will enter and see the wall,
  The Negro Race did not forsake.

A TINY SPARK

BY

CHRISTINA MOODY

Washington, D. C.
MURRAY BROTHERS PRESS
1910

PREFACE.

HIS little volume is composed of verses, written at different times, in my leisure hours, as an expression of the author's varying states of mind, or for the gratification of friends.

It makes no pretensions to literar y merit, but will find its aim accomplished if it should prove a pleasure to friends, or a means of leading a devout heart to a more cheerful confidence in God.

CHRISTINA MOODY.
(Age 16 Years.)

Washington, D. C.
December 1, 1910

DEDICATED

TO

MY MOTHER AND FATHER

INDEX.

A TINY SPARK

To My Dear Reader.

Don't criticize my writing
  Cause I ain't well trained you know
I hab al-ways been so sickly
  Dat I haben had much show.

Don't laff and ridicule me
  Cause 'twill make me feel ashamed,
For I knows dat I ain't great
  Nor neither have I fame.

Some of dese poems you'er reading
  Was written long ago,
When I was jist a little kid
  Of thirteen years or so.

Don't criticize my poems,
  'Cause I wrote 'em all for you;
I ain't had much training
  'Tis de best dat I can do.

And if you find's my book
  Ain't good as t'ought to be,
Jist leave it to my ignorance
  And don't you laff at me.

The Love of a Slave Mother.

Just between the dawn and daylight
  Down by the Swany River shore
Crept a slave mother with her child
  Clasped to her bosom tight.

She looked upon her and whispered
  "So Mas'er was gwine to sell you
And we's done run away.
  Now Mas'er won't see us no mo'
T'will de break of Judment day."

  She casted her eyes toward heaven
And sent up a silent prayer
  That Jesus the King of Glory
Would take her and baby there.

  Just as the Sun of heaven
Kissed the earth with its blessed light
  She whispered softly to baby
"Cling to yo' mother tight."

  Within that very moment
The sound of a splash was heard,
  And silence came over the waters
As though nothing had occured.

  But upon the morning breezes
Rose a soft and tender sound,
  It floated to her master's house
And lingered upon his ground.

"So Mas'er was gwine to sell you
And we's done runaway
And Mas'er won't see us no mo'
T'well de break of Judgement Day."

The Soldier's Letter.

Dear Mother, it gives me bitter pain
To break this news to you,
That I, your son, am dying,
But dying brave and true.

I know when you receive this
Your heart will break in twain,
But mourn me not, dear Mother,
For I do not die in vain.

Some of our bravest soldiers
Are lying cold and still,
They shed their blood most freely,
In the fight on San Juan's Hill.

Let your heart be filled with pride
For the Negro boys fought well;
They faced that fearful battle
Fearing neither shot nor shell.

I have not forgotten, dear mother,
How—the day I marched away—
You said, "My son, for mother's sake
Don't forget to pray."

I've kept your bidding, mother,
For I've prayed both day and night,
And on San Juan's bloody hillside
In the thickest of the fight,
Found my prayer ascending upward
To the King above the heighth.

I fear not Jordan's billows
Though they do fiercely roll;
I'm safe in Jesus, the anchor of my soul.
I can hear his voice a calling
I know my work is done;
Meet me in heaven, mother,
From your true and loving son.

Chillun and Men.

W'ats dat fretting mammy's chile?
You'se enough to set me wile.
Stop my work and play wid you?
Hum, dats a pritty ting to do.

Here's I got dis fish to fry—
Hush, honey don't you cry—
Dar now, dar now, shut right up.
Lause dat youngon's broke my cup.

Le' go dat po cat's tail—
Why I just soon be in jail—
Don't you know dat cat will scratch
Land of goodness give me dat match.

Set yo' se'f down in dat chair;
And you jest move, sur, if you dare;
  Take yo' hands off dat air fish--
  Holy smokes dar goes de dish.

Good ting my hands is in dis doe,
If dey weren't I'd whip you sho.
  Getting sleppy? well I guess,
  Lay down dar and take yo' res'.

Don't you lemme see you move,
Turn over dar take off dem shoes.
  Look what a mess dis room is in,
  Tings am stroned from end to end.

Above all tings I do declare,
Jest look'er yonder at dat chair.
  I never seed sich in all my life,
  Dat youngon's hacking it wid a knife.

Here comes Ben, well I be bless,
What'll he say about dis mess?
  Chillun and men, chillun and men;
  When a 'oman gits married
      Then hur trobles begin.

The American Flag.

Wave on, old Flag, with all thy might!
Wave on, and show thy colors bright!
  Wave on, oh, Flag of Liberty!
  You are welcome to wave in the land of the
    Free.

You've sparkled your stars, you've waved
    your stripes,
To wave you have tried in the stormest night
  Once all around you cannons roared like
    thunder,
  And shots fired through you rent you asunder
But on waved the threads, all left of thee,
Waved on until our country was free.

  God the mighty and the just
  Has given thee, oh Flag, to us.
You deserve more honor than we can give to
    thee
For you represent to us our Liberty.
  All we can do, is look at you and say,
  "You are the greatest of all Flags today."

The Negro's Flag and Country.

"Why do you write of the American's Flag,
  Of its stripes of red and white?
And why do you call a flag your own
  To which you have no right?

Why do you praise the white man's flag,
  When you have not one of your own?
And why do you love this country
  When this country is not your home?"

These words were said to me by a member of my race.
The fire was kindled within me as I looked him in the face.
  I call this Flag *my own*, because long years ago
  A war broke out for freedom and the land was full of woe.

The white man old and young fought with all their strength and might.
But they found the field was pretty hot, then the Negro joined the fight.
  The Negro shed his blood without a murmur or complaint,
  And though they faced many a hardship, their brave hearts did not faint.

My claim upon this country is sealed with Negro blood.
That swept many a battle field in royal crimson flood.
I claim it, yes! I claim it! because for many years.
We have mourned the loss of our heroes with bitter hearts and briny tears.

Give me back my death bound warriors, and I'll bow my head and cease:
But no! they are gone, yes gone forever, so let their bones rest on in peace.
Then sing it in the school house, then cheer the Negro's Flag.
Ring it in the school bell, don't let its banners drag.

Sing of the Negro heroes who fought in the days of yore;
Sing it until it echoes on the banks of eternity's shore.
The Negro's Flag and country, long may thy glory shine,
And know ye that I, a Negro, claim the Royal Flag as mine.

Advice From Uncle Enoux.

Mother, train yo' chillun jest de way yo'd hab
'em go,
'Cause jest like you bends de saplin, da't de
way its gwine to grow.
Father, teach yo' sons jest de ting yo'd hab
'em know,
'Cause de way you aims yo' arrow dat's de way
its gwine to go.

Now don't you tink yo' chillun is too good to
learn to work,
'Cause a little bit a hardship, now and den
aint gwine to hurt,
For dey's got one ting to learn, and dat is—
neber shirk
If dey's workin' in a office or a'diging in de dirt.

You may hab plenty money, and a plenty
something eat
And may leave it to yo' chilluns when you
lays you down to sleep;
And evyting at first will run right smooth
and sweet
T'well de money dat you left 'em gine to
sneak, and sneak, and sneak.

Den if you aint taught 'em nothing, but to set
and hold dey hands
Dey can't earn demselves a libing, and a'how
you spose dey can?
Den dey'll end up in de po' house, 'cause 'tis
jest is true and show
Dat de way you aim yo' arrow, dats de way its
gwine to go.

Alone.

I think 'twould been nice if mamma had stayed
And had not gone to heaven so soon;
And happy I'd been if my little brother Jim
Had not followed her to the tomb.

T'was just yesterday when they layed father away,
And left me in the wide world alone
Don't make the parlor cheerful,
Don't turn the gas light on,
For it brings back sad memories
Which pierce my heart like a thorn.

No mamma to read by the fireside,
No brother to kiss and chide,
No more smiles from father
I wish that I too had died.

If I should wander in the orchard,
Oh! my heart, what do I see?
Only our favorite play ground under the old oak tree.
But instead of mamma's hammock and brother's swinging chair.
Three newly made graves, side by side, lie there.

I Am Happy--Dat Is All.

When I see's de nice white snow
Den dar's fun fur me I know.
De winds may blow, and storms may rise,
And clouds may gather in the sky;
But I gits my sled and slicks de rounds,
And away I shoots across de ground.

When de rain come pouring down,
I trys to pout and trys to frown,
But when I looks up on de she'f
Dar's something dar dat takes my bref,
—Dat ol' Banjo.

When de wind does howl and blow,
What shall I do, whar shall I go?
Down by the fire I stretch myse'f,
Like a little birdy in her nest;
And while de wind does weep and wail
Grandpa tell me old time tales.

Oh! I's happy as kin be,
No kind ob weather troubles me,
I loves de Summer in its bloom,
I loves de Winter in its gloom,
I loves de Spring, I loves de Fall,
I am happy—dat is all.

What the Master Said.

"Suffer little children to come unto me,"
The Master said one day
I am the light, in Me is no darkness,
I am the only true way.

He that beleiveth and is baptized
Beyond this world his treasure lies;
And he that in My foot path-tread,
Sweet I'll make his dying bed.

Spring.

The violets at last have awoke,
Their underground cells they have broke;
The birds again are on the wing,
Singing of the beautiful Spring.

Leaves are hanging on the trees,
Dancing at every passing breeze;
And the sky is clear and blue—
Everything in Spring seems new.

The pretty dandelion with its golden head,
And the grasses and clovers have left their bed;
Mother Nature has made her call,
Now the Glory of God surrounds us all.

Ol' Man Rain, P'ease Go Away.

Rain, Rain, go away.
Us little chilluns wants to play.
Got to stay in de house all day,
If ol' Man Rain don't go away.

W'ats de use in powing down
Like you wants to see us drown?
Wish dat you would'en stay,
Ol' Man Rain, p'ease go away.

Got de place all soaking wet,
Front do' swolen so 'twont shet:
Can't you see you'se in de way?
Ol' Man Rain p'ease go away.

Mammy's cross as de ol' scratch,
Papy's techus as a match.
How long is you gwine to stay?
Ol' Man Rain, p'ease go away.

Fido he's a fussing
And a biting at de cat,
And I recon if dey keep on
Dey will end up in a scrap.

Wat's de use of keep on drapping
And a being in de way,
When you knows for yo' se'f,
Dat us chilluns wants to play?

Grandma setting in de corner
Smoking of hur pipe,
I just said one word to hur
   And she just made me kite.

You haden ought to bother
Round in tother fokes' way
And I wish to goodness,
   Dat yo'd 'pease go away.

Grandpap he's a squalling
And a'moaning wid de gout,
And mammy keeps on fussing
   'Twell she's most put me out.

Look! look! What dat I see?
Sun a shining through de tree,
Rain done took hur heels and flew,
Sky done turn from black to blue—
Look, de rain-bow's in de sky—
   Ol' Man Rain, good-by, good-by.

The Depth From Whence We Came.

My fore-parents were slaves,
  I'm not ashamed to say;
Though many a one disdains the fact,
  And fain would drive it away.

Why should we be ashamed to know
  Of the depth from whence we came?
When we see the progress of our race—
  They have risen from slavery to fame.

We once were crushed to the earth
  And bound with a heavy chain,
And a seal was put upon us
  "Thou shall lose and never gain."

How tight that chain did hold us,
  And the seal, how well it did last,
While the Negro toiled on and grew weary,
  The chain and the seal held fast.

For many long years did he toil thus,
  With no sign of deliverance near;
To God he prayed with patience,
  But it seemed that He did not hear.

The old men died and left the yoke
  For the younger ones to bear
The young men grew old and others were born
  With the chain of slavery to wear.

But before the earth was created,
  God saw the slave bound man;
He wrote in His holy scripture
  "Ethiopia shall stretch forth her hand."

After many years of slavery
  God's lightening was seen in the sky,
His voice was heard in thunder saying,
  "Let the Negro rise."

Lo! the chain was broken,
  And the seal was torn away;
The Negro saw in the heavens
  The dawn of his coming day.

He shook the dust from his shoulders,
  And stood face to face with the world
He has proved his grit and courage
  Though rocks at him were hurled.

He grasped every opportunity
  And rose in spite of all,
Whenever duty demanded him
  He did not need be called.

You have risen, oh Mother Race,
  So be thou not ashamed,
Let the once cursed name of Negro
  Stand for the word of Fame.

My Mother.

I have friends, yes I can't count them that
 have been so kind to me.
My relatives too have I that I love affectionately
But there is one I have not named, whom I
 love above all others
Who's name is sacred, sweet and charming—'tis my mother.

Her eyes are full of a mother's love,
They are soft and tender as those of a dove.
When she speaks I only hear sweet music ringing in my ear
No other hand can sooth my pain
Or drive sorrow back with fierce disdain
 But my mother.

No! I have not forgotten my father, who is
 loving, kind and good,
Who has always done as much for me as any
 father could.
His eyes too are tender, his voice is low and
 sweet,
He brightens our home with his loving deeds,
 his presence is always a treat.

But, my mother! She's my mother you
 know
No matter who else there may be,
And I just can't help from thinking
There is nobody like her to me.

23

The Child.

Precious to my heart is this sweet little child
Come my dear, just one kiss, rest here awhile.
Nestle closer to my breast,
Slumber there, oh! thou blessed
Fair little flower.
Thou little one knows no care,
Dwells in castles built of air,
Would there I too could share
Thy little bowers.

Resolve For Today.

Another day has dawned, another day has broke
To toil for the Master and to bear His righteous yoke.
And though the day be sulky, and dry for want of rain,
And our feet tired and weary, and our bodies full of pain,
We'll take the gospel plow and plow up the field of sin,
And we will sow seeds of kindness where the thorns of sin have been.

Manish Tom.

When little Tom was five years old
He received a watch of solid gold
  Said he, "I am a little man
  And as brave as any in this land."
But a'last, a dog came in sight
And put poor manish Tom to flight.

Our Faithful Guide.

I lay me down in peace to sleep and I think
    not of the morrow,
Yet I know not whether it will bring to me
    joy or sorrow.
  But still I slumber peaceful and leave it all
    to Him,
  Who rules the earth and heaven, mortal and
    immortal men.
And if we always trust Him with our tiny
    might
He'll safely lead and guide us through the
    day and night.

The Little Seed.

A little seed fell to the earth,
'Twas the seed of an apple tree.
'Twas too small to grow I could plainly see—
Why it was'nt as large as a pea.

But the little seed planned of days to come,
When his body would be great and tall,
But how could that be, when he was so wee,
He could scarcely be seen at all?

By and by the seed broke in twain,
'Twas the death of him I said,
But instead of death, a pretty stem
Lifted up his little green head.

The stem grew up with perfect grace
And looked with wondering eyes,
At the painting of Nature's wonderfull art,
Until he became very wise.

Little leaflets too came forth,
With beauty that can't be told.
So the seed that was wee, grew into a tree
'Twas a wonderful sight to behold.

The Christian.

I is on my way to heaben,
  Steady bound fur cannons shore.
I has turned my back on Satin
  I don't like dis world no more.

I has got de sword of truth
  Holding fast in my right hand,
And I's gwine to cut and slash old Satin
  Twell I reach de promis land.

Life I know won't be so smooth now
  Stumbling blocks is in de way.
But dey aint a gwine to hender
  If I ondly wach and pray.

Don't you tink by me a talking,
  Dat I's tink myself so strong,
Cause I aint, I's weak and sinful,
  But I knows de right from wrong.

I can't preach like brother Jacob
  Nor can I sing like sister Green
But I can tell anybody of
  The one on which I lean.

I can tell you how he suffered
  When he died on Calvry's tree:
I can tell ob how in Glory
  Jesus pleads for you and me.

I can tell ob wonderous mercy
  Dot he showed to my po' soal;
How he helt de hand of justice,
  Under mercy's sweet control.

How when I has most forgot Him,
  And wanders out in depth of sin,
How His voice so sweet and tender
  Calls me back to Him again.

So it aint no use in loving
  All these fadeing earthly things,
I hab set my heart on heben,
  And I'se gwine to meet de King.

Slack Religion.

Folks is getting mighty slacky,
  Dese days dey don't pray no mo'
  And when Jesus comes a knocking, dey jist turns Him from de do.'
Went down Sally's house las' night and she ups and says to me,
"Look'er here, sister Mandy Jinkens come go to de dancing bee."
  Den I turned in mazing wonder, sot my eyes on dat air gal
  And I said in soder whisper, "Show'ly you don't mean dat, Sall?"

Why 'twas jest last quarterly meeting dat you
shouted up so high,
Thought upon my word and honor, dat yo'd
showly touch de sky;
And all de benches round you was a gwine
right an' lef;
And now, Miss Sally Carline, has you layed
dat on de she'f?"
Den she walled dem great big eyes of her'n
and looked at me jest so,
And she got me kinder han'cap'ed 'twell I
coulden say no mo.'

Den she said, "Why, sister Jinkens, dancing
aint no harm
And I'm gwine to dance all I want to, 'twell
de brake of Judgement morn."
Now Sally Carline Johnson can go rite on hur
way,
But you bet yo' life dat Mandy aint a gwine
to git too gay
And I aint gwine to lose my 'ligon, and I
aint gwine git too prowd,
But I's gwine join my Jesus, when He comes
up on de cloud.

29

Mary Lue's Lover.

Sambo he aint true
        Bo! Ho! Bo! Ho!
He's gone to loving little Miss Drew
Jest de thing I thought he'd do.
        Bo! Ho! Bo! Ho!

I aint crying fur him you know
        Oh! Oh! Oh! Oh!
But he hurt my feelings so
I aint gwine speak to him no mo.'
        Oh! Oh! Oh! Oh!

I'll snub dat man as show's I live,
        Dat I will, Dat I will.
I'll go by him with Willie Till
Den I guess he'll hab a chill.
        Dat I will! Dat I will!

Guess he t'inks he's ac'ing smart.
        Oh me! Oh my!
I aint goin'er let him break my heart
By and by I'll have my lark.
        Oh me! Oh my!

Never seen him 'twell last May
Hate him worser every day
        Oh! Oh! Sam Bo!
I have lovers by de sco
        Bo! Ho! Bo! Ho!

I don't want him any mo
If he comes I'll shut my do'.
        Bo! Ho! Bo! Ho!
He ain't goner make me lose my grace
        Oh! Dear! Oh! Dear!

Here he comes I'll wipe my face,
Pin my dress Jane, do make haste.
        Oh! Dear! Oh! Dear!
Is that you Sam, well come right in
        Teehe! Teehe!

You're looking lonesome, how've you been?
        Teehe! Teehe!
How's de darling little Miss Drew,
Show'ly she aint jilted you?
        Teehe! Tehee!
I's been mighty lonesome Sam,
Glad you'se back, indeed I am.

To the Memory of Rev. George W. Lee.

"He is gone!" our elder deacon said,
  "He took his heaven bound flight,
The world looks on and says, 'He is dead,'
  But he lives in the land of light."

And while the deacon spoke thus
  Every eye was wet with tears,
For we had lost one of the noblest men
  That had lived in our country for years.

The deacon said, "Let us rise and in one great body pray
  The prayer our blessed Saviour taught his twelve disciples to say."
And our voices were lifted to heaven, in a mournfull and grief stricken tone,
  And God sent us down a blessing, from around the dazzling white throne.

We have lost a noble hero, who's place can never be filled,
  And though years may pass away, yet his memory will ever live.
'Twas in the morning he took his flight to the land of the blessed,
  And I know that Reverend Lee, was glad to go to rest;

For many a time I've heard him say, when death's chilly stream was passed,
  How he'd lay his head on Jesus breast, and cry, "I am home at last!"
So let him rest and mourn him not, since we know it will not be long
Ere we too shall follow in his steps, and join the happy throng.

My Prayer.

In the morning when I arise, a little pray I
pray:
"Lord keep my heart and tongue from wrong
Throughout the live-long day."
And when the evening shadows fall a little
song I sing:
"Oh! may this weary soul of mine, soon go to
meet its King."
And when the night comes and I lay me down
down to rest,
I pray a thankful prayer, for I know I have
been blessed.
And my soul within me whispers:
"Lord, watch thy humble child."
And I know my prayer is heard,
For I feel the Saviour's smile.

When I'm Dead and Gone.

When I'm dead and gone don' weep and wail
fur me
'Cause I's a gwine to heben to sing a Jubilee.
And when you carries me to de church, don'
bow yo' head and cry
'Cause I t'ink 'tis a blessed thing, dat man was
made to die.

I don't want to stay and suffer in this lowly land of sin
So when I's dead and gone to heben clear yo' throat and say, "Amen."
When you carries me to the grave, and lays my bones beneath de sod,
Jest remember dat my spirit lives above de world wid God.

Don' you drap yo' lower jaw, 'twell yo' face is two yards long,
Don' you drap yo' se'f in moaning, don' you sing no moanfull song;
'Cause way up yonder in glory around the glassy sea
My po' soul a gwine to shout a mighty Jubilee.

The Forsaken Mother.

I am all forsaken, an outcast all alone.
My children all have left me,
Their hearts have turned to stone.
My husband died and left me with little children four
And it was all that I could do
To keep poverty from our door.
There was Willie, Johnie, Fannie and Bess—
I worked for them and did my best.
Through honesty I raised them everyone,
'Twas a hard task, but alas it was done.

My children married and settled down.
Fannie went away to live,
But the others stayed in town.
I went to live with Bess,
The youngest of them all,
She said there was not room enough,
The house was very small.
I went to live with Willie,
But his wife said to me
That she thought there was not
Room enough in the house for three.
My feet were tired and weary,
My humble heart was sore,
As I slowly trudged along
To find my Johnnie's door.
But Johnnie said, "Mother you can't stay here,
For I rent my rooms, house rent is dear,
If it were not for that you could welcomely stay.
But you see for my rooms you are not able to pay."
Then, "Son," said I, "to the poor-house I must go."
And on I trudged to the poor house, with my heart full of woe.
"O, God, bless my children," the poor woman cried,
Then she casted her eyes toward heaven
And bowed her head and died.

Sam Found Something New and Mammy did too.

I wants somet'ing new to do,
I'se tired of workin' an' playin' too,
So I guess I'll git upon de she'f
An' pitch into t'ings an' he'p myse'f.

Corse I knows dat hit aint right
But my jaws feels likes dey wants to bite.
But how's I gwine to git up dar?
Oh, I knows, I'll git a cha'r.

Jist look—Lor's, dar's chicken pie;
I eat my fill, unless I die.
Dar's apple pie and ginger cake,
'Tis 'nuff to make your jaw bone shake.

Well, I guess I'll 'gin to eat,
I'll first start on de chicken meat;
And de pie nex' I t'ink I'll take,
And den I'll hab de ginger cake.

Dis am my lucky day, whoopee!
Oh! here comes mammy Lawdy me!
Wat' you doin' up dar, Sam?
War's my strap—lam! de! lam!

Stealin' eh! you rascul you,
You jist wait 'twell I git thro'.
Bip! Bam! "Oh! Mammy! wow!"
Bam! Bam! "Oh, Lawdy! Ow!"

"I aint neber goin' steal no mo' "
Bip! Bang! "You'll kill me sho'
Oh! Lawdy, hear my humble cry,
'Cause I b'lieve I's gwine to die."

Mary's Little Goat.

Mary had a little goat
With wool upon his back;
And every time the goat did wrong,
He got a little slap.

He followed her to school one day,
And butted all around,
After Mary got him home,
She whipped him good and sound.

She carried him to the sea-shore
And took him to the bay,
When the tide was coming in,
He'd butt the tide away.

She carried him for a motor ride,
To see the country fair,
He butt the chauffeur out the car
Away up in the air.

She carried him to the country
  To get a little fat,
He chased the cows and butt the pigs,
  And fought duels with a cat.

She carried him to a circus;
  So he thought he'd butt the clown
But he didn't stop a butting,
  'Till the tent was up side down.

So Mary took her goat
  And whipped him 'till he cried,
And gave him bread and water
  Until he up his heels and died.

Then Mary had his funeral,
  And she wept for her dead;
But late that night he rose again
  And butt her out of bed.

A Tale told by Grandma.

I was seting in de cabin do',
  One moon shin' summers night,
When I heard a mighty noise,
  An' I seen a mazzing sight.

Some soldiers was a coming,
  Jest a tearing down de road
And dey busted Mis'us do' in
  An' thro' de house dey poured.

Mis'us had hur bacon,
  All packed up in de wall,
But de soldiers broke de wall in
  And I clar' dey took it all.

Dey called out po' ol' Hanner,
  An' dey made her cook some meat
An' I can't begin to tell you,
  How dem Yankee men did eat.
Dey catched every chichen,
  An, dey killed every pig
An' Mis'us had histericks
  'Twell she far'ly danced a jig.

Den dey went in de garden
  An' dey striped de place right bare
Left de place a lookin'
  Like a syclone passed thro dar.
Den dey went in de barn,
  An' took de co'n and wheat
An' dey clared de hol' plantation
  Of eberyting dats fit to eat.

Dey took all of Mis'us wine,
  An' dey camp out on de place
An' de way dem soldiers carried on
  I tinks it am disgrace.
Some of 'em got toxicated,
  An' dey cracked de wo'ses jokes
An' dey laffed an' squarled an' hollered
  'Twell I frought dey sho' would choke.

'Twernt nobody on de place,
  Got a drap of sleep dat night
Ebery eye was so red nex' mornin'
  Woulden a thought dey had a white.
Ol' Mar'ser he had gone to war,
  So po' Mis'us she was lef'
Dout a soal fer to pertect hur
  But her own po' measely sef'

Well I neber was so sorry
  Fur a body in my life
As I was fur po' ol' Mis'us
  She was scared as little mice.
Why de way she ran across de yard,
  An' fell in Hanner's do'
Would of made you clar 'fore heben
  Dat she'd los' hur reason sho'.

Scared po' Hanner twell she hollered,
  Lowd enough to make you def'
Lawsy Mis'us w'ats de matter?
  Why you don't look lik' yo' sef'
You am fraid about dem soldiers
  'Twell you'se white as any sheet.
But don't worry honey
  You jest lay you down an' sleep.

But as I has formost told you
  'Twernt no sleep for us dat night,
We jest huddled up toget'er
  Watching fur de morning light.
Well atlas' when mornin' came
  An' de soldiers went away
Dey diden leave us vittles nough
  To las us thro' one day.

But de Holy Father knowed,
  An' he woulden let us starb,
So he sent us to a neighbor
  Dat de soldiers didn't rob
An' so my story's ended
  An' I aint gwine tell no mo,
So taint no use for to ax me
  Cause my answer will be no.

The Pie That Sister Made.

Mamma was eating a pie one day,
And 'twas a fly in it.
She did'nt know it and took a bite,
And down on the fly she bit.
My sister who made that pie was my mother's pet,
But after mamma bit that pie, she was no more, you bet.
My mother grabed a round out of the old arm-chair
And on my poor sister's bones she took a liberal share.

A Verse for Dark Days.

When the days are long and dreary,
And your soul is tired and weary,
And when your burdens seem too heavy to bear,
Just think of Jesus who is on the other side;
He is fixing you a home over there,
And remember this, that Jesus said, "Even tho' I go away,
I will send my spirit down, so watch ye here and pray."
So weary heart leap for joy, cease thy dark dispair,
And think of Jesus who is on the other side,
He is fixing you a home over there.

The Night is Fast Approaching.

Why stand ye hear and idle,
  When there's work enough to do,
And the night is fast approaching,
  Soon the sun will be hid from view?

Why not work whilst the Sun doth warm thee,
  For I warn you, it's beams will not last,
For the night is fast approaching
  And this day with its beauty shall pass.

Cease plucking fading flowers,
  Go! gather the golden grain
For the night is fast approaching,
  When the idler shall be slain.

Shake thy lazy spirit,
  Leap up in the strength of thy might,
For the night is fast approaching
  And the world shall have no light.

Go work with faultless courage,
  For the Master will pay thee well;
When the shadows of the black night falls,
  He'll save thy soul from Hell.

Love and Hate.

Two daughters had mother wisdom—
  The pride and joy of her life—
One was called Love and tenderness,
  The other Hate and strife.

Love was the sweetest creature
  That ever abounded on earth.
When the heart was filled with sorrow,
  She would change it into mirth.

But Hate was indeed the vilest,
  How poisenous was her breath.
She would crush the tender heart
  Until it longed for death.

But when Hate has been abusing,
  Love will always find a way
To sooth the tender aching heart,
  And take Hate's thorn away.

Samson No. 2.

I's brave as de bravest,
  I kin fight from sun to sun,
I can lick Jack Johnson—
  Yes lick him till he runs.

But my jints is kinder stiff,
  And I needs to limber up,
And I need a bit more practice,
  On dem things called upper-cuts.

Everybody says dat Jack
  Is mighty powerfull strong,
But I clair I could lick him
  If he ever catched me wrong.

ABOUT THE EDITORS

Henry Louis Gates, Jr., is the W. E. B. Du Bois Professor of the Humanities, Chair of the Afro-American Studies Department, and Director of the W. E. B. Du Bois Institute for Afro-American Research at Harvard University. One of the leading scholars of African-American literature and culture, he is the author of *Words, Signs, and the Racial Self* (1987), *The Signifying Monkey: A Theory of Afro-American Literary Criticism* (1988), *Loose Canons: Notes on the Culture Wars* (1992), and the memoir *Colored People* (1994).

Jennifer Burton is in the Ph.D. program in English Language and Literature at Harvard University. She is the volume editor of *The Prize Plays and Other One-Acts* in this series. She is a contributor to *The Oxford Companion to African-American Literature* and to *Great Lives from History: American Women*. With her mother and sister she coauthored two one-act plays, *Rita's Haircut* and *Litany of the Clothes*. Her fiction and personal essays have appeared in *Sun Dog, There and Back*, and *Buffalo*, the Sunday magazine of the *Buffalo News*.

Gayle Pemberton is William R. Kenan Professor of the Humanities at Wesleyan University. She holds a B.A. from the Universtiy of Michigan, and M.A. and Ph.D. degrees from Harvard University in English and American Literature and Language. She is the author of *The Hottest Water in Chicago: Notes of a Native Daughter* (1992) and numerous essays on African-American literature, film, and American culture.